Cana Society

A Macro Analysis

Harry H. Hiller

Department of Sociology
University of Calgary

Prentice-Hall Canada Inc., Scarborough, Ontario

To Beverly, Nathan, and Drew
— a family I am proud to be part of.

FC
97
H55

Canadian Cataloguing in Publication Data
Hiller, Harry H., 1942-
  Canadian society

Bibliography: p.
Includes index.
ISBN 0-13-113838-3

1. Nationalism — Canada. 2. National characteristics, Canadian. 3. Multiculturalism — Canada.*
4. Regionalism — Canada. I. Title.

FC97.H55 1986   971   C85-099648-1
F1021.H55 1986

© 1986 by Prentice-Hall Canada Inc.
Scarborough, Ontario

Prentice-Hall Inc., Englewood Cliffs, New Jersey
Prentice-Hall International Inc., London
Prentice-Hall of Australia Pty., Ltd., Sydney
Prentice-Hall of India Pvt., Ltd., New Delhi
Prentice-Hall of Japan Inc., Tokyo
Prentice-Hall of Southeast Asia (Pte.) Ltd., Singapore
Editora Prentice-Hall do Brasil Ltda., Rio de Janeiro
Prentice-Hall Hispanoamericana, S.A., Mexico

ISBN 0-13-113838-3

Production editors: Mary Land, Maureen Chill
Copy editor and proofreader: Terry Macli
Manufacturing co-ordinator: Sheldon Fischer
Typesetter: DSR Typesetting Ltd.

Printed and bound in Canada by Gagné Printing Ltd.

1 2 3 4 5 6 GP 91 90 89 88 87 86

Contents

Preface

Social scientists will generally employ a carefully defined focus when they study a significant phenomenon. The necessity to explain relationships between factors in order to account for behaviour lends itself to small-scale studies of interpersonal relationships or organizations at the micro level. Occasionally, efforts are made to generalize these studies to the national or comparative level, but often the results are glimpses or segmental portraits of one component of the total society.

This book moves beyond the local and segmental to the national and integrative. It is predicated on the need to present the larger picture, and explains the use of the word *macro*. In other words, it is possible to know a lot about local matters or to be knowledgeable about selected themes or issues while neglecting the larger context in which these affairs take place. The framework for the larger picture in this instance is the national unit. Painting with a broad brush, the goal is to bridge the localism and frag-mented knowledge of the reader with the specialized findings of cumulative scientific studies of selected phenomena and to present a comprehensive portrait of Canadian society. While there are clearly hazards in dealing with the complexities of human life at the macro level, the realities of everyday life as well as the expanding horizons of our social scientific knowledge are making this exercise both necessary and possible.

The organizational framework of this book revolves around questions and issues that are relevant to a societal analysis. *Questions* refer to matters that are themselves in doubt or dispute, whereas *issues* identify realities taken for granted and whose meaning engenders considerable debate. Thus, the concern over whether the population resident within Canada actually forms a society is considered a question because the reality of a national society cannot be taken for granted. On the other hand, while the matter of inequality in the society is commonly acknowledged, the implications of inequality are debatable. Therefore, inequality is considered an issue.

Four questions and three issues are presented here as the most critical themes in a macro-understanding of Canadian society. The first two chapters deal with macro questions: "The Question of Society" (Is there such a thing as a Canadian society?); and "The Question of Autonomy" (To what extent is Canadian society an independent social unit?). Chapters Three, Four, and Five deal with the societal realities of inequality, region-alism, and ethnicity, and attempt to explain why they are critical issues in

Canadian society. Chapters Six and Seven return to macro questions: "The Question of Uniqueness" (To what extent is Canadian society unique?); and "The Question of Identity" (Why is a national identity problematic for Canadian society?).

A minimal number of assumptions are made about the reader's knowledge of Canadian society. For example, over the years I have found that the federal policy of bilingualism is frequently misunderstood because little is known about the heritage of this policy except in general terms. Therefore a Landmark Canadian Documents section is included to acquaint the reader with the Report of the Royal Commission on Bilingualism and Biculturalism. Summary discussions of four other landmark documents are also included in the text.

At the beginning of each chapter, two other special features are included. The first feature may be thought of as an "Issue in a Picture:" it portrays an interesting aspect of Canadian society which should stimulate discussion, and may require more careful study and thought than one might first expect. The second feature is an historic quotation from an eminent analyst of Canadian society, published in a classic study. The reader may want to consult the study itself, or obtain biographical details about the author in order to find out what the specific contributions of the book or analyst were.

Another feature of the book is at least one insert in each chapter entitled "Real People." These are accounts of real incidents either experienced by me, or reported to me, which I think illustrate in a graphic fashion some of the issues raised in the text.

The study of a society undertaken here must of necessity be interdisciplinary in nature. Dealing with topics such as regionalism or national identity, for example, suggests the need for perspectives from a variety of disciplines; yet the material has been filtered through the eyes of a sociologist. Even though the framework for the study is the political unit of Canada, the focus is on its people and their relationships. This means that, in our use of the term *Canadian society*, the key word is *society*. Rather than introducing the reader to a discipline, however, this book aims to introduce the reader to a particular society and provides disciplinary concepts and ideas when suitable: it is predicated on the need to fill a void in the market whereby students can be introduced to a specific society rather than societies in general. Consequently, the orientation which I have developed is macro-sociological.

I have deliberately used the endnote citation method to foster smoother reading of the text. The endnotes themselves, however, are frequently longer than a simple citation and many contain comments, elaborations, or references to other works relating to the points made in the text. Students should be encouraged to use the endnotes for reference purposes.

Acknowledgements

I am deeply indebted to many who have made this book possible. First of all, I would like to thank my own students at the University of Calgary who have stimulated me with their questions. I also want to thank my students at Thebacha College in Fort Smith, Northwest Territories for giving me a truly northern perspective on Canadian society during two brief teaching stints on their campus. Gratitude must also be expressed to my colleagues Jim Frideres, J. Rick Ponting, Harvey Rich, and Gladys Symons for their insights in areas where my own knowledge needed supplementation.

Manuscript preparation, a tedious task at the best of times, was shouldered by Myrtle Murray and Lynn Meadows. The completion of this manuscript represents a special tribute to Mrs. Murray who has served as my secretary for many years. I will always remain grateful for her competent and cheerful service. The editorial guidance from Prentice-Hall — in particular from Marta Tomins, Terry Macli, Mary Land, and Maureen Chill — is also appreciated.

Most of this book was completed during a time in which I had heavy administrative responsibilities at my own university. Consequently, most of the writing took place outside of normal office hours. For this reason, I dedicate this book to my patient and understanding wife Beverly and our two children. Therefore, in a real sense, I may be the author but this has been a team effort. While I take the ultimate responsibility for the book and its contents, I remain humbly grateful for the contribution of all.

Harry H. Hiller

Introduction
What Is a Macro Analysis?

The logic of scientific method requires that the focus of analysis in research be as narrow as possible. Botanists who wish to study flowers do not examine every species available and then draw conclusions about flowers. Instead, they focus their study on a particular type of flower and then determine its characteristics and reactions to different environments. Similarly, sociologists who want to construct a theory of family structure do not draw conclusions by studying one example of each type of family in the world. Rather, the focus is first narrowed by doing an intensive study of a particular family structure in a particular location. This allows the sociologist to understand the dynamics of family interaction in the location selected for study. By narrowing the focus as much as possible, scientists can be sure that their conclusions are reliable and valid.

After examining a certain type of flower or a specific form of family, the scientist always aims to endow particular results with a general application. What does our study of flowers teach us about dry-land flowers in comparison to flowers of high altitude mountain regions? What does our study about families tell us about differences between single parent and dual parent families, or families in Scotland in comparison to families in Canada? In both cases, the unit of analysis is eventually broadened and our knowledge of flowers and families is enlarged.

Social scientists refer to society as though it were a meaningful unit of analysis. Yet the careful application of scientific method requires that studies first be conducted on specifically defined components of a society at the micro level. We are then left with a series of fragmented conclusions about different aspects of a society, which, when merged, can help us see the society at a general level. *Macro analysis is the study of social phenomenon in terms of society-wide aggregates.* For our purposes, the boundaries of the unit of analysis (i.e., Canadian society) are the geo-political borders of the country of Canada.

Early social scientists (e.g., Durkheim, Weber, Marx, Spencer) preferred the macro approach for they were interested in the broad scope of change which would occur over time in societies and civilizations. Later, social scientists believed that the essence of human action occurred in face-to-face interpersonal micro situations. Recently, there has been a renewed interest in the macro approach to global patterns of social relations.

Macro analysis involves more than working from the particular to the universal. It requires that special attention be given to the structural features of a society (class relations, region, the role of the state, and inter-societal relationships) which provide the framework or context around which the everyday life of a society is shaped. Rather than examining all facets of the society (e.g., family structures, crime rates), macro analysis should address only those features which contribute to the larger picture of what Canadian society is. In other words, macro analysis implies a *societal* analysis which, in turn, should enable us to return the flow of analysis from the universal to the particular. Once we understand a society at the macro level, we can develop a clearer understanding of the micro aspects of the society.

As long as political states serve as the basic unit of world order, it is both useful and imperative to study national societies. Furthermore, if we remain aware of the fact that these national societies are not simple and homogeneous, but complex and diverse, we can look for the emergent properties of society which provide it with form and character. The end result of macro analysis should complement the numerous micro studies available on particular aspects of society, and should also stimulate the desire for a thorough knowledge of the constituent features of society. Indeed, the macro approach is necessary both within Canada and elsewhere, if we are to understand the broader dimensions of any society.

1 The Question of Society

Canapress Photo Service

"Canada is not the only society which has been created by large numbers of human beings moving into vacant areas, but it is unlikely that any other society has resembled a huge demographic railway station".

— John Porter, a Carleton University sociologist, in his ground breaking study *The Vertical Mosaic* (1965:33).

IT MAY SEEM IRONIC that even though the Canadian state is over one hundred years old, the precise nature of Canadian society and its existence as an entity is still in question. In fact, the stormy years after the centennial birthday suggested more than ever that the concept of a Canadian society could not be taken for granted. While Quebec was contemplating what degree of distance from the rest of Canadian society was most appropriate, the Symons Report was concluding that Canadians knew little about their own society, and a Federal Task Force on Canadian Unity was scouring the country for clues about ways to create a more integrated and cohesive society. What kind of society is this that has been problematic for so long?

The use of the term "Canadian society" implies that it can be differentiated from other societies and that it has some measure of internal coherence. Yet there seems to be evidence to suggest that internal coherence in Canadian society has been in continual question. Repeated waves of immigration and emigration, British and American influences, French-English differences, a relatively sparse but clustered population in a vast territory, and uneven economic development are only some of the factors that have contributed to fragmentation rather than societal unity.

It is, therefore, by no means certain that there really is such a thing as a Canadian society. Does the strength of the various small scale sub-societies in Canada preclude any meaningful discussion about Canadian society as a whole? Do differences in the resident population overwhelm whatever may be held in common?

Canada exists as a nation by the political and legislative decree of the *British North America Act* passed by the British parliament in 1867. This legislative document created an independent national unit and we are compelled to raise sociological questions regarding the nature and character of the people and their interaction within her geographic and political borders. But does merely living within these boundaries create a society? If so, then why have Canadians been so preoccupied with the lack of national unity and the need for greater understanding? What is it about the people living within the political entity called Canada that contributes to a weak sense of society?

Certainly there are many things about Canada's population that make it unique among other national populations. Within the national boundaries there are various regional, ethnic, occupational, economic and environmental distinctions which all contribute to what is known as the *national character*.[1] But in what way can we speak of the population within Canada's borders as a society?

Historically, it has been customary to describe Canada not as one society but two: French-Canadian and English-Canadian. From this perspective, the differences between the two societies were so striking that the idea of a "single society" was almost meaningless. Using multi-cultural or regional categories, we might conclude that Canadian society is nothing but an amalgam of numerous sub-societies which make up the whole in the manner of a jigsaw puzzle. Let us assume, however, that national political boundaries force the population within these borders to interact and to be cognizant of each other at least in some minimal way, if only because they share a common territory and political system. Thus, we use the term "Canadian society" to refer to the total population contained within the politico-national unit.[2]

Describing a Human Society

Having raised the question as to whether the term "society" describes Canada's population appropriately, it is important to specify the basic characteristics of a society and then to determine the degree to which Canadian society exhibits these characteristics. From a sociological point of view, a human society must possess the following character-istics: locality, organization, durability and self-identification.

LOCALITY

A society requires that its members share a common environment or locality. A common territory encourages and facilitates interaction that binds together the many smaller groups within the area. Thus, living together in a common environment creates the potential for the forma-tion of a society.

Assessment: It is true that Canadians share a common territory, but this territory is large, often sparsely settled, and made up of ethnically diverse population blocs. Nevertheless, in spite of these factors, it is often thought that the experience of living in Canada will knit those who have come here into a common pattern of interaction. In other words, living in one geographic location (albeit a large one) should provide for the integration of all immigrants from other societies into one society — Canadian society.

The Canadian experience, however, has shown that a developing sense of society has been retarded by the dispersal of population over an extremely large territorial unit. Regionalism continues to divide the national population and remains a constant source of conflict.[3] Various forms of mass communication and transportation have reduced some of the effects of a vast territory, but other aspects of distance are much more difficult to overcome. For example, many Canadians may have little understanding of life in regions of the country which they have never visited. Other Canadians may have developed stereotypical attitudes about a particular region. Thus, the question of locality has impeded societal interaction and understanding in Canada.

ORGANIZATION

For a society to survive, its members must be organized in such a way that roles and tasks are distributed throughout the society. Such organization unites the society's members in a web of inter-relationships. In modern societies, this organization usually becomes very complex as policies are made and decisions are carried out by specialized individuals (e.g., customs officers, army personnel) on behalf of the entire society.

Assessment: In Canada, the various levels of government join with large corporations and community agencies to give organization and structure to the society. Furthermore, job specialization means that members of a society learn to depend on each other for goods and services. Many of these organizational dependencies and relationships, however, have been somewhat superficially constructed. Geography may have encouraged interaction in a north-south direction across the U.S. border rather than in an east-west direction across Canada. In order to establish and reinforce the organizational structure of Canadian society, the federal government has set up regulatory agencies and mechanisms such as tariffs and immigration rules which promote intra-societal interaction. Tariffs force consumers to turn to Canadian industries, and immigration laws monitor and control demographic behaviour.

The Federal Government has frequently used its powers to protect and expand a national societal organization in order to reaffirm the boundaries of the society. While the natural flow of corporate or organizational activity could proceed incognizant of national boundaries, federal rules and incentives are utilized to ensure the establishment of national organization.

DURABILILTY

A society requires that interactive organization be relatively permanent and durable. When generations of families have inhabited an area and interacted more or less continuously over a long period of time, a heritage of common behavioral patterns is likely to develop.

Assessment: Durability has been thwarted in Canada by fluctuations in immigration and emigration which have hindered the emergence of traditions. The absence, moreover, of a sense of societal history has impaired the development of group consciousness. Population turnover, coupled with lengthy periods of immigrant adaptation have made it difficult for Canada to establish durability as a society.[4]

Durability is enhanced through education systems which equip youth with an understanding of their society, its heritage, and development. Historically, anglophone schools have been particularly weak in societal socialization — partially because of a lack of materials dealing with Canadian society. In recent years, however, the emphasis has shifted from a traditional dependence on educational materials published abroad to Canadian materials which provide a Canadian perspective. This shift played an integral part in developing common reference points through which meaningful societal interaction can be facilitated.

SELF-IDENTITY

Finally, a society must be aware of itself as a unique and independent entity. Participants in one society must differentiate themselves from participants in another by an awareness of their society and a sense of belonging to it.

Within the international social world, members of Canadian society must be able to locate themselves by adopting the societal identity of being "Canadian." Customs, symbols, folk heroes, and important landmarks contribute to an awareness of societal identity. For example, the display of the maple leaf in public assists Canadians in differentiating their society from other societies and helps them to establish their own national identity.

Assessment: A collective Canadian identity has been slow to develop within the society. One of the most significant retarding factors has been the presence of two distinct societies within the state. For reasons which are discussed in Chapter 5, French-Canadian society has always had a well-developed conception of itself as a society in contrast to the more diffuse image of English-Canadian society. In addition, Quebecois have been apprehensive about English-Canadian intentions regarding an emerging national society. Francophones fear that these intentions may destroy Quebec society. For this reason, even the new more distinctive identity of Canada as a bilingual state has produced considerable controversy and dissension.

In addition to the idea of a dual society, the so-called hyphenated Canadian (Italian-Canadian, German-Canadian) terminology has persisted. Members of the society are frequently identified in terms of the society of their origin. While these social groupings of hyphenated Canadians may have given Canada the collective identity that it does possess, they have historically, reduced the society's ability to establish a self-identity which all members of the society can recognize and in which they can participate.

Perhaps no national population has all of these characteristics in combination to thereby constitute the "ideal type" society. It is clear though that Canada has particular problems in overcoming her spatial difficulties, developing the web of social organization that binds her members together, creating durable patterns of interaction among a permanent population, and fostering a sense of identification with the socio-political unit. The population within Canada may, therefore, continue to find it difficult to become a national society in a full sense of the term. Such a goal may never be desired, but the acknowledgement of these problems reveals much about the nature of Canada's population.

State, Nation, and Society

Societies were traditionally identifiable because their people were living in virtual isolation from other collectivities. The boundaries and distinctive social patterns of the society were easily discernible and the network of interrelationships could be simply traced. This conception of society changed as populations expanded, and as wars and economic relations between societies resulted in an intermingling of peoples. The advent of industrialization and the breakdown of the feudal world provided the context for deep thinking by early sociologists (e.g., Durkheim, Spencer, Weber) about the nature of society and its growing complexity.[5] The breakdown of the traditionally simple society provided opportunities to examine the difference between society and the state.[6]

A *state* is a political unit with the power to govern. Its emergence as a primary institution with sovereignty over other institutions was a significant development in human history. The state was given a special obligation to create, enforce, and interpret rules which would govern the behaviour of large numbers of people.[7]

As states expanded their sphere of influence, they increasingly gathered under their governing umbrella societies which reflected ethnic, racial, class, regional, linguistic or religious differences. In its attempt to be all-encompassing, the state embraced numerous sub-societies to form what we would now call a *pluralist society*; i.e., a society consisting of many meaningful sub-units. Personal submission to the state and its authority was frequently challenged by commitments to these sub-units, some of which had links beyond the political boundaries of the state. The state was, therefore, an instrument of human power which frequently welded people into political units irrespective of their own sense of society.

The characteristics of a society mentioned earlier produce a feeling among people that they belong together. This group consciousness is heavily dependent on the concept of *nation*. The word nation stems from the Latin word "nasci" which means "to be born" and originally meant a group of people born in the same place.[8] Similarity of birthplace (the objective dimension) provided the basis for fellow feeling (the subjective dimension) due to the sharing of common origin, traditions

The Sense of "Nation" hood in Quebec

the fleur de lis — the national flag
the maple leaf — the Canadian flag

Quebec City — the national capital
Ottawa — the Canadian capital

MNA (Member of the National Assembly) — elected member of Quebec legislature
MP (Member of Parliament) — elected member of Canadian parliament

and institutions.[9] The concept of nation is related to ethnicity because of the ethnic commonality of background and sense of belonging together. For this reason we can speak of the francophone community in Quebec as a nation and legitimately refer to the existence of a Quebec society. Increasingly, native peoples in the North are also discovering their camaraderie as expressed in their self-reference as the Dene Nation.

The equivalence of nation with state is, however, another matter. A state which is composed of one ethnic group is a *mono-ethnic state*, and, in this situation, state and nation are equivalent; i.e., a nation-state. States may, however, contain more than one nation due to the existence of two or more ethnic identities; e.g., Switzerland, Nigeria. Nation groups can also be participants in more than one state (e.g., the French in Belgium, France, and Germany). When states contain more than one ethnic nationality, they may attempt to create a new single nationality based on the political entity. In the medieval world, a multiplicity of languages and cultural traditions were common and were not incompatible with allegiances to the lord or king.[10] Only in the contemporary world is the unity of the nation-state inclined to demand undivided allegiance. This demand may result in nationalist movements which may challenge the state and serve as the basis for secession.

When several national/ethnic groups reside within a state, we refer to this as a pluralist society even though one group may dominate. Pluralist states hold people together through a mutual commitment to abide by the regulations of the state even though the emotional dynamic of togetherness is lacking. Nevertheless, changes and adaptations over several generations may contribute to a growing sense of nationality based on the identity of the state. As this occurs, it becomes increasingly possible to speak of a national society as circumscribed by the boundaries of the state.

In sum, a state is the organization of peoples into a political unit whereas a nation implies a more derivative condition of an ethnic identity which may or may not be politically organized into a state. This distinction explains why Canada has been described as "two nations warring within one bosom" and clarifies why the idea of a single national society is problematic.

Some states are held together more by regulation than the desire for integration.[11] The dominant anglophone model of Canadian society has been that whatever regulation was initially needed to make the state viable would eventually be replaced by the populist desire for more integration. The francophone perspective, on the other hand, has been to object to any loss of their ethnic identity in favour of a pan-Canadian identity. Clearly, the weak existence of a Canadian nationalism is rooted in the vague existence of a single Canadian society.

It may be that whatever sense of society exists at the federal level in Canada is based on a mutual acknowledgement of the authority of the state to be the final arbiter of grievances and to maximize mutual well-being.[12] At the same time, there does exist an evolving set of events and experiences that continue to sharpen the outlines and provide greater substance for a developing "Canadian" sense of society. This process will be the focus of Chapter 7.

Region as a Unit of Society

The question of whether people who live within the boundaries of Canada form a society might first be examined by using region as the unit of analysis. In contrast to the state which is a larger unit of analysis, region is a smaller unit which potentially is more reflective of local peoples, their history and their culture. While it may be difficult to identify a society at the level of the nation-state, perhaps it is easier to observe society in the context of region. At the very least, contrasting regions as a smaller unit of analysis should enable us to determine the extent to which the society of the nation-state is fragmented.

Regionalism is a recurrent theme in Canadian society. Geographers are most likely to draw our attention to regions as places affected by physiographic, climatic, or topographical factors that are related to where people live and how people live.[13] Geographers may also understand a regional society as structured around growth poles or central places which provide employment and opportunity.[14] Geographically understood, a region is a land area of physical territory that is in some way distinctive in contrast to other regions. Mountains, prairies, woodlands, coastal regions, and their respective supporting economies can be distinguished and boundaries established.

The anthropologist thinks of region in terms of culture and seeks to relate specific cultures to specific geographic environments. With some exceptions, sociologists have traditionally left the regional variable to geographers and anthropologists.[15] Perhaps the most troublesome aspect of region is that it is difficult to locate the social boundaries of region. Regions are seldom homogeneous social groupings, and differences within a region may be more significant than superficial similarities or traits. To discover that the average income of the population of a region is low in comparison to other regions may be less important than to know that there are significant disparities in income within the same region. In sum, for sociological purposes, a region may be too imprecise as a unit of analysis.

Yet there remains a lingering conviction that region is an important variable in understanding society. While it may be difficult to determine what aspects all residents of a region may have in common, it is clear that a combination of cultural and physical characteristics do make one area distinctive in some measure from another area. The sociologist looks for whatever characteristics of the population (e.g., ethnicity, occupation, income) seem to be held in common and contrasts them with other regions where population characteristics may be different. The sociologist might also look for attitudes and opinions that are identified with one area and then compare them with other regions. This approach suggests that a region can be considered to have a psycho-social dimension which essentially transforms the concept of region from geographic space into social space.[16] Sociologists look for objective indicators of region in the characteristics of the population and for subjective indicators in the attitude, identities, and feelings held by residents of a region.[17] In most instances, however, the identification of a region as a social construct is still largely dependent on geographic boundaries.

Differences in population characteristics or attitudes do not necessarily create regionalism.[18] It is only when these differences are specifically recognized as a differentiating feature from other regions that they can produce, reinforce, or sustain regionalism. In other words, *regionalism* has a political dimension that involves a consciousness of kind, a collective identity, and a defense of territorial interests.[19] Regionalism involves the politicization of regional concerns and the articulation of regional commitments. What has made region a critical factor in understanding Canadian society is not just that regional differences exist, but that the evaluation of these differences has led to the recognition of disparities which has in turn spawned heightened regionalism.[20] This process will be examined in greater detail in Chapter 4.

Before the dynamic relationship between regions can be discussed, it is important to determine the extent to which there are population differences between the regions of Canada. The nature of the commitment to region (i.e., regionalism) can be understood more clearly if we develop an understanding of the population differences between regions. This exercise will also provide a comprehensive picture of the components of Canadian society.

We are still left with the problem of determining what constitutes a region. The six traditional regional units in Canada are the Atlantic provinces, Quebec, Ontario, the Prairie provinces, British Columbia, and the Territories. Other than the Atlantic and Prairie regions, the other regions are established provinces — which may or may not be an adequate means of determining regionalism. There are also problems with assuming that, for example, Northern and Southern Ontario are essentially the same and constitute a region. What does lend some credence to the "province as region" argument is that provinces provide the political apparatus to create a collective-regional identity based on socio-political interaction within that unit. So while we cannot be totally satisfied with equating region with province, it is possible to use provincial units as the context in which regional differences in Canada can be identified. Provinces can be clustered, as long as we acknowledge that regional boundaries are more difficult to determine than simple provincial boundaries.[21]

It is possible, then, to begin with the assumption that the experiences, interests, and attitudes of Canadians will vary with the territory in which they reside. While regional differences in population and environmental factors may be identifiable, the ultimate question is whether these factors produce regional societies. Is there a Maritime or a Prairie society with unique and distinctive characteristics? If these regional societies do exist, are they obfuscated by the presence of sub-regional societies at a local or community level?

Clearly there is a hierarchy of human relationships from the simple, small-scale community to the complex large-scale society. We can expect the smallest most intimate relationship to be more important than the more distant and anonymous relationship. Society, region, sub-region, and community then form a continuum from lowest commitment to highest commitment. For that reason, we should not expect region to be a primary unit of group identity. That kind of collective consciousness is more likely to occur when region is politically transformed into regionalism.[22] For our purposes, it is only important to determine whether regional differences might serve as the basis for regional societies.

The branch of sociology that deals with the statistical study of human population is known as *demography*. Where the state is a country of enormous size, it is important to look for any demographic differences that exist between regions within that state. Regions then are important not because of some assumed homogeneity within the region but because of differences between regions. These regional demographic differences fall under four main headings: population distribution, population composition, population change, and internal population shifts.

POPULATION DISTRIBUTION

Perhaps the most basic fact about the Canadian population is that it is unevenly dispersed over its constitutent territory. While size of the territory is vast (9,922,330 square kilometres), no permanent settlement is found in approximately 89% of that land space due to factors of climate and terrain.[23] Consequently, much of the country is uninhabited.

The term that is used to describe the settled areas is *ecumene*, literally meaning "inhabited space." Traditionally, population settlement took place on land supportive of agricultural pursuits. These same locations, however, were also preferred by urban dwellers. Thus the 8% of the land surface available for farming also contains the largest urban populations. Figure 1.1 illustrates the size of the ecumene in Canada. In general, the ecumene consists of land adjacent to the American border, with a higher northern reach in the Western provinces than elsewhere. The largest cities are also located in these southern extremities of the country with the three largest cities less than one hour's travelling time from the U.S. border. Thus it is clear why north-south interaction across the border has frequently been less cumbersome than east-west relationships in Canada.

In spite of the fact that the ecumene spreads across the southern boundary of Canada, some segments of that ecumene are more densely populated than others. Figure 1.2 reveals that 61.8% of the Canadian population of 24,343,000 (1981) live in the provinces of Ontario and Quebec, 17.3% of the population are located in the three Prairie provinces, less than 10% can be found in the Atlantic provinces, and 11.3% reside in British Columbia. From an historical perspective (Table 1.1), it is significant to note that the Atlantic provinces have experienced a continuous erosion of their proportion of the population from 16.6% in 1901 to 9.2% in 1981. British Columbia, on the other hand, has experienced incremental growth from 3.3% in 1901 to 11.3% in 1981. Quebec has also experienced an erosion of its earlier population strength due to a declining birth rate, an exodus of anglophones, and the fact that this province has been a less popular destination for international immigration than Ontario and the West. While there was large-scale settlement of the Prairie provinces during the first few decades of this century, many of these immigrants later left their farms as a response to the mechanization of agriculture and greater urbanization.

FIGURE 1.1

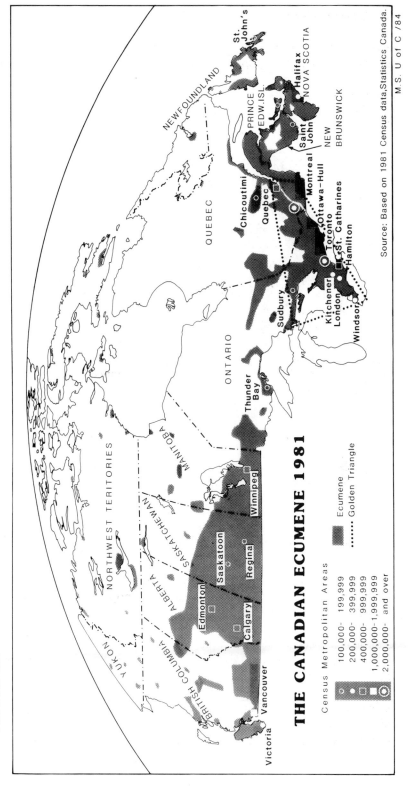

THE CANADIAN ECUMENE 1981

Census Metropolitan Areas

- 100,000- 199,999
- 200,000- 399,999
- 400,000- 999,999
- 1,000,000-1,999,999
- 2,000,000- and over

Ecumene
...... Golden Triangle

Source: Based on 1981 Census data, Statistics Canada.

M.S. U of C /84

FIGURE 1.2 **Percentage Distribution of the Population of Canada by Province, 1981**

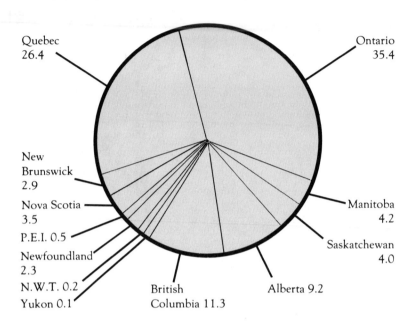

Quebec
26.4

Ontario
35.4

New
Brunswick
2.9

Nova Scotia
3.5

P.E.I. 0.5

Newfoundland
2.3

N.W.T. 0.2

Yukon 0.1

Manitoba
4.2

Saskatchewan
4.0

British
Columbia 11.3

Alberta 9.2

TABLE 1.1 **Percentage Distribution by Region of Population, 1901-1981**

	1901	1921	1941	1961	1971	1981
Atlantic Provinces	16.6[a]	11.4[a]	9.8[a]	10.4	9.5	9.2
Quebec	30.7	26.9	29.0	28.8	27.9	26.4
Ontario	40.6	33.4	32.9	34.2	35.7	35.4
Prairie Provinces	7.8	22.3	21.0	17.4	16.4	17.4
British Columbia	3.3	6.0	7.1	8.9	10.1	11.3

Note: [a] excludes Newfoundland

Source: Adapted from Statistics Canada, *Canada's Changing Population Distribution,* 1981 Census of Canada, Catalogue 99-931, Table 2.

Therefore, the 22.3% proportionate share of the population in 1921 was eroded in subsequent years and has been restrained from further erosion in recent years, primarily because of growth in Alberta. General tendencies throughout Canada towards industrialization and urbanization have particularly benefitted Ontario where one in every three Canadians reside.

TABLE 1.2   **Population Distribution and Land Area, by Province, 1981**

	Population	Land Area Square Kilometres (in thousands)	Population Density
Canada	24,343,180	9,205	2.6
Newfoundland	567,680	372	1.5
Prince Edward Island	122,510	6	21.7
Nova Scotia	847,445	53	16.0
New Brunswick	696,405	72	9.7
Quebec	6,438,400	1,358	4.7
Ontario	8,625,110	917	9.7
Manitoba	1,026,245	548	1.9
Saskatchewan	968,310	570	1.7
Alberta	2,237,725	635	3.5
British Columbia	2,744,470	893	2.9
Yukon	23,150	532	.04
Northwest Territories	45,740	3,246	.01

Source: Canada Handbook 1984, p. 43; and 1981 Census of Canada Catalogue 92-901, Table 1.

Differences in the distribution of the population can also be illustrated another way. Table 1.2 demonstrates that size of land surface varies considerably from the smallest (Prince Edward Island) to the largest (Northwest Territories). The land area of the Atlantic provinces is particularly small in comparison to the other provinces whose individual constituent area is larger than many countries in the world. Prince Edward Island is the only province completely occupied and therefore has the highest density. The large segments of unoccupied land in most other provinces that have significant proportions of their land surface in the north (but most of their population in the south) means that population densities are unusually low.

TABLE 1.3   **Population Distribution of Urban and Rural Dwellers, by Province, 1981**

	Urban		Rural	
	Over 500,000	Less Than 30,000	Rural Non-Farm	Rural Farm
Canada	41.2	15.8	20.0	4.3
Newfoundland	—	39.3	41.0	.3
Prince Edward Island	—	36.3	53.9	9.8
Nova Scotia	—	24.8	42.8	2.1
New Brunswick	—	20.5	47.1	2.2
Quebec	51.6	14.3	19.5	2.9
Ontario	44.3	13.0	15.1	3.2
Manitoba	54.9	12.7	19.4	9.4
Saskatchewan	—	18.6	23.2	18.6
Alberta	53.1	16.2	14.3	8.5
British Columbia	41.6	17.3	19.9	2.2
Yukon	—	64.0	36.0	—
Northwest Territories	—	48.0	52.0	—

Source: Computed from Statistics Canada, 1981 Census of Canada, Catalogue 92-901, Table 6.

The differences between the urban and rural distribution of the population is also quite revealing. Rural populations can be farm (primarily engaged in agriculture), or non-farm (rural but not dependent on agriculture as source of income). Table 1.3 indicates that, while 24.3% of the population can be considered rural, only 4.3% are engaged in agriculture. The highest proportion of the population engaged in agriculture is found in the Prairie provinces, and, even there, mechanization has meant that fewer people are needed to farm the land. The proportionately largest group of rural non-farm residents are found in the Atlantic provinces where many people live in small fishing villages. The preference for rural non-farm residence is also a phenomenon of urban growth and the desire for living space. Five provinces (Quebec, Ontario, Manitoba, Alberta, British Columbia) together contain over 85% of the Canadian people and are also the only provinces with urban centres over half a million. Over one-half of the population of Quebec, Manitoba, and Alberta are found in such large cities.

In general, the Atlantic provinces and the Territories are more rural and small town, while the other provinces are more urban, in spite of a

REAL PEOPLE 1

Elections and Population Imbalances

Burnaby, B.C.

It was a cool, damp day in February of 1980 when Mary Lou got in her car to drive to the office. Her car radio blared out the latest hit followed by the news. The newscaster reminded listeners that it was election day. Mary Lou knew that she had a busy day ahead of her but that she could vote on the way home because the polling stations were open till eight o'clock.

After a full day at the office, Mary Lou ran some errands and picked up some supper at a fast food restaurant. She decided to take it home and eat it there more leisurely. As she approached her driveway, the disk jockey made a comment about the election. "Oh no," she thought "I forgot to vote. The polls are still open though, so I guess I should go."

Then the news came on. Even though polls were open in the West, the media had already declared a victory for the Liberals based on the returns in Central Canada where the polls were now closed and where the majority of the votes were cast and the counting had already begun.

"What's the use" exclaimed an already exhausted Mary Lou. "It doesn't matter anyway." She parked her car and went into the house to relax.

Questions to Consider

What does this example illustrate about the effect of population imbalances? What are the implications of our belief in democratic majority rule for less populated regions? Should Mary Lou have voted anyway?

large rural component in some Western provinces. The highest level of urbanization, however, can be found in central Canada in what is known as the *Golden Triangle*. The industrial heartland of Canada, the area north of the American border and south of a line extending from Quebec City to Sault Ste. Marie, contains 58% of the Canadian population.

The demographic distribution of the population indicates an uneven dispersion of people throughout the country. We may also make the following demographic conclusions:

1. Most of the population lives adjacent to the American border on land suitable for agriculture (though such land extends farther north in the Prairie provinces).
2. History, climate, and industry have favoured the population growth and dominance of Ontario and Quebec particularly as represented by the Golden Triangle.
3. The smallest provinces have the highest population densities but also more rural and small town populations.
4. There is a slow westward shift of population toward British Columbia, and to some extent to Alberta, which is primarily urban in character.

POPULATION COMPOSITION

The uneven distribution of the population in Canada contributes to regional differences which are further compounded by other factors. Three such characteristics are ethnicity, language, and religion.

One of the most typical characterizations of Canadian society is that it is an ethnic mosaic. What is less frequently noted is that this mosaic varies with territoriality; i.e., the diversity of ethnic groups is rather unevenly dispersed throughout the nation. One of the fundamental reasons that regional cultures exist is the fact that the ethnic composition of the population varies considerably from locale to locale in Canada.

Table 1.4 displays something of the ethnic heterogeneity found in Canadian society. While persons of British descent make up the largest single ethnic group in Canada (40.2%), there is a considerable range in the proportion of this group from province to province. Newfoundland, for example, is dominantly British at 92.1% while Quebec is only 7.7% British but 80.2% French. A large percentage (38.3%) of the inhabitants of Saskatchewan are of British extraction, and only 4.9% of French descent, but a wide range of other nationalities are also present. While the Atlantic provinces are not nearly as ethnically diverse as the Prairie provinces, the French component of the population is much more visible in the Maritimes (particularly New Brunswick) than it is in the West. Italians are significant minorities in Ontario and Quebec, whereas Ukrainians are significant minorities in Manitoba, Saskatchewan, and Alberta. Persons of Asian and African descent are found in largest numbers in provinces with large metropolitan areas, and in particular British Columbia and Ontario. Native peoples are more likely found in the West and the North.

These regional variations can largely be explained through differences in settlement patterns. The Atlantic region was settled first by British and French colonists who also created what became known as Upper and Lower Canada through settlement along the St. Lawrence

TABLE 1.4 **Percentage Composition of the Population by Specified Ethnic Groups for each Province, 1981**

	British	French	Dutch	German	Ukrainian	Italian	Asian & African	Native
Canada	40.2	26.7	1.7	4.7	2.2	3.1	3.5	1.7
Newfoundland	92.1	2.7	.1	.3	a	a	.4	.6
Prince Edward Island	77.0	12.2	1.1	.7	a	a	.5	.4
Nova Scotia	72.4	8.5	1.6	3.9	.2	.4	1.3	.8
New Brunswick	53.5	36.4	.6	.9	.1	.2	.5	.7
Quebec	7.0	80.2	.1	.5	.2	2.6	1.5	.7
Ontario	52.6	7.7	2.2	4.4	1.6	5.7	4.3	1.0
Manitoba	36.9	7.3	3.3	10.7	9.8	.9	3.1	5.9
Saskatchewan	38.3	4.9	1.8	16.9	8.0	.3	1.5	5.7
Alberta	43.5	5.1	2.9	10.5	6.2	1.2	4.4	2.7
British Columbia	51.0	3.4	2.7	6.9	2.3	1.9	7.6	2.4
Yukon	43.6	4.7	1.7	5.7	2.8	.4	1.7	14.8
Northwest Territories	22.4	3.9	.7	2.5	1.3	.5	1.1	55.6

Note: a indicates less than .1%

Source: Computed from 1981 Census of Canada, Catalogue 92-911, Table 1.

and Great Lakes region. By the late nineteenth century, significant settlements had also been established in the Red River area of Manitoba and on the west coast in Victoria and Vancouver. Massive immigration from other European countries in the early twentieth century was required to populate the Western plains. It was this, and subsequent immigration, which altered the dominantly bi-ethnic composition of the Canadian population and which has resulted in greater ethnic diversity. Even more significantly, different locations in Canada possess considerably different mixes of these ethnic backgrounds in their population.

The fact that Quebec (a francophone society), is adjacent to Ontario (a predominantly anglophone society), serves as a basis for significant provincial differences. It is interesting to note that in Table 1.4, persons of British descent are the same size minority in Quebec (7.7%) as persons of French descent are in Ontario (7.7%). Clearly, this is an important demographic basis for differences between these two provinces. The fact that the largest ethnic group in the Yukon is British (43.6%) with only a small proportion of native peoples (14.8%) while the Northwest Territories has a much larger group of native people (55.6%) and smaller group of persons of British descent (22.4%), makes these adjacent northern territories very different as well. The wide range of European and Asian minorities in the West make this area very different from the British dominated Atlantic region. It is these ethnic differences that lead to significantly different regional cultures, and that make a sense of society at the national level difficult to obtain.

In some ways, ethnic differences may be exaggerated because immigrants usually adapt to the dominant Anglo-culture. The data in Table 1.4 does not tell us whether the respondent was a first, third or fifth generation immigrant, and later generation immigrants may have long forgotten their ethnic identity. Thus, ethnic descent may not be nearly as important as current ethnic identity.

One indicator of the salience of ethnicity might be the language most often spoken at home. Table 1.5 indicates that, with the exception of Quebec (where only 12.7% of the population speak English), English is clearly the dominant language in Canada. New Brunswick, neighbouring Quebec, has a significant one-third French-speaking minority, and the Northwest Territories has a more than one-third component of persons speaking native languages at home. In the Atlantic provinces (except New Brunswick), we find the highest percentage of people who speak English at home. Lastly, in the provinces west of and including Ontario, more people speak a language other than French — a reflection of the ethnic diversity of these regions. Thus, it can be said that the extent to which a language is spoken at home may indicate ethnic identity, and from this it can be concluded that there are significant differences between various areas of Canada.

TABLE 1.5   Percentage Composition of Language Most Often Spoken at Home (Home Language) by Province, 1981

	English	*French*	*Other*
Newfoundland	99.3	.3	.4
Prince Edward Island	96.6	3.1	.3
Nova Scotia	96.1	2.9	1.0
New Brunswick	68.0	31.4	.6
Quebec	12.7	82.5	4.8
Ontario	86	3.9	10.1
Manitoba	86	3.1	10.9
Saskatchewan	92.8	1.1	6.1
Alberta	91.7	1.3	7.0
British Columbia	91.7	.5	7.8
Yukon	96.1	1.0	2.9
Northwest Territories	63.6	1.4	35.0

Source: Computed from 1981 Census of Canada, Catalogue 92-901, Table 6.

TABLE 1.6   Percentage Composition of Ability to Conduct a Conversation in either Official Language, by Province, 1981

	English Only	*French Only*	*Both*	*Neither*
Newfoundland	94.6	a	2.3	a
Prince Edward Island	91.7	.2	8.1	a
Nova Scotia	92.3	.2	7.4	.1
New Brunswick	60.5	13.0	26.5	a
Quebec	6.7	60.1	32.4	.8
Ontario	86.7	.7	10.8	1.7
Manitoba	90.3	.3	7.9	1.5
Saskatchewan	94.6	a	4.6	.8
Alberta	92.4	.2	6.4	1.0
British Columbia	92.8	a	5.7	1.4
Yukon	91.9	a	7.9	.2
Northwest Territories	79.9	.1	6.1	13.9
Canada	66.9	16.6	15.3	1.2

Note: a indicates less than .1%

Source: Computed from 1981 Census of Canada, Catalogue 92-910, Table 4.

Official government policy is that Canada is a bilingual country. Table 1.6 reveals that with the exception of a significant minority of persons using native languages in the Northwest Territories, English or French can be spoken by most people. The Table also shows that people in English-speaking regions are most likely to speak English only, with a minority of people who are able to use both official languages. Conversely, areas where French is spoken (Quebec and New Brunswick) are much more likely to contain people who speak English as well. In Quebec, for example, although 80.2% of the population are of French descent, about one-third (32.4%) of the population speak both English and French. Thus, the likelihood of being able to converse in both official languages is much greater in francophone regions than in anglophone dominated areas. The fact that French remains the dominant language in Quebec will, however, continue to distinguish that region from the rest of Canadian society.

Another important aspect of regional differentiation is religious affiliation. Just as there is a relationship between ethnicity and language, so there is also a relationship between ethnicity and religion. Census data on religion obviously are not indicative of commitment or participation, but they do give us some measurement of religious preference. In this data we find further evidence of regional differences. For example, while 88.2% of the Quebec population is Roman Catholic, only 19.8% of the population of British Columbia is Catholic. Similarly, while Saskatchewan claims 27.5% of its population as United Church members, Quebec has only 2% affiliated with that church. The largest single religious body in Canada is the Catholic church (47.3%) and in locations where there are many people of French descent, the percentage of Catholics is considerably higher. Generally, the farther west from Quebec that you go in Canada, the lower the percentage of Catholics in the population. However, the sizeable number of Catholics in other parts of Canada is usually also tied to an ethnic heritage (e.g., German Catholics in Saskatchewan). The western part of Canada has a higher proportion of persons embracing a non-Christian religion or having no religion at all. Evidence of European immigration is reflected in the significant Lutheran presence in the West and the early immigration from the United Kingdom is revealed by the comparative strength of Baptists, Presbyterians, and Anglicans in the Atlantic provinces.

Variance in ethnicity, language, and religion among Canada's population gives us further evidence of the regional differences that are present in the composition of the society. Again, differences within regions may be as important as differences between regions and we should not conclude that regions represent a homogeneous set. It is clear, however, that different demographic patterns within the society contribute to regional patterns that distinguish parts of the society from

TABLE 1.7   **Percentage Composition of Population by Religious Denomination for each Province, 1981**

	Catholic	Protestant	United	Anglican	Presbyterian	Lutheran	Baptist	Eastern Non-Christian	No Religion
Canada	47.3	41.1	15.6	10.1	3.4	2.9	2.9	1.3	7.3
Newfoundland	36.3	62.6	18.6	27.2	.5	.1	.2	.1	1.0
Prince Edward Island	46.6	50.5	24.5	5.6	10.4	.2	5.0	.2	2.6
Nova Scotia	37.0	58.0	20.2	15.6	4.6	1.5	12.1	.4	4.0
New Brunswick	53.9	42.9	12.7	9.6	1.8	.3	12.8	.2	2.8
Quebec	88.2	6.4	2.0	2.1	.5	.3	.4	.5	2.1
Ontario	35.6	51.8	19.4	13.6	6.1	3.0	3.4	1.6	7.1
Manitoba	31.5	56.6	23.7	10.7	2.4	5.8	1.9	.8	7.3
Saskatchewan	32.4	58.3	27.5	8.1	1.7	9.3	1.8	.4	6.2
Alberta	27.7	56.0	23.7	9.1	2.9	6.5	3.0	1.7	11.5
British Columbia	19.8	54.7	20.2	13.8	3.3	4.5	3.0	2.9	20.5
Yukon	24.2	53.4	14.3	20.2	2.7	4.0	4.4	1.2	19.5
Northwest Territories	40.3	52.0	8.2	33.6	1.1	1.4	1.5	.6	6.4

Note: There are numerous other religious groups considered Protestant in addition to the five major Protestant groups named. For this reason, Protestants are also aggregated as a special category.

Source: Computed from 1981 Census of Canada, Catalogue 92-912, Table 1.

each other. These variations can be summarized in the following way:

1. Ethnicity, language, and religion exhibit a close regional correlation. A British heritage, Protestantism, and the English language are most likely in the Atlantic provinces, Ontario, and the West; a French heritage, Catholicism, and the French language are most likely in Quebec and the adjacent border region of northern New Brunswick. Thus, Quebec and northern New Brunswick are significantly different from the rest of Canada on these dimensions.
2. Earlier settled and more rural areas such as in Atlantic Canada tend to be more ethnically homogeneous than more recently settled rural areas in the West which are more ethnically and religiously heterogenous. In general, the area west of Quebec is much more heterogeneous on all three of these dimensions than the area east of Quebec.
3. Native persons are found primarily in the West and the North where many maintain their own languages. They are likely to be affiliated with either the Catholic or Anglican church.
4. Asians, Africans, Italians, those who speak neither English or French, and those who are non-Christians are more likely to be found in provinces with large metropolitan areas.
5. Bilingualism is more likely in areas where French is spoken than in areas where English is the primary language.

POPULATION CHANGE

Population Turnover. Our discussion so far has mentioned some of the dynamic changes in the Canadian population. We have noted that ethnic diversity is a significant characteristic of the population which resulted from immigration. This influx of people into the society has combined with an out-migration of people and has prevented the consolidation of a sense of society. It has been estimated that even though eight million people immigrated to Canada between 1851 and 1961, more than six million emigrated or left the country during that same period.[24]

Figure 1.3 illustrates how closely emigration has shadowed immigration through much of Canada's history. A large number of the emigrants were former immigrants who used Canada as a stop-off point for later migration to the United States in what is known as a *stepping stone migration*. These and other Canadians emigrated to the United States to take advantage of employment opportunities, particularly before industrialization became stronger in Canada. Quebecers in particular migrated to the New England states where they found work while still remaining reasonably close to home.[25] In recent years, migration to the United States has become much more difficult due to the tightening

FIGURE 1.3   **Levels of Immigration and Emigration by Decade, Canada, 1851-61 to 1971-81**

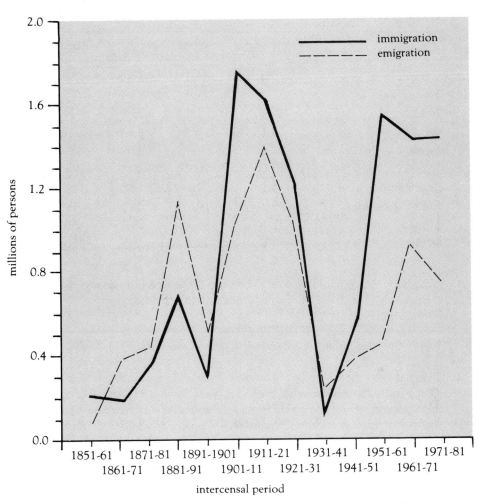

Source: Compiled from *Canada Yearbook 1957-58*, Statistics Canada, p. 160; Pierre Camu, E.P. Weeks, and Z.W. Sametz, *Economic Geography of Canada*, (Toronto: Macmillan Co. of Canada, 1964), p. 58; 1971 *Immigration Statistics*, Canada Manpower and Immigration, Table 2; and *1981 Census of Canada*, catalogue 91-208, Table 1 and Table 5.

of American immigration laws. Consequently, Statistics Canada has estimated that emigration from Canada to the United States has decreased while emigration to the United Kingdom and other countries has increased.[26]

It is also noteworthy that the source countries of immigration have

TABLE 1.8   **Percentage of Population Born Outside Canada for Selected Source Countries by Period of Immigration**

	Before 1945	1945-54	1955-69	1970-81
Germany	5.3	34.4	45.6	10.3
Hong Kong	.3	.9	23.1	75.3
India	.9	1.8	22.1	74.8
Italy	3.1	21.8	65.4	9.2
Japan	20.2	2.0	27.8	47.5
Norway	53.0	19.0	20.1	7.1
South America	1.1	2.2	18.3	77.1
United Kingdom	25.3	19.7	34.5	19.7
United States	32.3	6.0	23.3	35.0
USSR	36.6	45.2	9.3	8.6
Viet Nam	a	.1	1.8	97.8

Note: Rows do not add up to 100 because of persons born outside Canada who are Canadian through their parents citizenship.
a indicates less than .1%

Source: Computed from 1981 Census of Canada, Catalogue 92-913, Table 5.

changed over time.   If we examine Table 1.8, we notice that Hong Kong, India, South America, and Viet Nam are more recent sources of immigration, while countries like Norway and the U.S.S.R. are older sources of immigration. Germany was a post-war source of immigration, and migration from Italy was primarily a phenomenon of the 1960's. Thus, it can be concluded not only that immigration has repeatedly injected new populations into Canada but also that each wave of immigration brought people from different countries and that this has resulted in considerable societal diversity and flux.

Immigration also has its regional components. The smallest proportions of immigrant populations are found in the Atlantic provinces (Table 1.9). The regions with the largest number of immigrants are those containing the metropolitan cities. Consequently, Ontario has over one-half of all immigrants in Canada. Ontario and British Columbia both have over 23% of their population born outside Canada. Immigrants, therefore, seem to be attracted by urbanization and industrialization, and, given the uneven distribution of employment opportunities in Canada, it is not surprising that some regions of the society are growing through immigration more than others.

TABLE 1.9 **Percentage of Population Born Outside Canada, Percentage Born in Canada in the Province of Current Residence, and Percentage Immigrant Population, by Province, 1981**

	% Born Outside Canada	Of Those Born In Canada % Born Inside Province of Residence	% Total National Immigrant Population
Canada	16.1	—	
Newfoundland	1.7	95.7	.3
Prince Edward Island	3.8	84.3	.1
Nova Scotia	5.0	85.7	1.1
New Brunswick	a	86.2	.7
Quebec	8.3	95.9	13.6
Ontario	23.7	86.7	52.4
Manitoba	14.4	83.8	3.8
Saskatchewan	8.7	85.5	2.2
Alberta	16.5	64.7	9.4
British Columbia	23.3	60.3	16.3
Yukon	12.5	34.4	.1
Northwest Territories	6.1	60.4	.1

Note: a indicates less than .1%

Source: Computed and adapted from 1981 Census of Canada, Catalogue 92-913, Tables 1B and 2A, and Canada's Immigrants (Minister of Supply and Services, 1984), Chart 3.

Source of Growth. The movement of populations into a country (immigration) minus the movement of population out of a country (emigration) produces a rate of net migration. It has already been established that Canada has had a lower level of net migration because immigration has been somewhat counter-balanced by emigration. What then has been the primary source of Canada's significant population growth?

Natural increase is determined by subtracting the total number of deaths in an area from the total number of births in that same area. The data reveals that high fertility levels have been the primary source of growth. Canada appears to have recently completed the demographic transition of high growth rates due to high fertility levels. The theory

TABLE 1.10 Rates of Natural Increase and Net Migration by Province, 1931-1941 to 1971-1981

Province	1931-1941		1941-1951		1951-1961		1961-1971		1971-1981	
	Nat. Incr.	Net Migr.	Nat. Incr.	Net Migr.	Nat. Incr.	Net Migr.	Nat. Incr.	Net Migr.	Nat. Incr.	Net Migr.
Newfoundland	—	—	—	—	265	-29	222	-90	148	-65
Prince Edward Island	105	-28	121	-86	157	-96	127	-62	78	15
Nova Scotia	109	10	177	-72	183	-46	127	-59	73	-1
New Brunswick	132	-18	184	-64	196	-49	144	-85	93	0
Quebec	139	8	194	2	222	36	132	4	79	-13
Ontario	72	27	117	76	180	123	124	86	77	36
Manitoba	94	-53	116	-54	171	—	125	-55	85	-47
Saskatchewan	126	-155	107	-181	186	-80	137	-136	88	-44
Alberta	132	-47	139	26	236	109	162	38	113	202
British Columbia	46	118	114	236	172	160	101	190	72	155
Yukon and Northwest Territories	124	99	211	177	304	96	297	46	219	38
Canada	104	-1	146	24	198	64	131	36	83	38

Note: Rates are per 1,000 average population for the decade

Source: Statistics Canada, 1971 Census of Canada, Catalogue 99-701, Table 11, p.34; and computations for 1971-1981 supplied by Statistics Canada.

behind the demographic transition is that growth initially accelerates when improved medical care and nutrition cause mortality rates to decline. As modernization occurs, fertility rates will also drop and natural increase becomes less important as a source of growth. The transition occurs when the period of high fertility and low mortality produce a high rate of natural increase. The traditionally high fertility rates in Quebec have been reversed in recent years and the fertility rate in Canada has dropped. It is now assumed that Canada has completed the demographic transition.[27]

Table 1.10 shows that natural increase has been a much more important source of growth in Canada than net migration. However, even here there are regional variations. Quebec, which had a rather low level of net migration, depended heavily on natural increase to maintain the francophone share of the total Canadian population. The emphasis placed on high birth rates in Quebec has been referred to as the "revenge of the cradle" — a way of once more achieving the original balance between anglophones and francophones that had been disturbed supposedly by immigrants who were assimilating anglophone culture.

The more rural provinces (e.g., Prince Edward Island and Saskatchewan) were losing population through net migration but were also gaining population through significant levels of natural increase. On the other hand, provinces such as Ontario and Alberta had both a positive net migration flow, and a strong rate of natural increase to contribute to high population growth. Alberta and British Columbia have particularly benefitted from positive net migration flows. Internal migration will be discussed further in the next section but we should recognize that net migration produced only a total population gain of 2.4 million in the first one hundred years of Canada's existence as a country whereas growth due to natural increase was a dynamic 14.5 million.[28]

Aging. The high level of population turnover coupled with high rates of fertility has meant that Canada's population has traditionally been rather youthful. Table 1.11 shows that a high proportion of Canada's population is under twenty years of age. The drop registered for 1941 is a consequence of the depression and the return to high levels in 1961 is the result of the post-war baby boom. The lower levels in 1981 indicate completion of the demographic transition and lower fertility rates. The implications of lower fertility become clear when we consider that the proportion of the population in each age cohort over 20 is higher in 1981 than it was in 1901. The largest increase has been in the over 60 category and this reveals the aging of the population. Table 1.12 shows that one in every five Canadians will be over 65 by the middle of the next century. When we consider the problematic aspects of immigration and emigration in relation to societal cohesion, it is clear that an aging

TABLE 1.11   **Percentage Distribution of the Population by Five-Year Age Groups at Twenty Year Intervals, 1901-1981**

Age Group	1901	1921	1941	1961	1981
0- 4	12.0	12.0	9.2	12.4	7.3
5- 9	11.5	12.0	9.2	11.4	7.3
10-14	10.8	10.4	9.7	10.2	7.9
15-19	10.4	9.2	9.9	7.9	9.5
20-24	9.5	8.0	9.0	6.5	9.6
25-29	7.9	7.8	8.4	6.6	8.9
30-34	6.8	7.4	7.3	7.0	8.4
35-39	6.2	7.2	6.6	7.0	6.7
40-44	5.4	6.0	5.9	6.1	5.5
45-49	4.5	5.0	5.5	5.6	5.2
50-54	3.8	4.1	5.1	4.7	5.1
55-59	3.0	3.2	4.4	3.9	4.8
60-64	2.6	2.7	3.4	3.2	4.0
65-69	2.0	2.0	2.6	2.7	3.5
70+	3.1	2.8	4.1	5.0	6.2

Source: Compiled from Statistics Canada, 1961 Census of Canada, Col. 1, Part 2, Catalogue 92-542; and 1981 Census of Canada, Catalogue 92-901, Table 2.

population has positive benefits. Societal aging does give Canada an opportunity to develop a sense of permanence and durability from which a more integrated society can develop.

Population change has meant that Canadian society has been rather unstable for much of its existence. The reasons for instability can be summarized as follows:

1. Both immigration and emigration have been at very high levels and this has resulted in significant population turnover. Furthermore, different waves of immigration have had different sources and this has increased ethnic diversity. Regions west of Quebec have, in this century, received considerably more growth through immigration than regions east of Quebec.
2. While a high rate of natural increase through the demographic transition has contributed to solid population growth in all regions, natural increase has been a more important source of growth in Quebec and the Atlantic provinces. A recent decline in the rate of natural increase suggests that any significant population growth in Canada may require a more active immigration policy.

TABLE 1.12   **Percentage of the Population Over 65 and Percentage Increase in Number of Aged and Total Population by Decade, 1901-1981**

		% Increase Over Last Decade	
	% Over 65	Aged	Total Population
1901	5.0		
1911	4.7	23.6	34.2
1921	4.8	25.3	21.9
1931	5.6	37.1	18.1
1941	6.7	33.3	10.9
1951	7.8	41.5	21.8
1961	7.6	28.1	30.2
1971	8.1	25.4	18.3
1981	9.7	35.3	12.9
1991	11.1*		
2001	12.0*		
2051	18.2*		
1901-1981		770.6	353.6

* Indicates projections

Source: Adapted from Tables 1 and 2, *Sixty Five And Older: A Report By The National Council Of Welfare On The Incomes Of The Aged,* National Council Of Welfare, 1984.

3. The aging of the population is evidence of greater population stability from which societal coherence and tradition can be built. Because the Atlantic Region has been less dependent on immigration, a sense of society and regional history has developed more easily there.

INTERNAL POPULATION SHIFTS

The distribution and composition of the Canadian population has not been static over time for there has been a rearrangement of population within the borders of Canada. Through a voluntary form of migration known as *population drift*, individuals have chosen to relocate to more suitable surroundings. Migration might be prompted by a "push" such as the presence of a surplus population in relation to labour demands, or the "pull" of better opportunities elsewhere. An analysis of these "push" and "pull" factors helps us to understand why population rearrangement takes place.

Many persons might decide to relocate because their current location is unsuitable as a place to earn a living, carry on a career, or just as a place to live. It also follows that immigrants who do not know the country well may try several locations before settling down permanently. Shifts in employment demands, the policy of employer instigated transfers, and the long term trend toward urbanization have also been important factors in internal migration. Column 2 in Table 1.9 points out that the greatest population stability among native born is in Newfoundland and Quebec. The greatest instability is in the two far western provinces and the North. In other words, few people move to Newfoundland and Quebec and more people move into Alberta, British Columbia, and the Territories. For example, four out of ten residents of British Columbia were not born in that province.

Immigrants are an important component of the Canadian population and they are not included in the data just discussed, so it is important to examine net migration flows over time. Table 1.13 indicates that the Atlantic provinces have had a consistent, negative emigration from 1931 to 1981. Manitoba and Saskatchewan have also lost population through emigration. While Quebec has typically had a balanced migration flow, Ontario, the Territories, Alberta, and British Columbia have experienced strong positive net migration flows. In short, any internal rearrangement that has taken place between regions has led to population growth in Ontario, Alberta, British Columbia, and the North.

In most instances, population shifts have been a response to urbanization. The initial movement was from rural to urban within regions and, in later years, from urban to urban between regions. In 1871, only 19.6% of the population was considered urban whereas by 1981, 75.7% was urban. This suggests the magnitude of the rural-urban shift. The relationship between urbanization and industrialization meant that population would be attracted to those locations where employment opportunities were greatest. Thus developed the *Windsor-Quebec City urban axis* which contains about 55% of the national population, 70% of the manufacturing employment in the country, and an average income 10% greater than the rest of the nation.[29] Within this axis are the largest metropolitan cities of Toronto and Montreal and their satellite regions. Building from their initial (historical) advantage, their natural (resource base) advantage, and their central location in relation to national markets, they serve as natural magnets in population redistribution. Yet the data shows that Toronto, having passed Montreal in size, is increasingly dominating all of Canada. One analyst has suggested that Montreal and Vancouver have become regional centers.[30] Yet the data also shows that when regional population shifts do take place, Ontario, British Columbia, and Alberta cities are more likely recipients of such migration.

TABLE 1.13 **Percentage of Provincial Population in Census Metropolitan Areas over 100,000, 1981**

	CMA Population	% Provincial Population	% Growth from 1971
Newfoundland			
St. John's	154,820	27.3	17.5
Nova Scotia			
Halifax	277,727	32.8	24.7
New Brunswick			
Saint John	114,048	16.4	6.8
Quebec			
Chicoutimi	135,172		1.1
Montreal	2,828,349	43.9	3.1
Hull	170,579		14.3
Quebec City	576,075		19.9
Trois Rivieres	111,453		
	3,821,628	59.4	
Ontario			
Hamilton	542,095		8.7
Kitchener	287,801		26.9
London	283,668		- .8
Ottawa	549,399		21.2
St. Catharines-Niagara	304,353		.3
Sudbury	149,923		- 3.5
Thunder Bay	121,379		8.3
Toronto	2,998,947	34.8	14.1
Windsor	246,110		- 4.8
	5,483,675	63.6	
Manitoba			
Winnipeg	584,842	57.0	8.3
Saskatchewan			
Regina	164,313		16.8
Saskatoon	154,210		22.0
	318,523	32.9	
Alberta			
Calgary	592,743		47.0
Edmonton	657,057		32.6
	1,249,800	55.9	
British Columbia			
Vancouver	1,268,183		17.2
Victoria	233,481		19.2
	1,501,644	67.1	

Source: Compiled and computed from 1981 Census of Canada, Catalogue 95-943, Table 1, and 1971 Census of Canada, Catalogue 92-708.

The last aspect of urban-related migration has been the *counter-urbanization* trend which became evident in the 1981 Census.[31] More persons are moving to the rural fringe from the city than the reverse except in the Prairie provinces. This trend is away from the urban core to the satellite regions of urban areas.

Table 1.13 indicates that there is considerable regional variation in the rate of urbanization as it relates to large cities over 100,000 in Canada. Only 16.4% of the population of New Brunswick are in these metropolitan areas whereas 63.6% of Ontarians reside in such cities. Furthermore some provinces (e.g., Nova Scotia), have only one such city while Ontario has nine and Quebec has five. Some provinces (e.g., Saskatchewan) have only small cities while other provinces (e.g., Manitoba) each have one big city that accounts for more than one-half the provincial population. Resource development, government expansion, and the popularity of the coastal climate have led to recent growth in cities like Halifax, Ottawa, Calgary, and Vancouver.

Internal population movement changes the character of the society, creates regional resentments, fosters further population imbalances, and is symptomatic of underlying inequities within the society. Further, a comparison between regions with large metropolitan concentrations and regions of weak urban development suggests that the nature and substance of life varies considerably within the national society.

Internal population shifts can be summarized as follows:

1. Population movements within Canada have been in the direction of large metropolitan areas. Toronto in particular has assumed a dominant position in the national landscape.
2. Regions experiencing positive net migration flows are more likely to have larger cities and more cities. Regions experiencing negative migration flows have smaller cities and fewer cities.
3. The dominance of the Windsor-Quebec City urban axis remains unchallenged, but some new growth has occurred in the Alberta urban corridor and in southwestern British Columbia.

Assessing the Society within the Canadian State

A sense of society does not just happen; it requires time, structure, opportunity for interaction, and a growing collective consciousness. We can now summarize the factors that affect our perceptions of a Canadian society in evolution.

THE DEMOGRAPHIC FACTOR

Canadian society has experienced a large measure of population change. Population turnover through emigration and immigration; the fact that immigration came in numerous waves of different ethnic composition; the variation in the degree of assimilation of the residents; and the persistent shifting of population within the country due to urbanization, opportunity, and climatological factors, have contributed to the absence of a feeling of "belonging together" within Canadian society. Furthermore, bilingualism or multiculturalism may be politically useful policies but they reassert old loyalties and old traditions at the expense of Canadian loyalties and traditions necessary to give a society its own character.

THE REGIONAL FACTOR

The national society within the state is further divided by the fact that the continuous demographic changes already noted above have a regional context. The uneven distribution and redistribution of population groups; the early settlement of some areas and the recent settlement of other regions; the differences in population characteristics; and the differential in population gains and losses have produced numerous grounds for conflict within the societal unit.

When regional differences are transformed into an awareness of the meaning of these differences, then regionalism or a regional identity results. Cleavages based on ethnic, religious, or occupational factors often combine with inequalities in economic development to coagulate regional feeling. Jon Pammett's study of public orientation to region has reaffirmed that region is a major factor in personal identity.[32] About 60% of Canadians think of themselves in regional terms while 30% do not think regionally and 10% are not sure if they think regionally. There is, moreover, considerable geographic variation in the tendency to think regionally. Ontarians were least likely to think of themselves in regional terms and were more likely to feel close to the federal government. Residents of the four Western provinces were more likely to think in regional terms. In the Maritime provinces, people in Prince Edward Island and Nova Scotia show the greatest likelihood to identify with the Atlantic region. Perhaps somewhat surprisingly, Pammett's data suggest that the greatest regional consciousness comes from those who are younger, have higher incomes, and who are more geographically mobile. Clearly, region is a salient factor in Canadian life.[33]

THE NORMATIVE EVALUATION FACTOR

The analysis of regional differences and the identification of regional identities is easily presented as a societal problem. From this perspective, it is possible to conclude that regional differences ought to be eradicated and society-wide homogeneity and equality ought to be the goal. It is important to observe that regional analysis frequently produces passion and pronouncement. While regional variance is a fact of Canadian life that gives the society its character, the differences noted here and accentuated in Chapter 4 suggests that at least some aspects of regional analysis are problematic for a national society. In other words, regional study usually results in normative evaluations as to what Canadian society should be like.

. The focus on region makes it very difficult to assume that the interests of the state are always the interests of the regions.[34] It is not often that the state can appease all regional interests with the same policy. For example, what is in the best interests of the oil producing regions may not be in the best interests of the oil-consuming regions. The industrial strength of one region may be at the expense of another region that faces high unemployment and dependency on federal handouts. Anglophone Canadians may have lauded early federal policy which encouraged immigration in order to strengthen the national economy, and to claim the West in the face of possible American expansion. To francophone Canadians, however, this policy altered the bi-ethnic balance because an immigrant population would eventually embrace English culture and render the francophones a minority regional culture. In each of these instances, federal policy made in the "national interest" has negative effects on some regions. Therefore, regional analysis makes us acutely aware that a national society faces repeated challenges from regions whose best interests frequently contradict one another.

Bell and Tepperman have labelled this dimension of region in Canada as *conflictual regionalism*.[35] But they have suggested that there is also a *cooperative regionalism* — a basic commitment to the federal state and participation in its structures (e.g., law, parliament). Thus while regional disparities may seem to hinder the viability of the nation-state, regional differences play a significant role in giving Canadian society its unique form and character. In other words, while regionalism has divisive aspects for those concerned with creating a single sense of society, it is those same aspects which make the society what it is.

In addition, some regions may favour a decentralized federal system with strong regional identities while others may prefer a strong pan-Canadian society of the nation-state where a Canadian national identity dominates over regional loyalties. Indeed, there is evidence to suggest that commitments to region and state may not be exclusive and that it is possible to maintain both allegiances at the same time.[36] We will return to region in the context of national identity in Chapter 7 but, at this point, we should recognize that the significance of region depends on a subjective assessment as to what kind of society Canadian society should be.

Conclusion

Regional differences and regional disparities are not unique to Canada and are probably characteristic of all federal states. Yet in Canada, factors such as geographic size, population imbalances, ethnic commitments, and differences in economic development enhance the role that region plays in retarding the emergence of a more unitary national society. If we view Confederation as a union of convenience and of political and economic agreement rather emotive will and sentiment, then it ought not to be surprising that contractual arrangements are not conducive to the development of a sense of society.[37]

On the other hand, there does appear to persist an ephemeral ideal of societal unity as a significant ultimate goal.[38] Amidst population flux and diversity, there is emerging a more durable and stable population who have made their home in Canada for generations and who view themselves ethnically as "Canadian." Public expressions of regionalism may vary, but a commitment to the federal state continues. It is from this basic commitment that a society of the state — Canadian society —is becoming a more meaningful reality.

Further Exploration

1. Do you think people in your region have a sense of belonging? Does that sense of belonging conflict with or ever take precedence over federal objectives? Give concrete examples.
2. What do you think is *the* most important reason residents of Canada form a weak sense of society? Analyze why that reason is important and suggest policies which might overcome this weakness.
3. Watch your local newspaper for concrete examples of regionalizing events and perspectives as well as nationally integrating ones. Which kind dominates the news?

Selected Readings

Kalbach, Warren E. and Wayne W. McVey, *The Demographic Basis Of Canadian Society*, Second Edition, (Toronto: McGraw Hill Ryerson, 1979).

Beaujot, Roderick and Kevin McQuillan, *Growth and Dualism: The Demographic Development Of Canadian Society*, (Toronto: Gage, 1982).

Statistics Canada, Report on the Demographic Situation in Canada, (Ottawa: Statistics Canada, 1983).

Landmark Canadian Document I

Document: *Report of the Canadian Immigration and Population Study* popularly known as *The Green Paper On Immigration*, (Immigration Policy Perspectives, The Immigration Program 2, Immigration And Population Statistics, Three Years In Canada. Ottawa: Manpower And Immigration, 1974).

Issue: For many years, Canada's immigration policies had been expansionist, and aimed at making Canada an attractive place to settle. With new limitations on manpower demands in Canada, with the shift in immigration source from Europe to Asia, and with burgeoning population pressures in developing countries, new questions were raised about how many immigrants Canada should allow to enter and what countries they should come from.

Quotation: "[There are those who] compare the advantages Canadians enjoy with the living conditions of those in increasingly over-crowded and poverty-stricken countries abroad. They regard Canada's relative affluence, and abundance of opportunities, as constituting a moral obligation to keep the nation's doors open." (*Immigration And Policy Perspectives*, p. 16)

Context: In 1966, federal policy on immigration became explicitly linked to manpower needs in Canada through an elaborate selection system that required applicants to obtain a certain number of points to be eligible for admission. Outside of the point system, a category for admission existed for nominated or sponsored immigrants, which was based not on manpower demands but on respect for the family unit. Asian cultures in particular placed great emphasis on the extended family so that most applications in these countries were processed under the nominated or sponsored categories (e.g., 95% in New Delhi) which then by-passed the manpower criteria. Consequently, the overall skill level of immigrants to Canada was reduced, and the source of immigration to Canada shifted from Europe to Asia where over-population was a common problem. And even when the point system was applied, it frequently meant a brain drain of the most competent people away from developing countries.

Procedure: In 1973, the Minister of Manpower And Immigration announced a policy review of the immigration issue coordinated by a research team within the Department, but in which the views of organizations and individuals would be sought. Briefs and letters were received from religious, social action and educational groups, from business and professional associations, and from native peoples organizations and service organizations. These ideas were injected into government discussions at various levels and several documents known as the Green Paper resulted. These documents were not to announce policy, but to generate debate. Even so, they were generally perceived as expressing important elements of the government's thinking about immigration.

The Report: The Green Paper stated that immigration was a national problem because it accentuated regional imbalances, urban overcrowding, and could change the nature of Canadian society particularly because of its recent shift to non-white entrants. Furthermore, since the fertility rate in Canada was slightly below the replacement rate, it was suggested that immigration might be an important ingredient in the general rate of population growth for the future. But since most international migrants locate in our three largest cities, and it is in urban areas that intergroup conflict frequently becomes most pronounced, newcomers may become the focus for antagonisms that are socially disruptive.

An expansionist policy for wide-open immigration may no longer be appropriate; but how limited should a limited policy be when there are restrictions to Canada's absorptive capacity? Humanitarian sentiments to help the less fortunate must be tempered by the fact that even developing countries do not see out-migration as the solution to their problems.

The study noted that the dilemma was how to effect an immigration policy that reflected national interests so as to reinforce national sovereignty and unity, at the same time that it stressed the dignity of the individual and the immigrant's potential contribution to Canada — all in a humane and non-discriminatory manner.

Assessment: The Report raised two major questions: what should be the size and what should be the source of immigration? Both are critical questions but the Report provided little information on how to evaluate possible answers to these questions. For example, long term projections of the population needs for the country in relation to manpower demands would have been helpful in assessing size of the immigration stream. Furthermore, non-white immigration was implied as being problematic, and yet little was said about why and whether this was so, on how it might be reduced. In other words, and in spite of the government policy of multi-culturalism, the Report raised many fears about increasing the cultural plurality of Canada, then left those concerns for public resolution without adequate input. It is for this reason that some have argued that the Green Paper had racist undertones.

The Report was useful in that it raised the issue, however obliquely, about what kind of society Canadians wanted and how its members might relate to persons outside the Anglo-French, traditionally Christian, or European traditions around which Canada was built. Many of these overarching issues have still not been settled but a new immigration policy became law in 1978 (Bill C-24) that tied admittance more directly to current job demands in the country and accentuated a sensitivity to the global demands of refugees.

Further Reading: Assessments of the Green Paper from a variety of perspectives are contained in a special issue of the journal *Canadian Ethnic Studies* Vol. 7, No. 1, 1975. For a comparative description of immigration policies in the United States, Australia, and Israel, see Freda Hawkins, *Immigration Policy And Management In Selected Countries*. Ottawa: Manpower and Immigration, 1974.

ENDNOTES

[1]Don Martindale, "The Sociology of National Character," *The Annals of the American Academy of Political and Social Science* 370(1967):30-35.

[2]For a discussion of the potential of using the political or national entity as a unit of analysis in understanding human populations as societies, see T.B. Bottomore, *Sociology: A Guide to Problems and Literature*, Rev. Ed., (London: Allen and Unwin, 1971), p. 116.

[3]Lorne Tepperman discusses the divisive nature of regionalism in *Did Canada Have A Future? Sorokin's Prophecies Re-examined*. Eleventh Sorokin Lecture. (Saskatoon: University of Saskatchewan, 1980), p. 20.

[4]See Raymond Breton, Jill Armstrong, Les Kennedy, *The Social Impact of Changes in Population Size and Composition: Reactions to Patterns of Immigration* (Ottawa: Manpower and Immigration, 1974).

[5]For example, see Emile Durkheim, *The Rules of Sociological Method* (New York: Free Press, 1950), Chapter 4.

[6]S.M. Lipset, *Political Man* (Garden City: Doubleday, 1960), p. 2-4.

[7]R.A. Khan, James D. McNiven, and Stuart MacKown, *An Introduction to Political Science*, Revised Edition, (Georgetown: Irwin Dorsey, 1977), p. 22.

[8]Dankwart Rustow, "Nation," *International Encyclopedia of the Social Sciences*, Vol. 11, p. 7-14.

[9]Daniel Chirot, *Social Change in the Twentieth Century* (New York: Harcourt, Brace, and Jovanovich, 1977), p. 11.

[10]Oriol Pi-Sunyer, ed., *The Limits of Integration: Ethnicity and Nationalism in Modern Europe* (Amherst, Mass.: University of Massachusetts Research Report #9, 1971), p. 111.

[11]Ali Mazrui, "Pluralism and National Integration," in Leo Kuper and M.G. Smith eds., *Pluralism in Africa* (Berkeley: University of California Press, 1969), p. 345.

[12]For a discussion of this type of argument, see Donald Smiley, *Canada in Question: Federalism in the Seventies* (2nd Edition), (Toronto: McGraw Hill Ryerson, 1976), p. 218.

[13]D.F. Putnam and R.G. Putnam, *Canada: A Regional Analysis* (Toronto: J.M. Dent, 1970), and John Warkentin, *Canada: A Geographical Interpretation* (Toronto: Methuen, 1968).

[14]See N.H. Lithwick and Gilles Paquet, "Urban Growth and Regional Contagion," *Urban Studies: A Canadian Perspective* (Toronto: Methuen, 1968), pp. 18-39.

[15]The University of North Carolina is best known for its work in the sociology of regionalism in the 1920s-1940s. In particular, read the work of Howard Odum, Katherine Jocher, and Rupert Vance.

[16]Raymond Breton, "Regionalism in Canada" in David M. Cameron, ed., *Regionalism and Supra-nationalism* (Montreal: Institute for Research on Public Policy, 1981), p. 58.

[17]The subjective-objective distinction is made by Ralph Matthews in *The Creation of Regional Dependency* (Toronto: University of Toronto Press, 1983), p. 18.

[18]Matthews also argues that regionalism may be present even "when there does not appear to be much in the way of objective difference." See "Regional Differences in Canada: Social Versus Economic Interpretations," in Dennis Forcese and Stephen Richer eds., *Social Issues: Sociological Views of Canada*, (Scarborough: Prentice Hall, 1982), p. 86.

[19]For one discussion of the political aspects of region, see Mildred A. Schwartz, *Politics and Territory: The Sociology of Regional Persistence in Canada* (Montreal: McGill-Queen's University Press, 1974), p. 5.

[20]The comparative conception of disparities between regions is developed in Paul Phillips, *Regional Disparities* (Toronto: James Lorimer, 1982) and *Living Together: A Study of Regional Disparities* (Economic Council of Canada, 1977).

[21]For a discussion of some of the issues associated with regionalism in Canada, see Mason Wade, ed., *Regionalism in the Canadian Community, 1867-1967*, (Toronto: University of Toronto Press, 1969); and B.Y. Card, ed., *Perspectives on Regions and Regionalism* (Edmonton: University of Alberta Press, 1969).

[22]Alan Cairns has argued that instead of provincial governments being based on societies, the provincial governments mold their social environments to help create societies. "The Governments and Societies of Canadian Federalism," *Canadian Journal of Political Science* 10(1977):695-725.

[23]*Canada Yearbook 1980-81*, p. 1.

[24]Leroy Stone, *Migration in Canada: Regional Aspects* (Ottawa: Statistics Canada, 1969), pp. 22-26.

[25]cf. Yolande Lavoie, *L'emigration des Canadiens aux Etats-Unis avant 1930* (Montreal: University of Montreal Press, 1972).

[26]*International and Interprovincial Migration in Canada, 1980-81*. Statistics Canada, Catalogue 91-208.

[27]W.E. Kalbach and Wayne W. McVey, *The Demographic Bases of Canadian Society*, Second Edition, (Toronto: McGraw Hill Ryerson, 1979), Chapter 1. It is now accepted that variations in the birth rate are not solely related to industrialization and that other variables such as wars or depressions may intervene. In other words, the demographic transition theory is more complex than described here.

[28]T.R. Weir, "Population Changes in Canada, 1867-1967," *The Canadian Geographer* 2(1967):198.

[29]Maurice Yeates, "The Windsor-Quebec City Urban Axis" in Robert M. Irving, ed., *Readings in Canadian Geography*, 3rd ed. (Toronto: Holt, Rinehart and Winston, 1978), pp. 68-72. See also his *Main Street: Windsor to Quebec City*, (Toronto: Macmillan, 1975).

[30]Richard Preston, "The Evolution of Urban Canada: The Post 1867 Period," in Robert M. Irving, ed., *Readings in Canadian Geography*, pp. 41-42.

[31]*Urban Growth in Canada*, 1981 Census of Canada, Statistics Canada, Catalogue #99-942.

[32]Jon H. Pammett, "Public Orientation to Regions and Provinces," in David J. Bellamy, Jon H. Pammett, and Donald C. Rowat, eds., *The Provincial Political Systems: Comparative Essays*, (Toronto: Methuen, 1976), pp. 86-99.

[33]Another study which came to similar conclusions involved first year high school students. Both French-Canadian and English-Canadian students indicated a strong identification with their region. See Donald M. Taylor, Lise M. Simard, and Frances E. Aboud, "Ethnic Identification in Canada: A Cross-Cultural Investigation," *Canadian Journal of Behavioral Science* 4(1972):13-20.

[34]For a good discussion of the issues and remedies attempted, see Garth Stevenson, *Unfilfilled Union: Canadian Federalism and National Unity*, rev. ed. (Toronto: Gage, 1982).

[35]David Bell and Lorne Tepperman, *The Roots of Disunity: A Look at Canadian Political Culture*, (Toronto: McClelland and Stewart, 1979), pp. 185-197.

[36]David J. Elkins examined data that pointed out that Canadians may have multiple loyalties and, that with the exception of a separatist group in Quebec, loyalties to the nation-state need not necessarily erase regional attachments or vice versa. "The Sense of Place" in Elkins and Richard Simeon, eds., *Small Worlds: Provinces and Parties in Canadian Political Life*, (Toronto: Methuen, 1980), pp. 21-24.

[37]The contractual or mechanical basis of Canadian society is a point made by a number of people. For one example, see S.D. Berkowitz and Robert K. Logan, eds., *Canada's Third Option*, (Toronto: Macmillan, 1978), pp. 5-6.

[38]John Porter, "Canadian Character in the Twentieth Century" *The Annals of the American Academy of Political and Social Science* 370(1967):48-56.

2 The Question of Autonomy

Ford Motor Company of Canada, Limited

"Canada has ceased to be a nation, but its formal
political existence will not end quickly. Our
social and economic blending into the empire
will continue apace, but political union will
probably be delayed."

— George Grant, a social philosopher, in his widely read
Lament For a Nation (1965:86).

ONE REASON why the internal search for a sense of society is so difficult is related to factors external to the society. The efforts to strengthen "Canadian" corporations, or "Canadian" literature, or "Canadian" music, for example, have taken place in the presence of "foreign" corporations, literature, and music. The trend toward global interdependence among nations is also an external factor which has presented a special problem for Canada. In many ways, Canadian society is still searching for its independence. This is because Canada has been attached to older and more dominant societies for most of its relatively short history. This chapter will describe the nature, evolution and implications of these external influences for they provide a context in which to understand much of the conflict and cross-pressures existing in Canadian society today.

Colonialism as an Historical Process

Historically, Canadian society has always lived in the shadow of more powerful societies. These societies derived their power and international stature from military might, large populations, and concentrations of industrial, economic, technological, and educational strength. Canadian society actually emerged as a direct response to the power and influence of various world powers, for they supplied the people, goods, capital, and protection necessary for Canada's development. The early Anglo-Saxon inhabitants felt that Canadian society was in some way an extension of their own, more dominant, society. As a result, it was believed that Canadian native peoples should be pushed aside so that the new colony could be established.

Colonialism is the process whereby an imperial state maintains and extends its powers over a subordinate territory. The expansion of British and French power beyond their own national borders and around the world enabled both societies to participate in the molding of Canadian society. By initiating settlements in what is now Canada, they were able to establish and perpetuate their own national influences in a foreign land. After France lost control of Canada to Britain, British influence became more dominant in Canada.

The paternalistic relationship between the countries of origin and Canada was, therefore, established early and was perpetuated by Canada's refusal to join the American colonies in their rebellion against England. Canada thus retained her colonial ties and maintained an intricate set of dependencies. Whether these influences were economic, political, or cultural, the new society rejected autonomy in favor of sustaining colonial ties.

The first shift in colonial orientation for Canada was from France to Britain. Following the Second World War, however, the decline of the British Empire and the emergence of the United States as a world power prompted another shift in colonial status. Even though Canada had become an independent political entity with loose ties to the British Commonwealth, the cultural and economic strength of the neighbour country to the south drew Canada into a new form of colonialism. But where the earlier form of colonialism had been direct and formal, the new colonialism was less formal and less direct, though not necessarily any less powerful. The term *imperialism* is frequently used to describe this form of domination because the more powerful state seeks to extend its control beyond its borders by whatever means in order to retain its pre-eminent position. So, while colonialism implies political control, imperialism implies more subtle forms of influence and control. The extent to which nations react to and participate in such control varies over time and is dependent on other global events.

The analytical approach that views national societies in the context of global power differentials in known as *world systems theory*.[1] Basic to this theory is the idea that capitalism developed a world system of economic power which consisted of core societies, peripheral societies, and semi-peripheral societies. Core societies are highly industrialized and invest in societies weaker than themselves. Peripheral and semi-peripheral societies seek to emulate core societies through the adoption of economic, technological and political systems and processes. Despite this imitation, peripheral societies remain subordinate to the core economic powers who possess the capital needed for development. Because core societies need the markets, resources and labour of the weaker societies, they tend to assume an expansionist posture. France, England, and Germany were core societies at the beginning of this century, but were eventually replaced by the United States among capitalist countries and the U.S.S.R. among socialist countries. Canada is considered to be semi-peripheral because it has fallen under the economic and cultural influence of the United States as a core society. The world system approach, then, ties developments within Canadian society into an international framework.

From a sociological point of view, the significance of a subordinate position within the global system is that non-core societies are the recipients of a continuous transferring process known as diffusion. *Diffusion* is the transmission of economic forms, knowledge, traditions, or technology from one society to another. The originating society shares elements of its culture with the receiving society, so that the two societies become increasingly similar. Institutional and organizational linkages (e.g., unions, business franchises, professional associations, social clubs), serve as cultural pipelines from one society to another. Theoretically, diffusion is not a one-way process; through interaction with each other, societies share cultural traits to produce a homogenization of culture. But because of the strength of the core society in all aspects of its culture — whether economic, political or leisure — the direction of the flow of influence tends to be one-way in what is known as *penetration*. The core society absorbs from the peripheral society what it prefers and what it needs, but the strength of the influence is dominantly one way. Because the core society possesses capital, technology and information which other societies need, its position of dominance is retained.

THE STAPLES THESIS

Harold Innis, writing before world systems theory was proposed, pointed out that Canadian society was founded upon staple industries established for export to empire societies.[2] Whether it was the cod fisheries, trapping, lumbering, mining or agriculture, Canadian hinterlands were developed for exploitation by external markets. Canadian society, then, could be viewed as a series of resource-based communities centering around extractive processes and primary industries.

A protege of Innis, S.D. Clark, has described the impact this staple economy had upon Canadian communities which were developing on frontiers of economic expansion where staples were available.[3] Trade in staples such as fur and grain destined for European metropoles, was facilitated by transportation on the St. Lawrence River. This Canada-Europe Trade axis later became a Canada-U.S. axis as American industry and technology created new demands for Canadian staples. Innis felt that it was impossible to understand Canadian development without viewing its rich resources as a commodity in demand by more industrial nations.

Recent years have seen a renewed interest in the staples thesis because, although considered an industrial nation, Canada possesses a truncated industrial base which is still highly dependent on natural resources. In contrast to the resources described by Innis, the new resources include minerals like nickel, potash, hydro-electric power and of course oil and gas. Rex Lucas has identified 636 communities of a single industry in Canada.[4] Most of these communities were small (under 8,000 people), were resource-based (e.g., mining towns, pulp and paper towns, smelting towns), and often up to 75% of the labour force worked in a single industry. The dependence of many Canadians on resource-based employment means that the staple thesis is an important way of understanding the society and its dependence on external forces.

There are two aspects about a resource based economy that are important. First, much of the impetus, capital and technology for resource exploitation comes from core nations (particularly now the United States), and results in a high degree of foreign ownership. Second, resource-based economies are highly vulnerable to market demand. When market demand increases, boom conditions prevail;

when market conditions are poor or weak, poverty, unemployment, and displacement of populations result.[5] Thus a society that is heavily dependent on resource extraction for export will require a large blue collar work force and will lack the employment diversification necessary to maintain full industrial performance. In sum, when Canada depends on foreign markets for its manufactured goods it is exporting labour-intensive industrial jobs to other countries. The demands of core nations like Japan, the United States and West Germany require natural resources to maintain their industrial base and Canada needs those markets to maintain its productivity — even when productivity is dependent on non-renewable resources.

The autonomy issue is not solely a matter of economic penetration or dependence; it goes beyond that to include politics, education, entertainment and other aspects of culture. While many Canadians eagerly emulate what is occurring in core societies, others feel that such emulation is destructive of the society's own independence. Persons who are opposed to foreign influences that thwart Canadian independence and seek to reduce those influences are called *nationalists*. *Continentalists* are people who feel that because Canada shares the North American continent with the United States, it only makes sense for Canada to be closely integrated with that country. In addition, there are many residents of Canada who have ethnic ties outside of North America, and their scope may be even more international. In Canada, at least at the current time, the autonomy issue vacillates between the debates of the nationalists and the continentalists with the majority of the population preferring some middle ground depending on the matter at hand.

Foci of the Autonomy Issue

The Canadian dilemma is in determining how much foreign influence is acceptable. No society can be totally independent of other societies, but when is foreign influence harmful and when is it to be welcomed? Who is to decide when foreign influence is in a society's best interests? In what sectors of a society is foreign influence a more critical issue than other sectors?

A *shadow society* is a society whose sense of independence and uniqueness is obscured by the cast of continuous alien influences. Because Canadian society has lived so closely under the influence of more dominant societies for so long, developments since the 1960's suggest strong movements in the society to minimize that shadow. Most of these efforts have focused on three issues: foreign ownership, manpower importation, and cultural penetration.

FOREIGN OWNERSHIP

Foreign ownership is not a phenomenon that is unique to Canadian society, but among industrialized nations, Canada possesses a substantially higher proportion of such ownership. Beginning with the need for venture capital to exploit Canadian staple products for industrial needs in other countries, to the opening of Canadian subsidiaries of foreign corporations in sectors such as manufacturing, the issue of foreign ownership continues to be a matter of some debate.

There are two main ways by which foreign investment takes place in Canada: portfolio investment and direct investment. *Portfolio investment* means that foreign money enters the country in the form of a repayable loan or a bond which promises a fixed return on the investment but does not allow direct control over the operation in which the investment is made. *Direct investment*, on the contrary, means that foreign money enters the country through ownership or control acquisition as a share-

REAL PEOPLE 2

Staples and Insecurity

Uranium City, Saskatchewan

"Yup, I'm unemployed" drawled Frank as he leaned back in his rocker and closed his eyes. "They said it'd never happen. I came here to settle into something permanent and now look what happened.'

"I figured it was a good bet. Everybody knows the world needs uranium. Next to oil, it should be the hottest thing Canada has to offer right now . . . what with nuclear energy and all. There's gotta be a demand for it all over the world but they now say there ain't."

"What made our town different from all these others was that the government owned the company (Eldorado Nuclear) — not some foreign company. I figured they'd never shut us down 'cause they believed in Canada. If the government don't believe in Canada, who should? Well, at least I got time for fishing again — but I sure hate to have to move. I like these parts."

Questions to Consider

What does Frank's story illustrate about the lives of many Canadians? What difference would a multi-national corporation vs. a crown corporation have made?

holder. Majority ownership of shares can be obtained through either a controlling interest or a wholly-owned subsidiary. Through direct investment, foreign owners can possess decision-making power over a substantial proportion of the Canadian economy.

Prior to World War I, three-quarters of the foreign investment in Canada was British. Much of this investment was of the portfolio type but a recent study has pointed out that there was also a significant degree of direct investment.[6] By the Second World War and in the period immediately following the war, the nationality of that investment became American — primarily direct investment through the establishment of American subsidiaries in Canada. More recently, capital has entered Canada as portfolio investments particularly in the form of loans to finance government deficits.[7] The periodic pilgrimage of provincial premiers to the money markets in New York attests to this fact.

Generally speaking, while portfolio investment may result in a distressing drain of interest payments outside the country, it is usually viewed as preferable to direct investment because ownership and control is retained within the country. Direct investment, on the other hand, is a more clearly identifiable foreign presence. Foreign control of Canadian corporations appears to have reached its peak in the early 1970's and has now declined due to government and private acquisition.[8] For example, the purchase of Hudson Bay Oil and Gas by Dome Petroleum and the purchase of Acquitaine by the Canadian Development Corporation resulted in reclassification of these assets from foreign control to Canadian control.

There are several ways of measuring foreign control. Statistics Canada has estimated that, in 1981, 25.5% of all non-financial industries were foreign controlled.[9] When restricting the data to the top one hundred enterprises in Canada, foreign controlled corporations held 32.4% of the total corporate equity. Using corporate taxable income by country of control as another measure of foreign control, Table 2.1 suggests over 44% foreign control. The significance of this foreign control is not so much its proportion but its nationality and its sector concentration. The figures show that 73.9% of all assets and 80.7% of all profits among foreign controlled corporations were U.S. based, 10% of the assets and 8% of the profits were from British corporations, with the remaining corporations from either Japan, West Germany, France or the Netherlands. Furthermore, Table 2.1 indicates that foreign ownership is concentrated in two industrial sectors, mining and manufacturing. Whether the company is General Motors or Shell Oil, most of the large corporations in these two sectors of the economy are foreign owned.

Foreign ownership is not an issue in the areas of banking, transportation, utilities or communications. But it has been suggested that

TABLE 2.1 **Percentage Allocation of Corporate Taxable Income for Industrial Sectors by Country of Control, 1981**

	USA	UK	Other Foreign	Canada	Unclassified
Agriculture, Forestry, Fishing	3.4	—	1.6	75.4	19.6
Mining	66.3	.6	8.4	24.1	.6
Manufacturing	50.8	5.8	4.1	37.7	1.6
Construction	8.1	1.2	2.8	68.0	19.9
Utilities	12.3	.6	1.5	81.4	4.2
Wholesale Trade	18.3	2.8	9.4	63.4	6.1
Retail Trade	11.6	.5	.8	72.3	14.8
Services	23.4	.5	.4	50.4	25.4
TOTAL	37.4	2.9	4.4	48.4	6.9

Source: Adapted from Statistics Canada Catalogue 61-210, Corporations And Labour Unions Act, Report 1981, Part I Corporations, Table 8.

Canadian capitalists mediated the entry of foreign capital into Canada when they were unwilling to risk their own venture capital on struggling Canadian industrial companies or when they felt that the technology of foreign corporations made them superior capital risks. In either case, Canadian merchant capital supported the entry of foreign capital into the industrial sector.[10] Other reasons which explain how and why foreign capital entered Canada will be discussed later in the chapter, but it is important to note here that the benefits accruing from foreign capital investment were usually thought to outweigh any negative impact. For example, one study discovered that U.S. controlled firms were more likely to be profitable, were more likely to possess profit stability, and were less likely to incur losses than other foreign controlled firms and Canadian controlled firms.[11]

Large payments, in the form of dividends, interest, franchise fees, management fees and research costs are made annually to non-residents by corporations operating in Canada. Of all payments made to non-residents in 1981, 37.9% were for dividends, 24.1% for interest, 12.2% for royalties, 11.4% for professional services, and 6.2% for management fees for a total of $8186.1 million.[12] American-controlled corporations paid out 62.8% of this total to non-residents. Therefore, one of the first concerns that emerges from the foreign ownership issue is the export of large sums of capital outside the country each year. So while foreign capital was initially needed as a means of economic development, the export of profits made in Canada does not help the economy. Others would argue that the problem of foreign ownership is exacerbated by the fact that profits retained in the country to enlarge equity ultimately means that profits made in Canada are used to increase the size of the foreign controlled operation in Canada. Thus *retained earnings* are used to increase the foreign presence.

During the latter 1960's and early 1970's a number of studies, including the Gray report and the Task Force on the Structure of Canadian Industry, were commissioned to examine the issue of foreign ownership.[13] An organization called the Committee For An Independent Canada was established by persons interested in politics promoting economic repatriation and economic nationalism.[14] In the early seventies, the federal government established the Foreign Investment Review Agency (FIRA) to review and approve sales and transfers of corporations involving foreign capital. The Committee For An Independent Canada disbanded in 1981 and FIRA was reorganized in 1984 to be less restrictive and was renamed Investment Canada. However, the pressures exerted by these organizations have heightened public awareness of the foreign ownership issue. The matter continues to surface in formal and informal ways and helps to keep concerns about societal autonomy in the public eye.

MANPOWER IMPORTATION

For much of Canada's history, the country experienced both a "labour drain" and a "brain drain." The industrialization of the New England states created strong employment demands in the textile and manufacturing industries in that area and led many Canadians to immigrate to the United States. Other urban opportunities that occurred elsewhere in the United States (prior to the growth of industrial opportunities in Canada) contributed to the continual drain of population to that country. Furthermore, many of Canada's best students obtained their education at prestigious educational institutions in Britain, France or the United States and frequently remained in those countries. Even people who were educated in Canada took advantage of the more varied occupational possibilities in these core countries when given job offers. The same process of temporary/permanent emigration has been experienced in athletics, entertainment, the sciences, medicine and various forms of entrepreneurship. Attracted by the challenges of "making it" in more prestigious places, Canadians such as the economist John Kenneth Galbraith, American Broadcasting Corporation's news anchorman Peter Jennings, and comedian Rich Little left the country to pursue their careers elsewhere.

The 1960's was a time of enormous change in Canadian society. The post-war industrial expansion reached its apex, universities grew rapidly and student enrollment increased dramatically. The lack of adequate manpower in Canada resulted in a government policy of liberal immigration designed to encourage skilled migration into the country. Thus university faculty, medical doctors, scientists, accountants and others willingly migrated to Canada not only from the war-ravaged countries of Europe but also, because of the stresses created by the war in Viet Nam and urban social tensions, from the United States.[15] Throughout the rest of that decade and part of the next, Canada's manpower needs were met to a significant degree by immigration which some have nicknamed the "brain swamp" and "labour swamp."

However, just as the foreign ownership issue heightened awareness of foreign capital intrusion, so it raised the question of whether to continue the policy of importing foreign labour. The resident population of young university graduates sought employment opportunities in Canada and they pressured the government to be much more restrictive in approving immigration because the doors to emigration were now closed and because young people expressed a preference to remain in Canada.[16] During the 1970's, immigration rules were tightened considerably, and were tightened still further in the early 1980's as the recession increased unemployment. Immigration regulations now require extensive advertising for available positions in Canada first and over a protracted period of time, before employment of persons from outside the country will be permitted.

Government acquiescence to public demands for restricted immigration have put to rest some of the battles and controversies of the 1970's. Yet the lack of manpower in some specialized areas and the desire to import leading people with special talents, or merely the general desire for new people with new ideas, has created a new controversy concerning somewhat inflexible exceptions to that policy which the government currently allows. Corporations, professional sports teams, arts groups, religious organizations and the scientific community, constantly struggle with the issues raised by the availability of Canadian talent, their own organizational goals, and foreign expertise that they might like to acquire. Thus, if on the one hand, it is thought that Canadian society should be self-sufficient in supplying its own manpower, public debate is often intense when others argue for a less restrictive policy.

CULTURAL PENETRATION

At the root of the question about who should be given employment priority within the society lies a fundamental defense of, and concern for, a national culture. The concept of cultural penetration suggests that more dominant core societies flood Canadian society with foreign influence against the national will and in the face of little apparent defense. While there is a real sense in which this is true, the one-way diffusion process is ironically also welcomed. For example, Canadians enjoy American movies and American entertainers. Restricting access to these "foreign" aspects of popular culture would clearly be resisted. This creates paradoxical situations such as the Canadian Radio and Television Commission trying to increase the opportunities for "Canadian" artists and production at the same time that they also increase accessibility to cable networks which bring American television into Canada.

Clearly the proximity of the United States means that American cultural influences will be strong; but cultural influences from Britain or France or even farther afield make their presence felt as well. The real issue appears to be not so much whether these foreign components of culture should be allowed into Canada but whether their presence retards the emergence of an indigenous Canadian culture. For example, in 1976, a piece of legislation (Bill C-58) was passed by Parliament that took away the financial advantages of the huge American magazine *Time*, and gave tax advantages to *Macleans*, a Canadian news magazine. After considerable debate and controversy, *Time*, which was producing a Canadian edition of their magazine with a small insert of Canadian news, was dealt a severe setback when the government no longer allowed Canadian advertisers to deduct their costs of advertising in *Time*. This in effect channeled those advertising dollars toward the struggling Canadian magazine, and helped it become a viable operation. While some hurtled accusations of "dictatorship" and claimed loss of freedoms to the government, the government responded that *Time* was certainly still available for purchase in Canada in its American edition, but that it was important that Canadians should see themselves and others through their own eyes rather than through those of reporters and editors representing other societies with different agendas.[17]

Similar government policy has been established to encourage other aspects of Canadian culture. For example, symphony orchestras receiving federal grants (which are usually required for fiscal survival) must play a proportion of "Canadian" music and use "Canadian" artists in order to retain their funding. Thus while some complain that Canadian composers do not even vaguely compare with Beethoven or Bach ("so why must we listen to Canadian music"), others argue that unless Canadians give their own composers a chance, creative talent will be stifled within the society and Canadian culture will never be developed.

These are but a few examples of a counter-offensive that has become a trademark of Canadian soceity; i.e., government intervention even in the field of the arts and popular culture to strengthen Canadian culture in the face of foreign influence. This intervention, which has varied among different federal governments, generally focusses on increasing Canadian content. Whether it deals with the labour component in the manufacture of an automobile or the number of Canadian records played on a radio station, *Canadian content* refers to improving the proportion of Canadian participation in an activity. Even though government guidelines or regulations contain an element of forced choice which is obviously controversial, there is a long historical precedent for, and public acceptance of, this kind of intervention to maintain a significant Canadian cultural presence.

It is true that Canadian culture has traditionally been weak and poorly organized. Attempts to change this perpetual condition have focussed on internal measures to improve cultural productivity. These internal measures, however, are largely a response to the external cultural influences of other societies (particularly the United States), which are viewed as threatening to societal autonomy.[18]

Factors Constraining Self-Determination

The historical causes of dependency within Canadian society can be located in its strong linkages with core societies. As a young and expanding society possessing few indigenous traditions, Canadian society has endured repeated struggles while forging its own independence against rather formidable odds. In spite of trying to be the centre of its own universe, Canadian society is continually pulled like a satellite into the gravitational orbit of more dominant societies. Rocher notes that such satellitic status makes a society peripheral, unbalanced and inhibited.[19] Decisions made elsewhere and over which it has few controls impinge on the society. Efforts to exert controls are, at best, only partially effective, and feelings persist that the satellite society is inferior to the real centres of power and influence. Canadians repeatedly struggle with these feelings but the question is, what factors perpetuate this subordinate status? Four factors sustaining this dependency will be discussed.

THE ERA OF THE AMERICAN EMPIRE
It has already been suggested that Canada's relationship with core societies started with old-style colonialism through France and Britain and has proceeded to a neo-colonialism in its ties with the United States. What all three of these countries have in common is

a sequence of years in which they were a dominant global force. The concept of *empire* suggests groups of nations, people, states or territories united under the direction of a dominant power.[20] Throughout history, groups of states have been occasionally united under the influence of a more dominant state either through direct administrative and military subordination and/or through loose allegiances and mercantile ties. The Roman Empire, for example, tied a vast territory together through a common language, technological leadership, military strength, mercantile coordination, and rule of the seas. Similarly, the French settlement around the St. Lawrence River was part of an expansion of military influence and mercantile strength that saw France establish colonial ties all over the new world. Colonials taught indigenous peoples their language and drew their marketable products into the empire economy.

The British also experienced an era of empire expansion and influence that went far beyond their small island territory. With a strong naval and mercantile fleet they "ruled the waves" and the territories beyond them. The decline of the British empire has been followed by the rise of the American empire whose military, industrial and technological strength has made it a dominant global power, and, directly or indirectly, has brought much of the world under its influence. While some would label this influence imperialistic control, others note that the absence of absolute power requires the United States to negotiate with lesser states.

All empires have a core society that establishes and sustains directions of influence. The language of the core society becomes the major vehicle of communication among all societies within the empire. It dispatches its members to teach and train societies under its influence technologies and skills that will improve their productivity. It attracts promising leaders from other societies to be trained in its schools and absorb its culture. Through its technology and industry, it establishes interdependencies with other societies that provide markets or desired resources or products. Its marketing apparatus fosters the widespread distribution of its goods and its culture.

While some would argue that the American empire has begun to go into eclipse, there is no doubt that the United States is presently a core society. It has absorbed the best technologies developed elsewhere and promises prestige and handsome financial rewards to scientists, entertainers, athletes, and other leaders in their fields who participate in that society. As a centre of capital control, decisions made in the United States automatically affect other societies. Promising students from abroad are attracted to American educational institutions; these students then return to their own society as decision-makers and fre-

quently take American culture back with them. The distribution network is effective and elaborate, and American manufactured products
are available in many countries — a process known as *cocacolonization*.[21]
American influence is currently present throughout much of the world
and it is particularly strong in Canada because of the geographic proximity of the two countries.

It is important to stress the current position of the United States as a
dominant *world* power lest it be assumed that American influence is a
phenomenon unique to Canada. For example, one estimate is that on
the average, 30% of television programming in all industrialized countries is American, and 90% of the programming in developing nations is
American.[22] American cultural influence through books, magazines and
entertainers is intertwined with American capital, and technological and
military influence. American presidential elections or American space
launches are as newsworthy in Sweden and Germany as they are in
Canada. While the current global influence of the United States is
virtually a universal factor, Canadian society, for a variety of reasons,
engenders weak resistance to American economic and cultural penetration.

CONTINENTALISM

The presence of a global power (e.g., the United States) at one's border
might be considered a factor of special importance. It is natural for
bordering nations to establish both formal and informal patterns of
interaction over common interests. Californians love Banff in the
summer while Ontarians love Florida in the winter. Wheat farmers in
Kansas and Saskatchewan share common technologies and work styles.
Religious groups interact across the border sometimes with common
organizations.[23] Leisure organizations like Shriners, Masons and even
barbershop singing groups cross the borders. Americans and Canadians
both drive the same brands of cars. Fast-food franchises are similar and
sport leagues cross the border. There are many other examples of the
on-going integration of the two societies on the North American
continent.[24]

And yet the relationship is not one of equal sharing. Canadians are
frequently appalled at American ignorance of Canada even though, in
the global scheme of things, Canada is relatively unimportant. Canadian
society is affected by political and economic policies established in
Washington where decision-makers are frequently uninformed or minimize Canadian concerns. For example, the decision to allow interest
rates to rise in the United States forces interest rates to rise even higher
in Canada because of Canadian dependence on U.S. money markets. If
cars made in Canada to be sold in the United States (under the Autopact

Agreement) are not in demand in the U.S., unemployment in Canada results. A metaphor which has frequently been used to describe the relationship is that of the mouse and the elephant. The mouse (Canada) has an existence which is independent of the elephant (the United States), but must be ever alert to the movement of the elephant because virtually every move affects the mouse.

The existence of a common economic system, a common language (except for French), and as a consequence of the Cold War, common defense interests all contribute to greater continentalism. Some even foresee the possibility of free trade such as currently exists among members of the European Economic Community. A Senate committee found that 60% of Canadians preferred American television shows, and, even in Canadian newspapers, read not only hard news stories about the United States but human interest stories as well.[25]

Perhaps the newest form of integration between the two countries is the large-scale investment of Canadian capital in the United States. While historically Canadians have been reluctant to invest in unpredictable and innovative Canadian industry, and instead made portfolio investments in the United States, recent trends have seen direct Canadian investments in U.S. property and real estate developments such as shopping centres and office towers.[26] Because of limitations in the Canadian economy and the desire for corporate growth, Canadian subsidiaries in the U.S. have become quite active in cities like Minneapolis, Denver, and growth areas in the American south. For example, Montreal-based Northern Telecom expanded into the United States because it already controlled 70% of the Canadian market and was looking for new productivity gains. While such investments are sizeable, they are certainly not of the proportional magnitude of American capital flow into Canada. Nevertheless, it illustrates another aspect of continental integration.

Although continentalism, in many ways, is inevitable, it repeatedly raises the question of autonomy for a society unsure of its independence. In order to facilitate the east-west interaction across Canada rather than the north-south interaction which promotes continentalism, government intervention has again been a frequently-used vehicle, particularly in earlier stages of Canadian development. For example, the Canadian Broadcasting Corporation was established by the government with the explicit mandate to foster greater national understanding and knowledge of matters of general societal interest. Railroads (C.N.R./ Via Rail) and airlines (Air Canada) also represent a government mandate to facilitate communication within the society. Taking a *key sector approach* to the issue of foreign control, further government intrusions have been resisted as private enterprise activities in financial institutions, transportation and communications deemed vital to internal

Advertisements that Tell a Story

"Now . . . For your convenience. Open a U.S. Dollar Savings Account Here Today"
— *sign in the window of a trust company*

"Celebrate Canada Week, February 10-17"
— *ad in a Florida newspaper*

"This advertisement is directed to Canadian citizens and permanent residents only"
— *employment notice in the bulletin of a professional association*

"The Royal Visit . . . Get Your Souvenir Pictorial Book Today"
— *sign in a book shop*

"Here is a great buy this week. Canada No. 1 California tomatoes $1.52 a kilogram."
— *radio station ad*

unity have all been Canadian-owned. At the same time, however, public agencies such as the National Energy Board, the Canadian Radio-Television Commission, or the National Film Board have been established to ensure a significant Canadian presence in areas where countervailing influences were viewed as necessary to thwart continentalist pressures. In spite of these efforts, continentalism remains a perpetual dynamic within Canada and one with which the society must cope.

THE MULTI-NATIONAL CORPORATION

The third factor accentuating the issue of autonomy for Canadian society has been the emergence of huge multi-national corporations. Committed to profit and to their own expansion, these corporations cross national boundaries and make decisions that affect the economies and standard of living in whichever countries they operate. Multi-nationals, with their conglomerates and holding companies, effectively challenge the nation-state as the type of social organization most characteristic of the post-industrial world. Their capital growth, which expands assets and profits, facilitates the growth of power which can be expressed by providing employment and handsome benefits to employees as a reward for loyalty. The primary advantage of this form of organization is that the home office of the parent company is able to manipulate its resources from country to country in order to maximize its net gain. The nation-state attempts to establish the rules whereby it can control the multi-national operation in that country, but the fact that multi-nationals can transfer their resources to other, more coopera-tive countries, considerably reduces the control of the nation-state.[27] Thus for our purposes, the significant fact about multi-national corpo-rations is that they are *transnational*; i.e., they operate within national boundaries but follow an ethic in which profit transcends national concerns.

What are some of the ways a multi-national corporation can exer-cise its unique flexibility? It can move its capital or use its borrowing power to establish new ventures where local operations would be under-capitalized. It can use the profits generated in one country to subsidize an operation in another country. It can move its own pool of skilled labour or management to new locations. It can bargain with governments competing against each other for the establishment or expansion of new operations. More specifically, through the use of subsidiaries, the parent company can use its massive resources to reduce or destroy competition by underpricing other domestic operations or by purchasing the products of subsidiaries below market value while domestic competitors must purchase the product at market cost.[28] Because the multi-national is transnational, it can create a book loss in one country in order to reduce taxes there and shift funds and profits to a more favourable location. Thus, the desire of political units to retain or acquire the capital and technology of the corporation and the ensuing employment benefits for its citizens, leads to a general acquiescence by the nation state to corporate demands and needs. Some view these corporations as the newest form of imperialism while others see them as the most practical solution to world order because of the present plurality of many small interdependent nation states.[29] The 300 *Hypothesis* predicts that the global system of the future will be domi-nated by approximately 300 giant enterprises.[30] Regardless of the number of these corporations, it is clear that they have a power which threatens the autonony of, and sense of control by, national societies.

It is not surprising that, given the strength of the American eco-nomic empire, many of these multi-national corporations are Ameri-can. Of the 650 largest industrial corporations in the world, 358 are American.[31] Furthermore, given continentalist pressures, it is not sur-prising that 75% of the 194 dominant corporations in the American economy have between them a total of 391 subsidiaries in Canada. Of the 103 dominant manufacturing corporations in the United States 100 have Canadian subsidiaries, though again, not one each but a total of 304 subsidiaries. In addition, 56% of the dominant corporations in Canada are interlocked with dominant corporations in the United

States.[32] For Canada, then, multi-national corporations are largely U.S. based.

What problems do the multi-national corporations raise for Canadian society? One problem is the tendency towards *truncation*, i.e., a subsidiary seldom performs all the major functions which a major corporation requires for its operation. For example, scientific research, commonly referred to as R & D (research and development), or marketing are operations that are vital to the existence of the subsidiary but that are often centralized in one country by the parent firm. While the branch plant may provide employment for residents of Canada, truncation contributes to the technology gap and professionalization gap by minimizing the demand for such trained personnel in Canada. For example, a multi-national American-based tire company would more likely locate its research operation in the United States closer to its head office. Truncation might be tolerated in the early stages of a subsidiary's development, but once it becomes established, truncation perpetuates restricted professional employment growth in Canada.

Another problem with the multi-national corporation is that the government of the home office may attempt to put controls on the corporation's operations regardless of where it operates. This control is known as *extraterritoriality*.[33] While an internationally operating corporation may have no single national allegiance, its officers may be bound by regulations of their own country which can interfere with the interests of the country of the subsidiary. Several years ago the United States invoked a law called the *Trading With The Enemy Act* in an attempt to block the sale of Canadian-made locomotives to Cuba (the Montreal firm manufacturing the locomotives was owned by a majority shareholder corporation in New Jersey). While the sale eventually went through, this is an example of how jobs and general industrial expansion can be thwarted by an extension of the laws of foreign countries.

A third problem with multi-nationals is that Canadian subsidiaries may be prevented from increasing their productivity because they are prohibited from seeking export markets. Known as *export blocking*, the parent firm may not allow the subsidiary to compete for foreign contracts because either the parent firm or another of its subsidiaries does not want competition in a market that it also wants to enter. Given the fact that increased exports mean more jobs in Canada, lost exports mean lost jobs.

The federal government has sought to counter the slipperiness of multi-nationals not only by creating rules and regulations, but also by establishing incentives. One such incentive is the negotiation of a *Canadian content component* in certain contracts; i.e., we will buy your product if you use a certain percentage of Canadian labour or use materials produced in the country. A second method is to give *interest subsidies* to purchasers of Canadian products. The sale of 825 subway cars made by Bombardier in Montreal to New York City was successful largely because the Canadian government offered financing to New York at interest rates which were well below the prevailing prime rate. A related method used is to require any major Canadian project receiving federal financial support to maintain a certain level of Canadian-made materials and/or labour. This is known as *industrial offsets* because it gives specialized contracts to foreign companies with the proviso that the company turn other aspects of its business into Canadian production. Ironically, the sale of subway cars to New York was subject to a U.S. "Buy American" law which resulted in Bombardier establishing a subsidiary in Vermont.

One other method of controlling multi-nationals, which is currently under consideration, is a *unitary tax* that minimizes the advantages of bookkeeping shifts practiced by multi-nationals. The government determines what percentage of a company's business is done in its territory and then taxes the company based on that percentage of the parent company's worldwide profits. In all of these methods, the goal is to exert some control, in the national interest, over the adverse effects of the practices of multi-national corporations.

A fourth problem multi-nationals present to a society is that they often move their personnel between countries in response to the personnel requirements of the corporate structure. Transfers in and out of various countries is part of the corporate mentality of loyalty and devotion to the corporation. In her research, Levitt found that some Canadians were promoted through the ranks to managerial positions in subsidiaries around the world.[34] House, on the other hand, found that petroleum multi-nationals have tried to "Canadianize" their subsidiaries' management in this country as much as possible.[35] The point is that persons working for multinationals are likely to be good corporate employees who find no objections to the nature of their corporate structure as long as they are treated well. Thus, large corporations that operate transnationally establish their own set of loyalties which may or may not be in tune with national concerns and societal goals.[36]

A final dilemma presented to national societies by multi-nationals is their tendency to contribute to the homogenization of culture. The Gray Report speaks of the subsidiary as a "continuous transmission belt" of culture in general.[37] Examining the new values, beliefs, and other influences experienced by the city of Galt, Ontario, Perry discovered a "subculture of subsidiaries."[38] The duplication of products and commercials (especially advertising jingles), for example, contributes to cultural similarity. Why this has occurred will be clarified in the next section.

RELATIVELY SMALL POPULATION

The impact of continentalism and international corporatism is directly related to the fact that Canada has a population which is only one-tenth the size of the United States and which is dispersed throughout vast territory. This fact has produced collective feelings of comparative weakness in the presence of large scale capital, bigger organizations, and greater diversity and specialization in the society to the south. These feelings have left many groups open to the support of linkage with American organizations, and also makes foreign penetration that much easier.

At the economic level, the relatively small Canadian population means a small domestic market in which economies of scale sometimes cannot be practiced. Small Canadian industrial operations struggled to compete with American industries importing into Canada until the federal government approved the establishment of a *protective tariff* in 1879.[39] Regrettably, the establishment of a protective tariff did little to stimulate Canadian investment in the manufacturing sector. Canadian capitalists were reluctant to invest in relatively inefficient Canadian industries, and favoured investment in the finance, transportation and utility sectors of the economy. This left the door open for foreign capital to establish manufacturing *branch plants* in Canada which brought with them their proven product lines, technology, and experience. The protective tariff ensured that foreign corporations would have to service their Canadian market, through Canadian plants, to turn out product lines identical to those in the United States. This is known as the *miniature replica effect.*

Operating on a smaller scale because of the smaller domestic market, and insulated from competition because of the tariff walls, Canadian branch plants' production costs were higher than those of their American parents. However, the tariff gave Canadian producers an additional margin (the tariff charge), by which their product's price could be increased and yet still be competitive. Canadians, then, were likely to pay more for products identical to those produced in the United States; moreover, surplus products could not enter the world market because of these higher prices. But what was provided by the branch plants was employment for Canadians in the industrial sector which, as we have seen, became foreign owned with the agreement of indigenous capital.[40] In this context, Clement has referred to Canada as "a mature branch plant society."

The availability of similar products in both Canada and the United States helps to support cultural homogeneity. Smaller scale Canadian operations in the economic sector, or in social organizations or leisure activities, for example, frequently look to larger enterprises in the United States for cooperation in their mutual concerns. Emulating or modifying American procedures is frequently practiced in many sectors of society, and formal or informal ties are maintained. More than that, the branch plant organizational structure produces a *branch plant mentality* in which initiative, ambition and creativity is deferred to the more dominant society.[41]

The point of identifying the most critical factors constraining self-determination has not been to lay blame or even to determine the level of independence that is practical or desirable. But each of these factors represent a relatively enduring phenomenon which suggests that their influence will persist and serve as the basis for repeated reflection and conflict in the years ahead.

Foreign Influence Reconsidered

The extent to which foreign influence is problematic for Canadian society is open to much debate. While, occasionally, nationalist arguments provoke widespread support, the majority of Canadians have accepted the standard of living that has come with at least partial continental integration. Cuneo found that underprivileged groups (e.g., those with low education, low family income, older people, residents of Atlantic Canada) were most likely to support continentalism because they presumed they had nothing to gain by a change.[42] On the other hand, those clamouring most strongly for economic and cultural nationalism seemed to be those with the most to gain (e.g., the middle class). It is more than coincidental that the widest public concern for societal autonomy has come during the 1960's and 1970's when young university-educated persons were entering the workforce. The growth of the nationalist spirit will be examined more carefully in Chapter 7, but it should be noted that the issue of societal autonomy has no agreed-upon agenda or method of implementation; instead it serves as background matter in a variety of societal concerns.

Some have argued that criticizing foreign capital does not get at the root of the matter because corporations do not make decisions on the basis of the national good but, rather, on the basis of profit.[43] Others argue that the repatriation of the economy has been made a faulty panacea for all ills.[44] Still others have argued that integration theory is wrong to assert that sufficient interaction will lead to the breakdown of national attributes and the creation of a single polity. Instead, when two units interact with uneven capacity, a self-regulator in the smaller nation may inhibit the integrative process.[45] In fact, what we see in Canadian-American relations is just such a partial integration. One analyst has described Canadian-American relations as a *disparate dyad* because in spite of the inequality, Canada's goal has been to rearrange the nature of the relationship rather than terminate it, for termination would be unrealistic.[46] Thus, it could be argued that in continually seeking to control the nature of that relationship, Canadian society *is* expressing its autonomy.

The objective struggle to maintain that precarious balance between dependency and independence has had its subjective effects. The *cumulative impact hypothesis* suggests that all of the debate and controversy, as well as the realities engendered by Canada's marginal position over so many years, has produced a feeling of society inferiority.[47] These feelings reveal themselves in the mixed emotions of envy and admiration toward more dominant societies which serve as models, and also in the expression of hostility and antagonism in the struggle against subordination.

It is impossible to understand Canadian society without knowing of this perpetual search for autonomy. In fact, S.D. Clark has argued that in struggling to discover itself, the society has at least attempted to discover what it is not by distinguishing itself from American society.[48] This has resulted in a paranoiac form of nationalism based on a sense of persecution and powerlessness in which the positive content is lacking. But it is primarily this quest for control over its own destiny, by a society existing in a context in which that objective is extremely difficult, that ultimately brings positive content to the societal sense of independence. It is for this reason that the issue of autonomy continues as a vibrant societal concern.

Further Exploration

1. Some people think that one way out of the continentalism dilemma in Canadian society is to support economic continentalism alongside cultural nationalism. Assess the merits and problems of this position.
2. What staples are characteristic of your province? How do those staples tie your province into the world system?
3. Take a position on the foreign ownership question. Defend your position with whatever examples you can find and anticipate criticisms from people who hold other positions on the same issue.

Selected Readings

John Hutcheson, *Dominance and Dependency*, (Toronto: McClelland and Stewart, 1978).

Wallace Clement, *Continental Corporate Power*, (Toronto: McClelland and Stewart, 1977).

Landmark Canadian Document II

The Symons Report On Canadian Studies

Document: *To Know Ourselves: The Report of the Commission On Canadian Studies*, Vol. I and II. Ottawa: Association of Universities and Colleges of Canada, 1975. Volume III was published in 1984.

Author: Thomas H.B. Symons, former President of Trent University

Issue: A general feeling exists that Canadians are rather ignorant of their own country and society. Are Canadian educational institutions providing students with adequate knowledge of the elements of their own society?

Quotation: "A curriculum in this country that does not help Canadians in some way to understand the physical and social environment that they live and work in . . . cannot be justified in either academic or practical terms." (p. 13)

Context: Canadian universities experienced unprecedented growth during the 1960's. Undergraduate enrollment tripled during the decade and graduate enrollment increased six-fold. As disciplines, departments, and specialized courses grew, the lack of Canadian materials, or the ignorance of the existence of such materials meant that students were using the literature of other societies. For example, in sociology, the lack of undergraduate textbooks meant that students usually used American textbooks where features of American society were discussed (e.g., black-white relations), and little or nothing was said about the main features of Canadian society (e.g., French-English relations). Furthermore, expanded staffing needs in most disciplines meant that faculty had to be recruited outside of Canada, and these professors frequently possessed minimal knowledge of Canada. University administrators were also criticized for giving preference to the established areas of study and minimizing Canadian aspects (e.g., English literature might be considered more important than Canadian literature).

In addition to these factors within the university, it also needs to be pointed out that emphasis on the need for Canadian studies was part of the national mood of the late 1960's and early 1970's. Concern over the search for a national identity was linked with apprehensiveness over excessive foreign influence in many areas of national life from economic affairs to culture.

Procedure: At its annual meeting in Winnipeg in 1970, the Association of Universities and Colleges of Canada appointed a Commission On Canadian Studies which began its work in 1972. Hearings were held in more than 40 communities and the Commission received more than 1,000 briefs and over 30,000 letters. Public interest was high and the response was massive. Many universities, professional societies, and associations set up committies to study the issues and make recommendations to the Commission.

The Report: Instead of arguing that the need for Canadian Studies was linked to the need for a demonstration of patriotism, the Commission adopted a rationale based on the need for self-understanding as reflected in Plato's dictum "Know Thyself." The quest for self-knowledge was understood to be a basic societal need and, in its assessments, the Commission was looking for an "awareness factor" or "sensitivity" to the Canadian context or perspective within that acitivity.

The Report confirmed the suspicions of many, that Canadian Studies was being neglected in fields as diverse as art history, literature, economics, folklore, sociology, and the performing arts. They also determined that more government and private donor support was needed for Canadian archives development and audio-visual resources, and even for the promotion of Canadian Studies abroad.

The Report argued that universities should not only be concerned with the generation of knowledge but with service to the community that supported it. Since young people were interested in learning more about Canada, educational institutions should become actively involved in fostering this goal. It was also felt that new research emphasis should be given to studying those problems which are uniquely Canadian (e.g., environmental, social) and that assumptions and methodologies should be critically investigated before borrowing them from other countries. Persons training for the professions (e.g., architecture, business, etc.) should also be assisted to relate their craft more directly to the needs and uniqueness of their own society.

Debate: In retrospect, it may appear that knowing more about your country is a "motherhood" issue with which few would disagree. However, other issues lurked in the background generating considerable controversy. Some argued that knowledge and the principles of science were universal and that what was being advocated was academic nationalism.

Therefore, to talk about a Canadian approach to science was nonsensical. Others argued that the Canadianization of the university was a shallow mask for anti-Americanism among those caught up in the anti-Vietnam War mood and reacting to the sudden influx of American personnel and other influences. Still others argued that the real issue was excellence in the universities and promoting Canadian things because they were Canadian (e.g., W.O. Mitchell rather than Shakespeare) was very ethnocentric.

Assessment: One measure of the impact of the work of the Commission is that many changes in assumptions and perspectives have already taken place so that a current reading of some parts of the Report has an almost unbelievable ring to it. For example, in most fields Canadian texts and Canadian materials are much more readily available than they were in 1970. The Commission was largely successful in legitimating the need for "Canadian content" in the public mind and in university structures, whether in the performing arts, geography, or sociology. Other aspects of the Report still await more concrete action and in some cases still arouse debate.

The Report has been faulted for its dependence on impressionistic observations and some erroneous assumptions. This may be due to the lack of hard data to more accurately trace the cause and extent of Canadian Studies neglect. It has also been criticized for failing to show how the historical structures and context of Canadian universities (e.g., the poor facilities for graduate studies that existed in Canada for years, the heavy historic orientation to British academia, etc.), and the lack of university planning in Canada created the situation that produced the problems which the Report described. In spite of these and other criticisms, there is no doubt that the Report has provided a benchmark or touchstone for evaluating the extent to which research is being generated and students are being assisted to learn more about their own society.

Further Reading: An abridged version of the Symons Report, published in 1978 by the Book and Periodical Development Council, is available. Reviews of the Report appear in many disciplinary periodicals in the time period immediately following the appearance of the Report. Six reviews (one by a sociologist) expressing a range of sentiments are contained in the *Journal of Canadian Studies*, 11 (1976) and 12 (1977). Also see "What did Symons say? A retrospective look at the Commission on Canadian Studies," *Canadian Issues*, 2 (1977), 1.

ENDNOTES

[1]See Immanuel Wallerstein, *The Modern World System*, (New York: Academic Press, 1976) and Daniel Chirot, *Social Change In The Twentieth Century* (New York: Harcourt, Brace, and Jovanovich, 1977) for discussions of world systems theory. For its adaptation to Canada, cf. Lorna R. Marsden and Edward B. Harvey, *Fragile Federation: Social Change In Canada* (Toronto: McGraw Hill Ryerson, 1979).

[2]H.A. Innis, *The Fur Trade In Canada* (Toronto: University of Toronto Press, 1930); *The Cod Fisheries* (Toronto: University of Toronto Press, 1940); *Problems of Staple Production In Canada* (Toronto: Ryerson Press, 1933).

[3]S.D. Clark, *The Social Development Of Canada* (Toronto: University of Toronto Press, 1942).

[4]*Minetown, Milltown, Railtown: Life In Canadian Communities Of A Single Industry* (Toronto: University of Toronto Press, 1971). For a further discussion of some of the problems produced for human populations by big industry in small towns, see Roy T. Bowles, ed., *Little Communities And Big Industries: Studies In The Social Impact Of Canadian Resource Extraction* (Toronto: Butterworths, 1982).

[5]For illustrations of these problems in the mining industry, see Wallace Clement, *Hardrock Mining: Industrial Relations And Technological Change At Inco* (Toronto: McClelland and Stewart, 1980).

[6]Donald G. Paterson, *British Direct Investment In Canada, 1890-1914* (Toronto: University of Toronto Press, 1983).

[7]Richard Starks, *Industry In Decline* (Toronto: James Lorimer, 1978), p. 71.

[8]*Corporations and Labour Unions Act Report for 1981*, Part I Corporations, Statistics Canada Catalogue #61-210, p. 21.

[9]The data reported here are taken from the above-named report.

[10]This argument can be found in a number of places including Patricia Marchak, *In Whose Interests: An Essay On Multinational Corporation In A Canadian Context* (Toronto: McClelland and Stewart, 1979), p. 101; Wallace Clement, *Continental Corporate Power* (Toronto: McClelland Stewart, 1977), p. 79; and R.J. Richardson, "Merchants Against Industry: An Empirical Study Of The Canadian Debate", *Canadian Journal of Sociology* 7(1982): 279-295, who argues that merchant capital and industrial capital merged.

[11]Daniel M. Shapiro, *Foreign And Domestic Firms In Canada* (Toronto: Butterworths, 1980), p. 74.

[12]These data were computed from *Corporations And Labour Unions Act Report for 1981, Part I Corporations*, Statistics Canada Catalogue #61-210, Table 9.

[13]M.H. Watkins, *Foreign Ownership And The Structure Of Canadian Industry*, Report of the Task Force On The Structure Of Canadian Industry, (Ottawa: Privy Council, 1968); Gray Report *Foreign Direct Investment In Canada* (Ottawa: Information Canada, 1972). See also A.E. Safarian, *Foreign Ownership Of Canadian Industry* (Toronto: McGraw Hill, 1966), and a good introductory discussion in Malcolm Levine and Christine Sylvester, *Foreign Ownership* (Toronto: General Publishing 1972).

[14]Abraham Rotstein and Gary Lax, *Independence: The Canadian Challenge* (Toronto: The Committee For An Independent Canada, 1972), and *Getting It Back: A Program For Canadian Independence* (Toronto: Clarke Irwin, 1974).

[15]See Erick Jackson, ed., *The Great Canadian Debate: Foreign Ownership* (Toronto: McClelland and Stewart, 1975).

[16] As manpower importation relates to universities, see Robin Matthews and James Steele, *The Struggle For Canadian Universities* (Toronto: New Press, 1969); as it relates to other areas, see Ian Lumsden, ed., *Close The 49th Parallel: The Americanization Of Canada* (Toronto: University of Toronto Press, 1970).

[17]Reader's Digest was initially also the target of Bill C-58 but it was exempted on the ground that it was not news-oriented. For a discussion of some of the issues in this debate, see Isaiah Litvak and Christopher Maule, *Cultural Sovereignty: The Time and Reader's Digest Case In Canada* (New York: Praeger, 1974), and M. Patricia Hindley, Gail M. Martin and Jean McNulty, *The Tangled Net: Basic Issues In Canadian Communications* (Vancouver: J.J. Douglas, 1977), Chapter 2.

[18]For a good review of the issues, see Janice L. Murray, ed., *Canadian Cultural Nationalism* (New York: New York University Press, 1977).

[19]Guy Rocher, *A General Introduction To Sociology* (Toronto: Macmillan, 1972), pp. 513-514.

[20]The concept of empire developed here has been influenced by the work of George Grant who has applied it to Canada's relationship with the United States. See his *Technology And Empire: Perspectives On North America* (Toronto: House of America, 1969) and *Lament For A Nation* (Toronto: McClelland and Stewart, 1965), p. 8. See also John Hutcheson, *Dominance And Dependency* (Toronto: McClelland and Stewart, 1978), Chapter 3.

[21]Kari Levitt, *Silent Surrender: The Multi-National Corporation In Canada* (Toronto: Macmillan, 1971), p. 112.

[22]Hindley, Martin, McNulty, *The Tangled Net*, p. 171.

[23]See Harry H. Hiller, "Continentalism And The Third Force In Religion", *Canadian Journal Of Sociology* 3 (1978): 183-207.

[24]For a good review of the issues drawing the two countries together from energy and culture to trade and the environment, see H. Edward English, ed., *Canada-United States Relations* (New York: Praeger, 1976). For two contrasting lay accounts of how Canada should relate to the United States, see D.K. Donnelly, *CanAmerican Union Now!* (Toronto: Griffin House, 1978) and Andrew Lamoire, *How They Sold Our Canada To The USA*, Second Rev. Ed., (Toronto: New Canada Publications, 1976).

[25]Report of the Special Senate Committee On Mass Media, Vol. III, 1970, p. 131.

[26]Susan Goldenberg, *Men Of Property: The Canadian Developers Who Are Buying America* (Toronto: Personal Library, 1981). At one point in the early 1980's, Oxford Development Group of Edmonton controlled about 40% of the downtown office space in Minneapolis. *Calgary Herald*, August 28, 1981.

[27]For a discussion of these points, see George Modelski, ed., *Multinational Corporations And World Order* (Beverly Hills: Sage, 1972), pp. 20-24.

[28]Patricia Marchak, *In Whose Interests*, p. 102. See also her Second Edition of *Ideological Perspectives On Canada* (Toronto: McGraw Hill Ryerson, 1981), particularly Chapter 8 expressing her pessimism about the role of multinational corporations.

[29]C.S. Burchill, "The Multi-National Corporation: An Unsolved Problem In International Relations", *Queen's Quarterly* 77(1970): 3-18.

[30]Fouad Ajani, "Corporate Giants: Some Global Social Costs", in George Modelski, ed., *Multinational Corporations And World Order*, p. 109.

[31]Patricia Marchak, *In Whose Interests*,, p. 46.

[32]Wallace Clement, *Continental Corporate Power* (Toronto: McClelland and Stewart, 1977), p. 162, 179.

[33]A.A. Fatouros, "Multi-National Enterprises And Extraterritoriality", *Journal Of Contemporary Business* 1(1972):36.

[34]Kari Levitt, *Silent Surrender*, p. 108.

[35]J.D. House, "The Social Organization of Multi-National Corporations: Canadian Subsidiaries In The Oil Industry", *Canadian Review Of Sociology And Antropology* 14(1977): 1-14.

[36]For an interesting study of seven multinational corporation in Canada, see I.A. Litvak, C.J. Maule, and R.D. Robinson, *Dual Loyalty: Canadian-U.S. Business Arrangements*. For a reverse study of Canadian multi-national corporations, see I.A. Litvak and C.J. Maule, *The Canadian Multi-Nationals* (Toronto: Butterworths, 1981). See also Ahmed Idris-Soven, and Mary K. Vaughan, eds., *The World as a Company Town* (The Hague: Mouton, 1978).

[37]*Foreign Direct Investment In Canada*, Chapter 12.

[38]Robert L. Perry, *Galt U.S.A.: The American Presence In A Canadian City* (Toronto: Maclean-Hunter, 1971), p. 36.

[39]J.H. Dales, *The Protective Tariff In Canada's Development* (Toronto: University Of Toronto Press, 1966), particularly Chapter 6.

[40]This is essentially the argument of Wallace Clement most clearly presented in his *Class Power And Property: Essays On Canadian Society* (Toronto: Methuen, 1983), Chapter 3.

[41]See Rex Lucas, *Minetown, Milltown, Railtown*, p. 338.

[42]Carlo Cuneo, "The Social Basis Of Political Continentalism In Canada", *Canadian Review Of Sociology And Anthropology* 13(1976): 55-70.

[43]See Jorge Niosi, *Canadian Capitalism: A Study Of Power In The Canadian Business Establishment* (Toronto: James Lorimer, 1981); Gary Teeple, ed., *Capitalism And The National Question In Canada* (Toronto: University Of Toronto Press, 1972).

[44]John G. Craig, "What Is A Good Corporate Citizen?", *Canadian Review Of Sociology And Antropology* 1 (1979): 181-196.

[45]Denis Stairs, "North American Continentalism: Perspectives And Policies In Canada", in David M. Cameron, ed., *Regionalism And Supranationalism* (Montreal: Institute For Research On Public Policy, 1981), p. 95.

[46]Naomi Black, "Absorptive Systems Are Impossible: The Canadian-American Relationship As A Disparate Dyad", in Andrew Axline et. al.,

Continental Community: Independence And Integration In North America (Toronto: McClelland and Stewart, 1974), pp. 92-108.

[47]Rocher uses both marginality and ambivalence to describe the relationship and feelings of the colonized for the colonizers. *A General Introduction To Sociology*, Chapter 14.

[48]"Canada And Her Great Neighbor", *Canadian Review Of Sociology And Anthropology* 1(1964): 197. Glen Frankfurter has argued that English speaking Canadians created an imaginary ideal Britain to which they could be loyal as a means of distinguishing themselves from the United States. *Baneful Domination*, (Toronto: Longmans, 1971).

3 The Issue of Inequality

Canapress Photo Service

"Many Canadians are reluctant to admit that their country has a class structure. . . . But this does not dismiss the other evidence of the class division of the population which exists in terms of inequality of wealth, opportunity and social recognition. These barriers are not the horizontal ones of geographical regions or distinctive ethnic cultures but the vertical ones of a socio-economic hierarchy."

— Leonard C. Marsh, one of Canada's first social researchers, in his classic study *Canadians In and Out of Work* (1940:403).

IT HAS NOW BEEN ESTABLISHED that a major dilemma for Canadian society is how to deal with *external* forces that impinge on the society. As a nation, Canada is part of intricate global power relationships that affect everyday life in the society. This chapter looks at the differential power relationships that exist *within* the society, for many of the conflicts and issues which occur within Canada reflect the inequality that exists among its residents.

There are differing degrees of wealth, power, and prestige present in every society. This suggests that the phenomenon of ranking is a common occurrence. Sociologists refer to a society that possesses either a formal or informal hierarchical gradation of persons as a *stratified society*. A geologist may study how subsurface layers of sediment and rock combine to produce relatively enduring strata. Similarly, a social scientist can explore how the dimensions of ranking evolve within a society to produce a system of *social stratification*.

The study of Canada as a stratified society is important for two reasons. First, the notion of human equality is deeply imbedded in the ideology of modern Western democracies. Even so, we may not always be certain as to what equality means, and our everyday experiences make us realize that people are not equal in the roles that they play, in the responsibility and capabilities that they have, or in the rewards that they obtain. Consequently, whether we like it or not, inequality does exist, and we must measure its reality against our ideals. Secondly, inequality is real in its consequences. Greater responsibilities and capabilities, and greater rewards are intimately related to power and control, and the absence of such responsibilities and rewards indicates very little control. Therefore, by analyzing the structure and consequences of ranking within Canadian society, the tensions and struggles between different groups within the society can be illuminated. Also, because ranking is so closely tied to the work world, life chances, and the quality of life of each member of the society, it is a fundamental base from which to understand that society.

Perspectives on Inequality

What do a Rolls Royce, a house on the wrong side of the tracks, an annual winter vacation in the Caribbean, unemployment, a boarding school education, and a minimal hourly wage have in common? They are all symbols of social inequality. When these distinctions are added to our own perceptions of what qualities are preferred and honoured in a society, we become aware of vast differences that exist among people in terms of the rewards — money, respect, or influence — which a society may offer.

There are two basic explanations as to why inequality exists: the functional approach and the conflict approach.[1] The functional approach suggests that a stratified society is not only natural but it is inevitable given the differential rewards and opportunities found within the society. The key notion here is that people attain the class position they deserve. In other words, individual merit or achievement explains why differences in salaries or prestige are generated. Inequality is viewed as a motivating factor in serving the functional needs of a society.

Criticisms of the functional view suggest that inequality is not so much natural as it is traditional or even hereditary. Merit or achievement is always qualified by where you start out. If you are born into a home with an unemployed father, living in low-cost housing, and are surrounded by family and friends who have a pessimistic view of the world, how can you be faulted if you have little ambition or feel that the odds against which you struggle are too formidable? Compare such a person to one who has parents who are both professionals, who own property, and who inculcate values of optimism and advancement. Do the two persons have an equal chance to attain the position they deserve? What about people who have not earned their substantial rewards and yet have inherited large sums of money? Are janitors paid less than movie stars because they are really less important to the functioning of a society? In sum, the functional view more or less justifies the inequality that already exists by ignoring other factors that affect an individual's ability to respond to opportunities in the society.

While the functional approach places great emphasis on the individual, the conflict approach places its emphasis on the shared nature of inequality. Class formation occurs when people become aware of the characteristics that they share with others in a similar condition. This usually revolves around the ownership of private property or ownership of the means of production. Those who are the owners are the bourgeoisie; the non-owners are the proletariat. Members of a society become increasingly aware of which one of the two classes they belong to (i.e., class consciousness develops). The dominant ideas and beliefs in the society can be viewed as ideologies that sustain the class structure of inequality. Inevitably, according to the conflict approach, a class struggle must occur, and this struggle challenges the dominant class and its exploitation of the labouring class.

Criticisms of the conflict view of inequality suggest that just as the functionalist approach appears to be a rationale for inequality, so the conflict view appears to be a rationale for social change. The antagonism between these two opposing groups, as the original advocate of this perspective Karl Marx had envisioned it, has been muted by the fragmentation of the non-owners of the means of production into subgroups or class fractions which may be in opposition to each other. The large middle class present in industrial societies where corporate capitalism prevails can be viewed as being dependent on bourgeois power. This power, however, is mediated through bureaucratic structures in which the middle class provide "expert" information or technological expertise, and in which rewards are substantial enough to improve their standard of living. Finally, it can be argued that in a society where individualism prevails, many people resist adopting a perspective that requires class action or group views of class condition.

The functionalist view explains inequality on the basis of differences in *individual* abilities and tasks. The conflict view explains inequality in terms of *group* differences in power, capital accumulation, and the conflict which develops when groups struggle to preserve or rearrange their relationships. Without choosing which view is correct, or speculating as to how either position can be modified to accommodate contemporary social realities, it is important to note that they provide the framework for much of the contemporary debate about why inequality exists and what the class structure of Canadian society should be like. What evidence is there that indicates that Canadian society is a stratified society?

Indicators of Ranking

The most visible indicator of rank in everyday life is income, or wealth. You have probably established a connection between income and education and occupation. We frequently see people with little or no education in low paying occupations and, conversely, we see people with considerable education in high paying positions. The relationship between income, education and occupation is not always so directly associated — a real estate agent with a high income may not have had a high level of education. Generally speaking, however, the three dimensions of income, education, and occupation are perceived as good objective indicators of where one might be placed in a society's ranking system. What evidence is there that a differential of these qualities exist?

INCOME
Because income is directly related to purchasing power — which in turn determines standard of living and life-style — a person's income level is an important indicator of social stratification. Table 3.1 shows how income is unequally distributed within the population. If total income was distributed equally, each quintile's share in Row A would amount to 20%. The data show, however, that the lower the quintile, the lower its share of aggregate income. For example, the quintile with the lowest earnings possess only 4.5% of the aggregate income whereas if income was distributed equally, they would receive 20% of the income. Conversely, the quintile with the highest income earns 42.5% of the aggregate income — more than double their share.

TABLE 3.1 **Percentage Distribution Within Income Quintiles of Families and Unattached Individuals, Canada, 1982**

	Lowest Quintile	Second Quintile	Middle Quintile	Fourth Quintile	Highest Quintile
Income Share (A)	4.5	10.7	17.3	25.0	42.5
Source of Income (B)					
wages and salaries	25.8	52.3	72.7	81.5	77.8
self-employment	0.8	4.7	4.6	4.0	6.8
transfer payments	61.4	28.0	11.8	6.5	3.3
investments	6.5	9.0	7.0	5.6	9.7
other money income	5.5	6.0	3.9	2.4	2.4

Source: Compiled from Statistics Canada, 1982 Income Distributions, Catalogue 13-207, Tables 74 and 75.

Table 3.1 also shows that the sources of income vary. Persons in the lowest quintile receive most of their income from transfer payments; e.g., old age assistance, family subsidies and other forms of government assistance. The largest groups in this category are female single-parent families, elderly persons, and families in which the husband did not work. In contrast, the quintile with the highest income receives most of its income from employment and investments. Husband and wife families in which both spouses work made up a majority of this quintile, although it should be noted that such dual-income families are also becoming larger groups within other higher income quintiles.

The picture which emerges, then, is that of a population with a wide range of available incomes. Underemployed and unemployed persons, the elderly and lone-parent families have the lowest incomes, while dual-income, highly professional, and well-educated salary holders have the most substantial incomes.

EDUCATION

In an industrial society, differences in the level and type of education obtained by its members are a significant factor in stratification. Because industrialization demands a high level of specialized training and job expertise, education is thought to be the key to success in the system. This perception suggests that a better education leads to a better occupation, and that this should generate higher income. Accessibility to education and actual attainment, then, becomes the basis for further ranking within the society.

TABLE 3.2   **Percentage Distribution of the Population by Degrees, Certificates, and Diplomas, 1981**

	Persons 15 years and over	Persons 25-44 years old
No degree, certificate, or diploma	51.1	36.4
High school certificate only	19.4	21.0
Trade or college certificate	19.7	28.9
University certificate or degree	9.8	13.7

Source: Compiled from Statistics Canada, 1981 Catalogue 99-938, Chart 13 and Table 2.

TABLE 3.3   **Median Income for Families by Education and Sex, Canada, 1982**

Educational Level	Median Income
university degree	$45,282
post-secondary certificate/diploma	34,281
some post-secondary	32,932
some high school	28,511
0-8 years schooling	22,747
Sex	
male head of household	$31,482
female head of household	15,192

Source: Compiled from Statistics Canada, 1982 Distribution of Income, Catalogue 13-207, Table 7 and Table 12.

Table 3.2 demonstrates that there is indeed a wide range of levels of educational attainment. Twenty-nine point five percent of the population 15 years old and over have some type of post-secondary education including 9.8% with university degrees. On the other hand, 51.1% of this group have not even completed high school. We should note that these data include many young people still in the educational process, and many older people for whom educational opportunities were not as accessible when they were young. A different picture emerges if we look at the post-war "baby boomers" in the 25-44 year age group. In this group, the proportion with some post-secondary education rises dramatically to 42.6% though there is still a significant percentage (36.4%) who have not completed high school. If education is important in order to succeed in an industrial society (the number of bachelor degree holders increased by 42% from 1976-1981), then these wide ranges of educational attainment can be viewed as an important basis for hierarchical differentiation. Table 3.3 indicates that higher education is indeed linked to higher income.

OCCUPATION

Occupation is an important means of locating people within the stratification system because a person's occupation provides clues to a whole series of facts about an individual. We know that some occupations require particular kinds of credentials while others do not, and we know that remuneration and lifestyle vary from one occupation to another.

Table 3.4 displays the distribution of occupations in the Canadian population. The largest segment of the labour force is in skilled and semi-skilled rather than professional, managerial or unskilled occupations. Less than one-fifth (13.7%) of the labour force are in unskilled manual occupations. Reflecting a higher level of formal education, 8.5% of the workforce are considered professionals. The data in the table implies that differences in work modes create groupings of occupational categories with characteristics considerably different from other occupational groupings. This implication becomes even stronger when we consider subjective assessments of differences in rank.

SUBJECTIVE ASSESSMENTS

Differences in income, education and occupation in the population are not just curious artifacts; they combine to produce personal (i.e. subjective) perceptions of differences in rank. While one study demonstrated that people are frequently inaccurate in assessing their own social position, this can be explained by the tendency toward self-enhancement and the intervention of ego-effects.[2] It is, however, also clear that a consciousness of inequality and ranking within the society occurs at an early age. Baldus and Tribe have demonstrated that by Grade 6, most children have learned not only to classify people, but have developed ideas that people in the higher classes are to be esteemed while people in the lower classes are less likely to be successful in life.[3]

It has already been noted that the conflict position argues that persons who share a common class position develop a class awareness or class consciousness. Max Weber went somewhat beyond these ideas and made a distinction between class and status. Whereas class tended to be directly related to economic factors such as property, money and power, Weber added another dimension, namely *status*, in which

TABLE 3.4 **Distribution of Males and Females in the 1981 Labour Force by Socioeconomic Category and Mean Prestige Scores**

Socioeconomic Category	Percentage Labour Force			Mean Prestige Score
	Male	Female	Total	
Self-employed professionals	.7	.1	.8	78.6
Employed professionals	4.6	3.1	7.7	68.0
High-level management	3.1	.8	3.9	67.7
Semi-professionals	2.2	3.4	5.6	56.7
Technicians	1.3	.5	1.8	67.2
Middle management	2.8	1.1	3.9	64.8
Supervisors	1.9	1.4	3.3	46.3
Foremen	3.1	.2	3.3	51.0
Skilled clerical-sales-service	2.7	7.9	10.6	47.7
Skilled crafts and trades	10.7	.6	11.3	40.3
Semi-skilled clerical-sales-service	5.2	11.7	16.9	34.2
Semi-skilled manual	8.2	3.1	11.3	32.4
Unskilled clerical-sales-service	1.3	3.0	4.3	29.7
Unskilled manual	10.3	3.4	13.7	24.7
Farm labourers	1.0	.3	1.3	23.3
Farmers	.2	0	.2	40.9

Source: Compiled from 1981 Census of Canada, Statistics Canada, Catalogue 92-917, Table 1 using categories established by Peter C. Pineo, John Porter, and Hugh A. McRoberts, "The 1971 Census And The Socio-economic Classification Of Occupations," *Canadian Review of Sociology And Anthropology* 14(1977): 97-102. Mean prestige scores are adopted from Table III of this study. Some changes in occupational classifications from 1971 to 1981 may have altered these scores.

specific reference was made to the degree of prestige or honour assigned to persons in society.[4] Status then represents the end result of the ranking that takes place within a society. Grabb and Lambert found that economic considerations were dominant among Canadian perceptions of class differences. It is, however, interesting that the lower social strata were more likely to favour exclusively economic criteria whereas the upper social strata were more likely to include other factors (e.g., attitudes, lifestyle, education, and sophistication) in their perceptions of ranking differences.[5] Through their own research, Pineo, Porter, and McRoberts have produced prestige scores for occupational categories, revealing the actual existence of a ranking system in Canadian society. Table 3.4 shows the range in prestige scores from the highest, held by professionals, to the lowest, held by manual workers and labourers.

Does the evidence of inequality cited here support the functional or the conflict perspective? The answer revolves around whether people who share similar characteristics (on the dimensions of ranking which we have cited) are merely a statistical category, or whether they actually possess a group consciousness. If we just place individuals or families into categories based on income or education and view them as artificial constructs, there is no implication that they are anything more than a statistical aggregation. On the other hand, if groups of people can be perceived as sharing both economic interests and a similar view of the world, in contrast to those with different interests and world views, there then exists the possibility of social class conflict. In Canadian society, notions of class solidarity are repeatedly challenged by individual ideals of reward based upon merit and achievement. It is also true, however, that people frequently do build both loose and formal alliances with those having common economic interests.

Other Dimensions of Inequality

Three other dimensions of inequality have received considerable attention in Canadian society. They are the dimensions of gender, ethnic affiliation and region.

GENDER INEQUALITY
Table 3.4 indicates that there are major differences between occupations pursued by males and females. Women are generally found in skilled and semi-skilled, clerical, sales, and service occupations, or in jobs requiring manual labour (see also Table 3.5). Consequently, their incomes (Table 3.3) and prestige rank are lower than those of most males.[6] While women are also represented in certain categories of professional occupations, the gender-based segregation of women into certain work roles has, for the most part, continued.

Much of the work women do (e.g., housework, child rearing) is related to traditional roles of women and is not recognized as being formally a part of the labour force. In addition to carrying on their work in these roles, however, women have entered the "official" labour force in increasing numbers. This increase has come from personal choice or as a result of financial necessity. In 1971, women composed just under

TABLE 3.5 Major and Expanding Occupations for Canadian Women, 1981

Major Ten Occupations For All Women	Expanding Occupations For Women	% Increase Over 1971
secretaries and stenographers	Social workers	308
bookkeepers and accounting clerks	Computer analysts/ programmers	538
sales	University teachers	210
tellers and cashiers	Physicians/surgeons	240
waitresses and hostesses	Engineers	573
nursing	Psychologists	239
elementary/kindergarten teachers	Lawyers/ notaries	656
general office clerks	Biologists/Related	306
typists and clerk typists	Economists	422
janitors and cleaners	Agriculturalists/Related	412

Source: Adapted from Canada Update, Vol. 1, No. 5, May 1983.

35% of the labour force, but by 1981, their representation had increased to 41%. Many of these jobs had low pay, low opportunity for advancement, and frequently were also part-time or seasonal.

As more women enter the labour force, they will increasingly want employment that is personally satisfying and challenging, as well as tangibly rewarding. Table 3.5 suggests that women's participation in the labour force has expanded among more professional and skilled pursuits. The high percentages, however, mask a low starting point and so perhaps are not as significant as they seem. While the reasons for gender inequality are too complex to discuss here, it is clear that trends towards professionalization, dual income families and female-headed households have the potential of restructuring, at least to a point, traditional conceptions of women's role in the ranking system.[7]

ETHNIC INEQUALITY

Perhaps one of the most typical forms of differentiation commonly acknowledged in Canadian society is that of ethnicity. Ethnic background or ethnic affiliation is commonly used to distinguish between people. What is less commonplace is the awareness that ethnicity also has a vertical dimension; i.e., each ethnic group has its own placement in the status hierarchy.

In 1965, John Porter, a sociologist at Carleton University, published a book, entitled *The Vertical Mosaic*, which has become a Canadian classic. The underlying theme of the book was that ethnicity was intimately related to the stratification structure in Canada. The cultural mosaic of Canada was not random, argued Porter; some ethnic groups possessed a more favourable position in the society than others. Porter ties this ethnic hierarchy to the early settlement of the country and particularly to French-English relations. When the British and French first settled in Canada, there was a tendency to recreate a stratified society similar to that of the homeland. After the British defeated the French, the two culture groups existed side by side with their own individual structure of social organization; the British, however, retained the dominant position. Nevertheless, Quebec social structure remained relatively intact with doctors, lawyers, and the clergy occupying the highest levels of social standing in a largely agrarian community. British farmers also retained their rural social structure. The major hierarchical difference that could be observed was in the areas of commerce, trade, and administration where persons of British descent held overwhelming control.

With the onset of industrialization and the shift away from an agricultural economy, the entrenched English-Canadian upper class became the industrial leaders not only in English Canada, but also in Quebec. The situation was further exacerbated by the fact that the Quebec educational system emphasized classical studies and was not designed to prepare its students for technological occupations. As a result, the British were considerably overrepresented at the professional, administrative, and financial levels of the Quebec labour force. Similarly the French were overrepresented in the agricultural, primary, and unskilled occupations in that province. When the French moved to the urban areas, they formed a convenient working class or "oppressed majority" under English-Canadian control.[8] The implications of this kind of class subordination will be discussed in Chapter 5, but at this point it should be noted that, virtually from the beginning, ethnicity and class position combined in such a way that persons of French descent shared a social status which was lower than that of the English. Dofny and Rioux speak of this convergence of class consciousness and ethnic identity as ethnic class or *eth-class*.[9] This focus on ethnic differences in ranking may have ignored class differences among English-Canadians, but it did sensitize Canadians to the fact that ethnicity was an important component of the stratification of Canadian society.

The addition of other ethnic groups to the society through immigration contributed to greater complexity in ethnic stratification patterns. It is important to note that it is federal government policy that determines which ethnic groups are preferable immigrants, and a change in qualifications for admittance can significantly affect the nature of ethnic representation.[10] The government, then, determines which ethnic groups will be admitted and what work they are likely to do. For example, when East Europeans entered the country in the 1920's, they were largely rural peasants encouraged to settle remote western farm-lands (e.g., the Ukrainians in northern Saskatchewan), whereas the immigration of Asians in the 1970's consisted mostly of skilled and professional persons destined for urban centres.

TABLE 3.6 **Hierarchy of Selected Ethnic and Racial Groups in English and French Canada (Mean Rank)**

	English Canada Mean Rank	*French Canada* Mean Rank	
English Canadians	83.1	77.6	French Canadians, English Canadians
English	82.4	72.4	French
		71.0	English
Scots	75.2		
Irish	69.5	56.5	Scots
		55.2	Irish
French	60.1	51.2	Italian
Dutch	58.4		
French Canadian	56.1	49.7	Dutch
		45.3	Belgian
Belgian	49.1	40.5	German
German	48.7	40.0	Ukrainian
Ukrainian	44.3		
Poles	42.0	38.0	Poles
Greeks	39.9	33.5	Greeks
Russians	35.8	33.2	Russians
Japanese	34.7		
Chinese	33.1	27.8	Japanese
		24.9	Chinese
Negroes	25.4	23.5	Negroes

Note: Pineo lists the rankings for many other ethnic groups and only a few are listed here.

Source: Adapted from Peter Pineo, "The Social Standing of Ethnic and Racial Groupings," *Canadian Review Of Sociology And Anthropology* 14(1977):147-157.

The term used to refer to the class position at which immigrants enter a society is *entrance status*. Because of the central position of those of British descent, a status hierarchy developed with that group at the top. Table 3.6 demonstrates the existence of a hierarchy in both English and French Canada where the British and other western and northern Europeans have the highest ranks. In general, the farther the group of ethnic origin is from this European geographic area, the lower its rank. Note also that in contrast to the English, the French give equally high scores to French-Canadians and English-Canadians. This verifies the existence of a French-Canadian conception of Canada as a nation with two equal founding groups. The anglophone conception, on the other hand, seems to emphasize English dominance. In sum, immigration into Canada normally reinforces class differences previously existent among ethnic groups in which the British maintain their relatively high class standing as an ethnic group.

However, recent research has suggested that the ethnic component of stratification may now be overplayed. One argument is that ethnicity is more likely to be a determinant of status among foreign born, because among those born in Canada, ethnic status has less influence on occupational attainment. Secondly, whatever advantage the English have over the French may be greater for older persons than younger persons, and this suggests some type of convergence between generations in the two groups. Thus, ethnic stratification may already have weakened somewhat and may continue to weaken over time.[11] Another argument is that ethnic affiliation is only one factor among other factors affecting social status, and that it is a mistake to suggest that it is a fundamental cause of inequality.[12] While some change is likely to have occurred, it is not likely that ethnicity has been obliterated as a dimension of inequality.

REGIONAL INEQUALITY

Mildred Schwartz has described regionalism as a form of "institutionalized inequality" between the various parts of the Canadian entity.[13] While this inequality may be a consequence of the power relationships between regions, regions may also be viewed as a consequence of the class structure that cuts across regions.

The traditional view of regional inequality is that some regions have more people, more industry, and more resources than others, and this creates a differential in power. But this statement does not explain why inequality developed in the first place, or why it continues.

The *political economy perspective* (the view that economic power is the key to understanding the structure of a society) suggests that those who own and control the means of production, the capitalist class, enlarge their activities in those locations where profit-making potential is the greatest.[14] Profit-making, in turn, is more likely to occur in places closest to markets, adjacent to pools of cheap labour, proximate to other members of the decision-making capitalist class, and at transportation nerve centres. These factors have encouraged *centralization* and *concentration* of business activity which has helped produce regional differences in wealth. There are vast hinterland resources in outlying regions of Canada, and these resources are important to the industrial economy of central Canada and foreign markets. Extraction of these resources requires a hinterland working class whose employment cycle is heavily dependent on forces not only external to their region but also external to their class position. In other words, decisions by the economic elite, who have interests in other regions or countries, effectively control the nature and existence of resource-based jobs. Mine or mill shutdown, in deference to the escalation of activities in other regions from whom competitive pressure has been felt, or in the face of reduced market demand by industrialized regions, is the threat continually faced by workers in the resource industries.

Whenever the concentration of corporate capitalism occurs in a location, it will develop its own infrastructure of manual workers, its middle class of technocrats and managerial workers, and its capitalist class of owners with higher levels of income for that area. This development will effectively increase regional disparities in income. Poorer regions will experience a drain of their best people to regions with greater income potential. When hinterland economic activity requires participation by corporations from the centre, persons from the industrial heartland are sent to the hinterland as managers and supervisors, and this also constrains outlying regions from providing little more than manual labour with little opportunity for advancement. The centralization of capitalist activity, then, both reflects and contributes to regional class disparities.

At the descriptive level, Table 3.7 reveals that regional differences are reflected in median income levels. The Atlantic region, Quebec, and the Prairies (minus Alberta), all show median incomes below the national average. As the centre of oil and gas activity, Alberta represents an anomaly, with an inflated income level due to the demands for a necessary industrial resource. Ontario and British Columbia are both above the level of median income for the nation. The flooding of Alberta with migrants in the late 1970's and early 1980's reflected an attempt by persons, from areas where incomes were lower, to improve their economic situation. Even though this trend was short lived (it ended in 1982), most internal migration in Canada has been to the two or three metropoles (Toronto, Montreal, Vancouver). It is in these places where capital has been concentrated, cities have grown, and industrialization has been strongest.

TABLE 3.7 **Median Income for Families and Unattached Individuals by Province, 1982**

Canada	$24,041
Atlantic	20,437
Newfoundland	22,438
Prince Edward Island	19,595
Nova Scotia	20,143
New Brunswick	19,738
Quebec	22,254
Ontario	25,578
Prairie	24,618
Manitoba	21,205
Saskatchewan	22,368
Alberta	27,154
British Columbia	25,130

Source: Adapted from Statistics Canada, Distribution of 1982 Income, Catalogue 13-207, Table 2.

In general, core regions in Canada are likely to consist of highly urban industrial areas, and hinterland regions are peripheral to the core.[15] A *metropolis* is a centre of political and financial power, and it is from here that the elite engage in decision-making that affects the rest of the society. The *hinterland* essentially plays a supporting role, in relation to the metropolis, by providing raw materials and labour as needed. The relationship between the metropolis and hinterland is *symbiotic*: one needs the other, though the relationship is unbalanced. The metropolis tends to dominate and exploit the hinterland (to the benefit of the metropolis.) Regions may appear to be in opposition to one another but this is primarily because the decision-making elite of one region is in a position to exercise control over subordinate regions. Thus, behind many conceptions of superior regional power held by inferior regions, there is the perception that their fate is being controlled by sinister powers in dominant regions. For example, the farmers' movements of the West in the 1920's and 1930's were built out of regional percep-tions of elite control identified as the "Bay Street Barons" in Toronto. Similarly, Pierre Vallieres viewed francophone Quebecois as "white niggers" because of their subordination to the anglophone industrial elite.[16]

Region then can be understood not only as a demographic or

territorial relationship, but as a class relationship. Regions can be analyzed in terms of their own common class basis (e.g., the petit-bourgeois farmers of the West), in opposition to elite control that happens to be located in Central Canada (e.g., control of credit, markets, transport policy).[17] Or, regions might be examined in terms of their own class structure, so that interregional elite structures are discovered and accommodations are made between them which help to maintain the hierarchical relationship between regions. Struggles for control of a regional resource (e.g., fishing) by large extra-regional capitalist entrepreneurs in competition with regional capital or local residents also reflect the class context of regionalism.[18] The dynamics of regionalism will be the subject of Chapter 4, but it must be noted here that inequalities based on region are an important dimension of Canadian society.

Social Mobility

The suggestion that class position is not fixed, and that at least some people may experience a change in class position, can only be true when a society possesses a relatively *open class system*. In contrast, a *caste* system is found in a society where people are locked into a class position and there is virtually no opportunity to change one's social position while a member of that society. In such a society, status is *ascribed* or assigned. In more open class societies, status is *achieved*; i.e. a status position has been earned through personal efforts. Even in more open societies such as Canada, there is an ascriptiveness to status as a consequence of parental background, age, sex, race or even ethnic origin. To be born in a working class home does not prevent a person from dreaming of being president of a major corporation and perhaps even eventually attaining that goal. Unfortunately, however, the likelihood of that status transformation occurring is not great.

   Social mobility is the term used to designate movements or shifts by persons in the stratification system. In a society where the boundaries separating social strata or occupational groups are not permanently hardened, any change in social position produces what is known as social mobility. While mobility may be either upward or downward (i.e., vertical mobility), it is most common in our society to speak of upward mobility. If it occurs in one person's lifetime, it is known as *intragenerational mobility*; if it occurs between parent and child, it is known as *intergenerational mobility*. When someone changes occupations or roles that have similar status, we refer to that as *horizontal mobility*.

EDUCATION AND SOCIAL MOBILITY

In an industrial society, education is viewed as the primary mechanism for generating social mobility. Regardless of the status of your parents, it is argued, you can, through your own efforts, obtain the educational credentials to become a lawyer, or a nuclear engineer, or anything else you want to be. This view of a stratified society suggests that class position and social mobility are predominantly related to personal achievement. If this is the case, personal initiative should be the only variable quality that determines rank in the stratification system.

It has already been shown that ascribed characteristics, such as sex and ethnicity, serve to moderate tendencies for social mobility. Although education is a factor in social mobility, there are two arguments why achievement may not be considered a simple panacea for improving class or status position. The first argument is rooted in the historical position of education in Canadian society (the macro view); the second argument concerns itself with the home background of the student, and events which transpire in the schools (the micro view).

The Macro View. Based on data gathered in the 1950's, John Porter's *The Vertical Mosaic* stated that Canadians did not experience the kind of upward mobility that they should have had in the post-war period. This was largely because of a general societal failure in education.[19] The expansion of the urban labour force through industrialization in the post-war period created numerous new occupational opportunities which, argued Porter, could have led to considerable upgrading of the labour force. Post-war Canada, however, possessed a traditional and rather elitist conception of education, and because that conception encouraged advanced education for only a small number of people, social mobility was reduced. The dilemma was further accentuated by perceptions that the United States had better opportunities for advancement which led to a *brain drain* and *labour drain* of those particularly eager for upward mobility.[20]

The labour force needs that resulted found a rather quick resolution through immigration, noted Porter. When Canada needed skilled and professional people, it was much easier to import them through preferred immigration regulations (a so-called brain gain) than to insist on educational reform. Thus Canada was both donor and recipient in what has been labelled the *brain trade*.[21] The emigration of some of the most highly skilled persons, coupled with the additional demands for new skilled and professional persons, should have meant greater opportunities (i.e., upward social mobility) for the population already resident in Canada; but because of large-scale immigration, the potential for social mobility was greatly reduced. Porter conservatively estimated that between 1950 and 1960, immigrants filled 50% to 60% of the new, skilled jobs which were the result of the nation's industrial development. At that time, advanced educational opportunity was neither encouraged nor made available to everyone; the social structure remained relatively fixed as the result of *mobility deprivation*. There was more movement in and out of the stratification system than there was movement within it. Instead of immigrants entering Canada primarily at the lower social class levels and pushing the resident working class up the social strata, skilled immigrants filled the specialized needs of the work force because of the lack of preparation for mobility by the resident population.

It is important to note that Porter was *not* saying that no upward mobility occurred, or that immigrants (particularly skilled immigrants) were detrimental to Canadian society. Even though urbanization was producing a massive shift from manual to white collar occupations (i.e., from farm worker to office worker) in the Canadian labour force, this was not vertical mobility in itself. Obviously some mobility did take place once the necessary skills were acquired; but what disturbed Porter was that immigration was used as a convenient substitute for educational reform, and this substitution retarded both the demand for education and the development of fuller educational participation. In addition, a potentially dynamic social structure remained relatively static because Canada was not a "mobility-oriented society."[22]

Porter analyzed the evidence in the early 1960's just as educational change really began to occur in Canada. Throughout the 1960's and even into the 1970's university attendance increased dramatically, and post-secondary schools of technology were built. Post-secondary enrollment almost tripled by 1970 with close to 20% of the 18-24 year old age group enrolled at post-secondary institutions. In addition, the rate of increase in the number of undergraduate students was 10-15% annually and graduate enrollment increased sixfold.[23] Therefore, even though skilled and professional immigrants were still given entrance priority, the Canadian labour force was in a much better position to compete than before. In fact, by the middle of the 1970's, the interest in upward mobility and employment among Canadians produced a move to reduce immigration to its barest minimum. Nevertheless, in spite of these changes, and in spite of the fact that other factors besides education affect the extent of mobility, Porter's analysis demonstrates the importance of accessibility to advanced education and its relationship to immigration policy, both of which play influential roles in the potential of social mobility.[24]

The expansion of educational opportunities was based on the *human capital theory* that a better educated labour force would be a more productive one. Consequently, the emphasis on the last two decades has been on improving accessibility to education. It was thought that post-secondary educational institutions in particular should be conveniently located, relatively inexpensive, and more institutions should be available so that more students could be admitted. Governments poured large sums of money into educational endeavours so as to build human capital which would then have a positive effect on employment and the Gross National Product. In spite of the existing class structure, the idea was to create *equality of opportunity* so that mobility could take place.

Equal opportunity suggests that all people have an equal chance to take advantage of opportunities. In reality, by virtue of difference in family background, personal aptitudes, and personal circumstances, some people are more able than others, to take advantage of opportunities presented. The absence of *equality of condition* suggests that mobility through equal opportunity will be restricted or modified by other factors.

The Micro View. The analysis of equality of condition has resulted in a clearer picture of the factors that lead specific individuals to take advantage of educational opportunity. One perspective emphasizes the role of schools themselves (particularly junior and senior high schools), in sorting students into program streams. While such sorting is normally perceived to be done on the basis of intellectual capacity and aptitudes, research has found that the most important factor standing behind these performance criteria is family expectations. For example, if the home environment minimizes learning, that environment has a strong negative influence on academic performance. The family also exerts a significant, albeit indirect, influence on program selection in that a person's concept of his or her own ability is related to the socio-economic status of the family. Thus the role of the school in streaming students is strongly associated with family influences.[25]

Taking up where he left off at the macro level, John Porter and his associates have delved further into how the choice of higher education is related to social class. Table 3.8 shows that aspirations of Grade 12 students are highly related to the socio-economic status of the father. Fifty-one percent of those with parents of highest status aspired to go on to university and only 11% wanted to go to work. The lower the social status, the less likely it is that the students will be interested in attending university, although education is indeed viewed as a mechanism of upward mobility for some students of lower social class background. Note also that, the higher the social class, the more likely it is for parents to expect their child to obtain a higher education. The fact that at lower class levels, the work/university percentages are almost equal suggests that while for some going to work may be preferred, and may even be a necessity, for others at this level advanced education is thought to be a way out of that class position.

TABLE 3.8   **Educational Aspirations after High School of Grade 12 Students and Educational Expectations of Parents of Grade 12 Students by Socio-Economic Status of Father**

| | Socio Economic Status | | | | | |
| | I
(high) | II | III | IV | V | VI
(low) |
			(percent)			
Aspirations of Students						
go to work	11	11	15	13	24	26
graduate from university	51	42	35	36	22	24
Expectations of Parents						
expect child to go to work	4	7	14	19	28	31
expect child to go to university	64	60	53	39	29	32

Source: Adapted from M.R. Porter, J. Porter and B.R. Blishen, *Does Money Matter? Prospects For Higher Education In Ontario* (Toronto: Macmillan, 1979), Table 2.3 and 2.7.

Porter, Porter, and Blishen conclude that, at least in Ontario, the education system is reasonably meritocratic though it is modified by social class.[26] They note that the decision to embark on a path leading to university is made very early, and is more likely to be modified only among those of lower class background. The barriers to higher education are predominatly financial and cultural. Education may be the way in which some disadvantaged persons overcome their origin, but education and attainment is also the way parents transmit their status to their offspring.[27]

It has been suggested that post-war Canadian society has experienced its own quiet revolution in terms of the large numbers of people who have become middle class.[28] The conflict perspective minimizes this assertion by noting that the position of this middle class is indeed precarious, and that the middle class is only a "dressed-up" version of the proletariat. On the other hand, the functionalists are quick to accept the mobility potential of education as evidence of the meritocratic system at work. Clearly, for middle class people, education is the primary means of maintaining class position rather than the means of furthering social mobility.[29] Education, except for those in poverty or among elite groups, makes its strongest claim by mediating both the ascriptive influence of parental values and the personal role of achievement.[30] In this way, the education system helps maintain the class system as well as provide a partial means for modifying one's place in the class system.

REAL PEOPLE 3

Equality of Condition?

The students were sitting in the waiting area somewhat impatient to see the University Loans Officer. It seemed to take forever and there were lectures to attend and readings to do.

"If they don't give me a loan, I'll have to quit even though I just started," blurted out Bill to no one in particular. "My Dad got laid off and my Mother works as a waitress. How can I improve myself when they can't help?"

"Oh, quit your griping," lamented Jules. "You at least have a Dad. Nobody encourages me at all. I'm the only kid from my high school class to even think of going to University. Some of them even bet me I won't make it through the first term!"

"You guys are lucky", mumbled Carl from the corner chair, peeping from behind a magazine, "I wouldn't be here except my Dad expects me to come. The old boy could afford to pay my way . . . he's a lawyer . . . but he wants me to make it on my own. That's the only way I'll make it in the family firm."

"You make me sick . . . You and your sports car. I suppose you'll get a loan and I won't", muttered Bill. And he turned the other way.

Questions To Consider

What does each student tell us about his family background? What are their individual chances of graduating? What does this scenario reveal about prospects for upward mobility?

The stories of individuals who experience significant upward mobility frequently blind us to the fact that for the majority, class position remains rather constant. Even so, the vagaries of unemployment and technological change, or of achievement and aptitude within a capitalist system, creates some fluidity in the class system that prevents it from hardening. Improvements in the standard of living ought not to be confused with large-scale changes in class position; but they do create images of at least some mobility and thus cause the existing structure of class inequities to be more publicly acceptable.

Social Power

Stratification and inequality imply not only that some people have higher incomes and better education, or have bigger homes and fancier cars, but that with this differential in indicators of social status comes variations in power and control. Because money is a scarce resource, those who have it and use it can, directly or indirectly, control those who do not have it but need it. There is, then, a *relational* aspect to inequality where groups of people who receive more have advantage over those who have less, and can compete more successfully against them.

Power implies control over the decisions that affect other people. Power can be formalized, through positions of authority, or it can be informal, such as through ownership of property or shares. Decisions can be made by *elites*, simply defined as people in power roles. Or groups (e.g., labour unions, farmer coalitions) may attempt to participate in the decision-making process in a more *pluralist* model of decision-making.

The perspective most used in the analysis of power in Canadian society is known as *political economy*.[31] Built from the conflict model, this perspective begins with how people earn their living (the economic), and then explores the conflicting social relations that develop out of this process (the political). Some people accumulate capital (the capitalist class), others work for wages (labourers), while still others are self-employed (the petite-bourgeoisie).[32] This perspective maintains that those who possess capital hold the power, and the exercise of that power will automatically be exploitative of workers unless challenged. Studies in political economy can be either liberal or Marxist. What they all have in common is a focus on how power is used or experienced in a stratified society.

Persons at the highest levels in a stratified society can be identified as the *power elite*. In a capitalist society, they are the persons who possess capital and utilize it in a manner affecting many others in the society. The second half of Porter's *The Vertical Mosaic* established the power roles of elites in Canada, and pointed out that these elites possess similar social characteristics. Porter is able to identify elites in a variety of sectors of the society from the economic elite to the media, political and bureaucratic elite. For example, in studying the economic elite, Porter determined that in the early 1950's there were 985 men holding directorships in 170 dominant corporations, banks and insurance companies. He noted that it was largely this same group which held most of the common stock (and thus received most of the dividend income), meaning that both ownership and management were concentrated in the hands of a few individuals rather than widely dispersed to many shareholders.

The social homogeneity of this economic elite developed through a number of factors. First, members of this elite recruited internally to serve on each other's boards of directors through what is called *interlocking directorships*. Second, Porter constructed biographical sketches of this elite and discovered that family continuity was a dominant pattern. Third, many members had a university education, and many had attended the same private schools as youngsters. Fourth, persons of British descent were dominant in this group with very few persons of French-Canadian descent or Catholic affiliation included. Fifth, the economic elite socialized among themselves through memberships in private clubs and held prominent board positions in charitable organizations, educational institutions, and trade associations.

The economic elite is clearly the most fundamental segment of the elite, but Porter recognized that other elites also have important decision-making roles. The elite of organized labour had the highest proportion of foreign-born of all elites, the lowest level of education, and tended to come from working class backgrounds. The political elite and the federal bureaucratic elite were very similar in having the highest proportion of native-born, having the highest percentage with university education, and tending to be of British, Protestant, and professional backgrounds. Ontario as a region was overrepresented in this elite. The mass media elite was a smaller group in which ownership was shared among only a few families. The media in French Canada were an exception because they were independent of syndicates and chains. And lastly, Porter identifies the intellectual and religious elite — a much less homogeneous group.

Recent research has focussed more on the segments or fractions within the capitalist class. The goals of industrial capital (e.g., manufacturing) and commercial capital (e.g., mercantile/financial) have sometimes been in conflict, and these segments have sometimes sought alliances with each other. These two capitalist fractions can be further divided into Canadian and foreign capital. Using these criteria, Wallace Clement, one of Porter's students, distinguished between three types of elite; the *indigenous elite* of Canadian-controlled corporations, particularly in transportation, finance and utilities; the *comprador elite* of native-born directors and management personnel of foreign-controlled corporations operating in Canada (particularly in resources and manufacturing); and the *parasite elite*, largely outside of Canada, who control the multi-national corporations operating in Canada.

Bringing Porter's 1950's data up to 1972, Clement analyzed the corporate elite and concluded that through the growth of complex subsidiaries, the number of dominant corporations had been reduced from 170 to 113.[33] Interlocking directorships were again a dominant feature, and, of the 113 dominant corporations, there were 1,848 directorships interconnected with the Canadian Imperial Bank of

Commerce, the Bank of Montreal, the Royal Bank, the Canadian Pacific Railway, and Sun Life most closely interlocked. Significantly, 29% of this total elite of the 113 dominant corporations held 54% of all directorship positions. The integration of the Canadian elite with the American elite, and Canada's possible consolidation with the continental economy will be discussed in the next chapter; suffice it to say that Clement found that concentration of power was tighter and access into the elite was more difficult in Canada than in the United States.[34]

Another update of the Porter study by Dennis Olsen focussed on the state elite.[35] Olsen noted that the state elite composed of politicians, judges, and senior federal and provincial bureaucrats (e.g., deputy ministers) had become a large group who remained in continual interaction with each other through what Olsen called "executive federalism." Most members of this elite were from the middle class and received their mobility impetus through education. While the political and bureaucratic elite was much more open and accessible than the economic elite, they were still predominately a male group of British descent. Among members of the political elite, 58% had backgrounds in law, and one-half of the bureaucratic elite had social science degrees. Unlike members of the economic elite, however, politicians, and at least some senior level bureaucrats who are politically appointed, have relatively short careers and this reduces the degree of their elite entrenchment. Nevertheless, it is the political and bureaucratic group that makes policy decisions that are enforceable by law.

EVALUATION OF ELITISM

Some people view elitism as an inevitability. The *iron law of oligarchy* suggests that there will always be a tendency, in every society, for a small elite to dominate the masses.[36] The reason for this is that people tend to accept passively the flow of power to a few persons at the top. For believers in democracy, however, the long-term perpetuation of elite decision-making weakens general belief in equality and also reduces public participation in decisions affecting the lives of many people.

On the other hand, some argue that far too much has been made of elite control. A focus on boards of directors of corporations, for example, may miss the fact that persons who serve on boards exercise little formal control. Corporate board meetings are short and infrequent, and the directors are often only advisors. So while real power may be legally vested in the board, the actual control is held by managers, owners and those who prepare corporate information.[37] In addition, there is the argument that elites are neither monolithic nor completely impenetrable. The maturation of Canadian capitalism may for example, give rise to the emergence of new elite factions which may compete against established elites (and each other) rather than form a common class front. Moreover, a distinction has been made between the idea of a *strategic* and a *core* elite, the former made up of those who have achieved key functional roles, the latter of those who have inherited wealth and status. While access to the core elite remains virtually closed, the strategic elite appears to be more open to persons of demonstrated competence and skill.[38]

There is also some evidence which might point to the role of the strategic elite in changing the overall ethnic composition of the upper strata of society. For example, while francophones were previously underrepresented in virtually every elite, there has been increasing francophone participation in the federal bureaucratic and political elite, and there may even be emerging a stronger French-Canadian economic elite.[39]

In concluding this discussion, we should note that although many observers are concerned with "access" to the elite, others find the mere existence of an elite distressing. We will return to this issue at the end of the chapter.

Poverty

We have already seen in Table 3.1 that the quintile of the Canadian population with the lowest incomes receive only 4.5% of the aggregate Canadian income. But at what income level do we define someone as poor?

To answer this question, it is important to distinguish between absolute poverty and relative poverty for these two measures make use of different assumptions of what constitutes poverty. *Absolute poverty* pertains to the income level needed for basic subsistence (i.e., food, clothing, shelter). The poverty line might be adjusted to the location of residence where costs may be higher or lower, but the basic measurement is still the provision of subsistence needs. Anyone not having sufficient income to provide for these needs is considered poor. One problem with this definition of poverty is that what one person considers an absolute necessity, another person considers a luxury. The notion of *relative poverty* addresses this problem by establishing a minimal standard of living for a family within a given community. If, for example, a car is a necessity for transportation to work or school, or for participation in community activities, then the inability to afford a car indicates relative poverty. Generally speaking, Statistics Canada analyses of poverty are based on absolute conceptions of poverty while the Canadian Council on Social Development utilizes more relative conceptions of poverty.[40]

Using the absolute definition of poverty, about 17% of all households are below the poverty line, including 32% of all unattached individuals, and 10% of all families.[41] Using the relative definition, 27% of all households are below the poverty line, including 41% of all unattached individuals and 22% of all families. There might be added a further category of "near poor" who are just over poverty lines but whose economic situation is only marginally better. The number of poor unattached individuals has increased due to unemployment and a rise in the number of widowed elderly. Families that have both spouses working are more likely to have improved their economic situation, whereas single-parent families are more likely to be poor. The highest incidence of poverty is to be found in large cities and in the Atlantic provinces, and where the head of the household is either under 24 or over 65 years of age. In another study, T.J. Ryan suggested that children who learn behaviour that perpetuates poverty early in life find it hard to extricate themselves from it later in life.[42] The circle of poverty does therefore seem to reinforce itself.

Considerable controversy was raised in 1971 when the Senate released its special report on poverty. In this report, the Senate attempted to come to grips with what constituted poverty, how many Canadians were impoverished, and what should be done about it. Four members of the staff doing research for the Committee wrote their own account, entitled *The Real Poverty Report*, after resigning in anger.[43] Arguing that the Senate was not really interested in structural reform, but only in tinkering with the system, the authors proposed a more sweeping reform of the socio-economic system that engenders poverty. A more recent report also argued that in order to eliminate poverty, changes must be made to the minimum wage, rates for social assistance must be increased, and a guaranteed annual income established.[44]

The State and Inequality

In contrast to the United States, Canada has historically been much more active in the use of government programs to reduce inequalities. While this is true in the area of social legislation, such as family allowance and medical care, it is also true in the industrial sector through the establishment of government-owned businesses called *crown corporations* (e.g., Petro-Canada, provincial hydro companies, Potash Corporation of Saskatchewan). Several contextual factors are responsible for this approach.[45] First, the state has felt obligated to provide basic services in a young and sparsely populated country when venture capital was lacking or deemed inappropriate. Second, awareness of the necessity for industrial development in Quebec and then other regions has produced government intervention to ameliorate regional inequalities. Third, the presence of large blocks of foreign capital in the country has produced a nationalist awareness engendering a demand for some larger domestic presence. Fourth, the dependence on resources as an export commodity has led to a desire to reverse this dependence and to build an initial industrial base. In addition, there is also a desire to control the rapid depletion of non-renewable resources.

New constitutional guarantees of rights and freedoms represent federal attempts to reduce inequalities of age and sex among individuals across the nation. These guarantees, however, seem to ignore long-standing inequalities that have a regional component. In 1937, the Rowell-Sirois Royal Commission on Dominion-Provincial Relations advocated a more equitable distribution of social-service benefits because of the income and employment inequality that existed at that time. By 1957, the government had established *equalization grants* which redistributed tax revenues so that regions of Canada with incomes lower than the national average would be able to provide education and health facilities at the same level as regions with higher incomes. Sensing that a more comprehensive program of development was needed, the Department of Regional Economic Expansion was created in 1969, but its successes have been limited because of dependence on heavy government tax incentives. As Acheson pointed out, the net effect of these efforts was that underdeveloped areas virtually became "client-states" of the federal government. This was a consequence of their dependence on federal handouts through either grants or transfer payments such as unemployment insurance, or income supplements to raise the standard of living of their residents.[46] Matthews labels this same phenomenon *transfer dependency*.[47]

Because many of the attempts by the federal state have generally sustained regional inequalities rather than eliminated them, provincial governments have increased their intervention into the economy as a means to improve provincial economic development. Provincial governments have used their powers and finances to create new job opportunities for the expanding middle class, provided tax incentives or loan guarantees to save jobs or create them, and established mechanisms to take advantage of new technologies.[48] While government goals have shifted between supplementing the private economy to greater state direction of the economy, there does seem to be a move in the direction of joint ventures between public and private capital.[49]

In spite of federal or provincial state interventions, however, inequalities still exist. Whether this means that the state is merely an instrument of the capitalist class (and thereby not really interested in equality) or whether governments are still in search of more effective programs for reducing inequalities is a matter of some debate.[50]

Implications of Inequality

The use of the term "inequality" suggests that we all agree that equality is the normative or moral condition. The fact is, however, that Canada remains a stratified society and there is no ideological consensus on whether that inequality is necessary or unnecessary or, indeed, on the meaning of "equality" itself. (To believe in equality at the ballot boxes, for example, is certainly not the same as to believe in equality in economic matters.) At the same time the reality of individual differences must be integrated with our conceptions of what Canadian society should or could be.

Marchak has distinguished three different views of Canadian social structure.[51] The first one is that the goal of society should be fundamental equality through challenges to elite control in a *socialist* model. The second view is a *conservative* model which asserts that a hierarchical ordering of a society is natural, inevitable and necessary. The dominant ideology in Canadian society has been the *liberal* model which accepts a stratified society because of its belief in individualism, yet modifies the excesses of the capitalist system by making some provisions for the most disadvantaged. Marchak fears that with the increasing concentration of global capital (as multi-national corporations support the shift from competitive capitalism to monopoly capitalism), inequality will become even a more critical problem. In any case, the search for a just society appears to be an unending one.

One analyst has argued that Canadian elite studies imply that Canadians are "politically impotent and submissive" and "undisturbed" by the inequalities that exist in their society.[52] Such a view does not seem to conform to reality, although it is not clear how strong the social conscience of Canadians at any social class level really is when it comes to structured inequalities. At the very least, one can expect continuing conflict as groups with competing interests challenge each other and as new strategies for a just society are proferred. In this sense, social class analysis reveals much of the dynamic of the tensions and struggles within the society and thereby remains a useful tool to understand these conflicts as they occur.

Further Exploration

1. Which dimension of inequality is most problematic for you? What suggestions do you have for reducing it?
2. Discuss current examples of the metropolis-hinterland conflict in Canada.
3. Discuss one method used by the state to reduce inequality and analyze its success in doing so.

Selected Readings

Forcese, Dennis, *The Canadian Class Structure*, Second Edition, (Toronto: McGraw Hill Ryerson, 1980).

Harp, John and John R. Hofley (eds.), *Structured Inequality In Canada*, (Toronto: Prentice Hall, 1980).

Hunter, Alfred A., *Class Tells: On Social Inequality In Canada*, (Toronto: Butterworths, 1981).

ENDNOTES

[1] For a review of these approaches and their critics, see Alfred A. Hunter, *Class Tells: On Social Inequality In Canada* (Toronto: Butterworth, 1981), Chapters 2 and 3.

[2] John Goyder and Peter Pineo, "The Accuracy of Self-Assessment of Social Status", *Canadian Review of Sociology and Anthropology* 14 (1977): 235-45.

[3] Bernd Baldus and Verna Tribe, "The Development of Perceptions and Evaluations of Social Inequality Among Public School Children", *Canadian Review of Sociology and Anthropology* 15(1978): 50-60.

[4] "Class, Status and Party", in H.H. Gerth and C.W. Mills, *From Max Weber: Essays in Sociology* (New York: Oxford University Press, 1958).

[5] Edward G. Grabb and Ronald D. Lambert, "The Subjective Meaning of Social Class Among Canadians", *Canadian Journal of Sociology* 7(1982): 297-307.

[6] L.N. Guppy and J.L. Siltanan, "A Comparison of the Allocation of Male and Female Occupational Prestige", *Canadian Review of Sociology and Anthropology* 14(1977): 320-330.

[7] Cf. Marlene Mackie, *Exploring Gender Relations: A Canadian Perspective* (Toronto: Butterworth, 1983). See also Paul Phillips and Erin Phillips, *Women and Work: Inequality in the Labour Market*, (Toronto: James Lorimer, 1983); and Pat Armstrong and Hugh Armstrong, *The Double Ghetto*, Revised Edition, (Toronto: McClelland and Stewart, 1984).

[8] S.H. Milner and H. Milner, *The Decolonization of Quebec*, (Toronto: McClelland and Stewart, 1973), Chapter 3.

[9] Jacques Dofny and Marcel Rioux, "Social Class In French Canada", in Marcel Rioux and Yves Martin, eds., *French-Canadian Society*, Vol. I, (Toronto: McClelland and Stewart, 1971), pp. 307-318.

[10] See Anthony Richmond, *Post-War Immigrants in Canada* (Toronto: University of Toronto Press, 1970), pp. 3-26 for a brief sketch on immigration policy.

[11] These are essentially the findings of Monica Boyd, "Status Attainment In Canada: Findings of the Canadian Mobility Study", *Canadian Review of Sociology and Anthropology* 18(1981): 657-673.

[12] A. Gordon Darroch, "Another Look At Ethnicity, Stratification, And Social Mobility In Canada", *Canadian Journal of Sociology* 4(1979); 1-25.

[13]Mildred A. Schwartz, *Politics and Territory: The Sociology Of Regional Persistence In Canada* (Montreal: McGill-Queens University Press, 1974), p. 336.

[14]This argument is developed in some detail by Carl Cuneo, "A Class Perspective On Regionalism", in Daniel Glenday, Hubert Guidon and Allan Turowetz, eds., *Modernization And The Canadian State*, (Toronto: Macmillan, 1978).

[15]For a presentation of the metropolis-hinterland thesis, see Arthur Davis, "Canadian Society and History As Hinterland And Metropolis" in Richard J. Ossenberg, ed., *Canadian Society: Pluralism, Change And Conflict* (Scarborough; Prentice-Hall, 1971), pp. 6-32.

[16]For one account of the agrarian reaction, see John A. Irving, *The Social Credit Movement In Alberta*, (Toronto: University of Toronto Press, 1959). Pierre Valliere's book is entitled *White Niggers of America*, (Toronto: McClelland & Stewart, 1971).

[17]For an example of this kind of regional class analysis, see Peter Sinclair, "Class Structure And Populist Protest: The Case Of Western Canada", *Canadian Journal of Sociology* 1(1975): 1-17.

[18]Ralph Matthews, "Class Interests And The Role Of The State In The Development of Canada's East Coast Fishery", *Canadian Issues: Journal of the Association For Canadian Studies* 3(1980): 115-124.

[19]John Porter, *The Vertical Mosaic* (Toronto: University of Toronto Press, 1965), pp. 38-59.

[20]For an excellent discussion of the nature and significance of the brain drain, see Walter Adams, ed., *The Brain Drain* (Toronto: Macmillan Co. of Canada, 1968); also K.V. Pankhurst, "Migration between Canada and the United States" in *The Annals of the American Academy of Political and Social Science*, 367(1966): 53-62.

[22]For an assessment of John Porter's analysis of class, mobility, education and power in Canadian society, see a special issue (No. 5) of the *Canadian Review of Sociology And Anthropology* 18(1981) in memory of John Porter.

[23]Economic Council of Canada, *Seventh Annual Review*, 1970, pp. 56-61; and Max Van Zur-Mehlen, "The Ph.D. Dilemma In Canada". In Sylvia Ostry, ed., *Canadian Higher Education In The Seventies*, (Ottawa: Economic Council of Canada, 1972), p. 79.

[24]Michael D. Ornstein argues that the extent of mobility must be related to features of the labour market such as employment opportunities or the hiring and promotion policies of corporations. "The Occupational Mobility Of Men In Ontario", *Canadian Review Of Sociology And Anthropology* 18(1981): 183-215. See also Harvey Rich, "The Vertical Mosaic Reconsidered", *Journal of Canadian Studies* 11(1976): 14-31, who argues that Porter described an archaic rather than contemporary view of Canadian society.

[25]Sid Gilbert and Hugh A. McRoberts, "Academic Stratification And Education Plans: A Reassessment", *Canadian Review Of Sociology And Anthropology* 14(1977): 34-47.

[26]John Porter, Marian Porter and Bernard R. Blishen, *Stations And Callings: Making It Through the School System*, (Toronto: Methuen, 1982), pp. 311-315.

[27]Monica Boyd, "Status Attainment In Canada: Findings of the Canadian Mobility Study", *Canadian Review of Sociology And Anthropology* 18(1981): 670.

[28]S.D. Clark, "The Post Second World War Canadian Society", *Canadian Review Of Sociology and Anthropology* 12(1975): 25-32.

[29]Edward B. Harvey and Ivan Charner, "Social Mobility and Occupational Attainments of University Graduates", *Canadian Review Of Sociology And Anthropology* 12(1975): 134-149.

[30]John C. Goyder and James E. Curtis, "Occupational Mobility In Canada Over Four Generations", *Canadian Review Of Sociology and Anthropology* 14(1977): 303-319. For a good review of the recent evidence relating stratification to accessibility, see Paul Anisef and Norman Okihiro, *Losers & Winners: The Pursuit of Equality and Social Justice in Higher Education*, (Toronto: Butterworths, 1982).

[31]For discussion of the political economy tradition in Canada, see Wallace Clement and Daniel Drache, *The New Practical Guide To Canadian Political Economy* (Toronto: Lorimer, 1985).

[32]For a review of this class analysis, see Wallace Clement, "Canadian Class Cleavages: An Assessment And Contribution", in his *Class, Power and Property: Essays on Canadian Society*, (Toronto: Methuen, 1983): 134-171.

[33]Wallace Clement, *The Canadian Corporate Elite: An Analysis of Economic Power*, (Toronto: McClelland and Stewart, 1975).

[34]Wallace Clement, *Continental Corporate Power*, (Toronto: McClelland and Stewart, 1977), Chapters 6-8.

[35]Dennis Olsen, *The State Elite*, (Toronto: McClelland and Stewart, 1980).

[36]Robert Michels, *Political Parties: A Sociological Study Of The Oligarchical Tendencies Of Modern Democracy*, (New York: Free Press, 1966).

[37]See for example, D.E. Dimick and V.V. Murray, "Career And Personal Characteristics Of The Managerial Technostructure In Canadian Business", *Canadian Review of Sociology and Anthropology* 15(1978): 372-384; and Terence H. White, "Boards of Directors: Control and Decision-Making In Canadian Corporations", *Canadian Review of Sociology and Anthropology* 16(1979): 77-95.

[38]Merrijoy Kelner, "Ethnic Penetration Into Toronto's Elite Structure", *Canadian Review of Sociology and Anthropology* 7(1970): 128-137.

[39]See Jorge Niosi, *Canadian Capitalism: A Study of Power In the Canadian Business Establishment*, (Toronto: James Lorimer, 1981). For a discussion of the issue of francophone participation in the federal bureaucracy, cf. Christopher Beattie, Jacques Desy, and Stephen Longstaff, *Bureaucratic Careers: Anglophones and Francophones In The Canadian Public Service*, (Ottawa: Information Canada, 1972); and Christopher Beattie, *Minority Men In A Majority Setting*, (Toronto: McClelland Stewart, 1975).

[40]A.W. Djao, *Inequality And Social Policy: The Sociology Of Welfare*, (Toronto: John Wiley, 1983): 83-84.

[41]These data were obtained from David R. Ross, *The Canadian Fact Book On Poverty, 1983*, (Toronto: James Lorimer, 1983), pp. 7, 12-17.

[42]T.J. Ryan, *Poverty And The Child: A Canadian Study*, (Toronto: McGraw-Hill Ryerson, 1972).

[43]*Poverty in Canada: Report of the Special Senate Committee on Poverty*, (Ottawa: Information Canada, 1971), and Ian Adams, William Cameron, Brian Hill, Peter Penz, *The Real Poverty Report*, (Edmonton: Hurtig, 1971).

[44]*Not Enough: The Meaning and Measurement of Poverty in Canada*, (Ottawa: Canadian Council on Social Development, 1984).

[45]G. Bruce Doern and Richard W. Phidd, *Canadian Public Policy: Ideas, Structure and Process*, (Toronto: Methuen, 1983), Chapter 1.

[46]T.W. Acheson, "The Maritimes and 'Empire Canada' ", in David J. Bercuson, ed., *Canada And The Burden Of Unity*, (Toronto: Macmillan, 1977), p. 103.

[47]Ralph Matthews, *The Creation Of Regional Dependency*, (Toronto: University of Toronto Press, 1983), pp. 69-76.

[48]Since 1970, provincial crown corporations have grown much faster than federal corporations. See Allan Tupper and G. Bruce Doern, eds., *Public Corporations And Public Policy In Canada*, (Montreal: Institute For Research On Public Policy, 1981), Chapter 1.

[49]S.D. Berkowitz, "Forms Of State Economy And The Development Of Western Canada", *Canadian Journal of Sociology* 4(1979): 309.

[50]cf. Leo Panitch, ed., *The Canadian State: Political Economy And Political Power*, (Toronto: University of Toronto Press, 1977).

[51]M. Patricia Marchak, *Ideological Perspectives On Canada*, Second Edition, (Toronto: McGraw-Hill Ryerson, 1981).

[52]Menno Boldt, "Images of Canada's Future In John Porter's *The Vertical Mosaic*", in Wendell Bell and James A. Mau, *The Sociology Of The Future*, (New York: Russell Sage Foundation, 1971), pp. 190-191. For another critique of Porter, see James L. Heap, ed., *Everybody's Canada: The Vertical Mosaic Reviewed And Reexamined*, (Toronto: Burns and MacEachern, 1974).

4 The Issue of Regionalism

H.H. Hiller

"The economic history of Canada has been dominated by the discrepancy between the centre and the margin of western civilization. Energy has been directed toward the exploitation of staple products and the tendency has been cumulative"

— Harold A. Innis, acclaimed University of Toronto political economist, early leader of the social science community, and originator of the staples thesis, in his *The Fur Trade in Canada* (1930:385).

The issue of region has continuously retained its centrality as a fractious issue in Canadian society. Typically region is viewed as a geographical concept with low social relevance. Yet just as inequality tells us something of the structure of a society and how members of a society relate to one another, so region also engenders group differences which divide and distinguish members of a society. Even a cursory understanding of Canadian society suggests that it makes a difference whether you live in Grand Falls, Newfoundland; Trois Rivieres, Quebec; Regina, Saskatchewan; or Victoria, British Columbia. The climate, the economy, the history, and the type of people found in an area create differences in how we think, not only about ourselves, but also about other regions displaying different characteristics with whom we must interact in a national framework.

Chapter 1 presented some of the problems of defining a region, and the reader may want to review that material. In that chapter, our concern was to show the demographic differences between areas in Canada. Now we turn our attention to the dynamics of regionalism, and seek to explain why regionalism is such an important factor in Canadian society. The chapter concludes with an illustrative discussion of three Canadian regions: the West, the Atlantic region, and the North.

Regionalism as a Social Indicator

The concept of region implies the idea of space and, therefore, is always related to geography. Typically, we look for areas with similar topographical features and note how these areas are distinguished from one another by mountains, bodies of water, or changes in foliage. Regions can then be demarcated by types and amounts of precipitation, variations in temperature, soil conditions, and plant life.

But, if geography is a critical basis for identifying a region, the nature of soil conditions and variations in temperature, for example, have a major role to play in the attractiveness of that space as a place to live, and the economic ability of that space to support a population. Thus, if the first dimension of regionalism is geography, the second dimension is economic; i.e., what do people do to earn a living? The rocky soil of much of the Atlantic region does not allow the grain farming typical of the Prairies. Similarly, the landlocked Prairies do not support the fishing and marine industries common to the Atlantic area. The importance and economic value of what people do to earn a living shapes the nature and quality of their lives, and gives a region a distinct identity. Social institutions (e.g., grain growers or fish co-operatives, manufacturing unions, etc.) which grow up around these economic activities help to produce a regional culture, a similar view of the world, a folk culture of customs and traditions, a common history, linguistic idioms, and, consequently, a personal attachment to an area and group identity.

While homogeneous regions may exist in theory, or have been historically easily identifiable, modern societies are far too complex to establish simple regional distinctions. People outside of Central Canada usually think of Ontario as the industrial heartland of the nation, and yet, Ontario also possesses a strong mixed farming sector. Similarly, the stereotype of the Prairies as a wheat farming region ignores the fact that Prairie people are now primarily an urban people. The point is that changes within these regions, as a consequence of urbanization and other socio-technical changes, have blurred the simple distinctions that may have once existed between regions. Nevertheless, it is still possible to say that the dominant oil and gas industries of Alberta and Saskatchewan, for example, give those provinces a significantly different cast from the strong manufacturing sector of Ontario and Quebec. Similarly, the mining, lumbering and shipping industries of British Columbia clearly distinguish that region from the Prairies, and help to explain why the Prairies and British Columbia resist being lumped together as one Western region. Regions are seldom easily distinguished, but differences in the economic components of a region do combine with other factors (e.g., a sense of history or ethnic composition) to suggest the existence of regional cultures.

It is perhaps inevitable that the sheer vastness of Canada and its different phases of settlement would make regionalism a significant factor in this society. In Chapter 1, it was noted that demographic differences produce unique population matrixes that can form the basis for regional societies. But regionalism is far more than population differences, differences in land formation, soil composition, dialects, or linguistic expressions; regionalism is also a consequence of a *comparative relationship* among regions. In contrasting one region with another part of that national society, not only do differentiating characteristics become clear but *power relationships* become obvious. Thus, if one region of a country has a strong manufacturing sector and another region has virtually no manufacturing, that fact reflects a relationship between the two regions that must be explored and explained. Since all units within the national whole operate within a common framework, *regionalism is the product of how those units relate to one another.*[1]

It is not without significance that the first modern sociologists to take up the study of regionalism were prompted in their investigations by the negative comparisons made in distinguishing their region from other regions in the national whole. Sociologists Howard Odum and Rupert Vance at the University of North Carolina noted how the American South in the 1920's and 1930's had not participated in the industrialization characteristic of the North.[2] Their study of the regional South led them to seek both a material and cultural renaissance of the South because of the comparative disadvantage with the North. The descriptions of the history, folklore, topography, religion, and economy of the South became even more significant because of what they meant about how the South compared to other parts of the United States.

This observation has equal application to Canadian society. The significance of a region's character lies in its relationship to other regions, and it is precisely the perceived disadvantage that some regions feel that has provoked greater interest in regionalism as a major factor in Canadian society. The political economy of one region is intimately related to national forces that are themselves reflections of the political economies and power relationships of other regions. It is interesting to note that industrial expansion in the American South in the last few decades has reduced regional distinctiveness and regional identities.[3] The same cannot be said of Canada, however, where the acknowledgement of regional economic disparities within Canadian society has perpetuated regionalism as a divisive element.

The analysis of economic regionalism is important because it informs us about the nature of the relationships between regional units but this does not imply that only economic factors are important. Historical factors and social-psychological factors are also critical, and have profound effects on the emergence of regional identities. It is only when regions are compared and contrasted that we see why the segmentation of Canadian society into regional units is of such importance.

Explanations for the Persistence of Regionalism

Geographic and economic factors are the underlying components of regionalism, but a dynamic rather than static perspective requires that regions be understood in relation to other regions or loci of power. How can this approach help us explain the existence of regionalism in Canada? Six individual explanations can be isolated for analysis.

CULTURAL DISTINCTIVENESS
The question of whether each region in Canada possesses its own culture is open to much debate. Certainly, the ethnic concentration of persons of French descent in Quebec has given that region a cultural quality all its own. Furthermore if we look to the history of the settlement of other regions, it is possible to observe that the timing and initial composition of settlement also provided some of the enduring characteristics of these regions. The very early settlement of the Atlantic region by persons predominantly of British origin and the much later settlement of the Prairies by persons of mixed European origin

obviously have important consequences for the culture of each region. This is particularly true when these regions are separated from each other by several thousand miles.

A *culture* refers to the complex of beliefs, morals, customs, laws, and habits which people share as a consequence of their group experiences. Culture also includes material aspects such as art, technology, and objects which represent a people's expression of their struggle with their physical and socio-economic environment. Where spatial distances or barriers exist between regions, regional cultures are more likely to persist.

As each region's population tries to adapt to its own topographical and climatic features, and responds to its own economic challenges, it produces its own unique matrix of traits; such traits are reflected in its literature, folklore, self-understanding, and perception of itself in relation to other regions of Canada. The media frequently pick up symbols of regional character (e.g., pictures of the idyllic fishing village of Peggy's Cove, the skyscrapers of Toronto in the shadows of the CN Tower, the Prairie grain elevator surrounded by flat land and open skies) which help perpetuate regional images. Institutions, traditions, and social movements develop as an expression of regional concerns and interests, and these characteristics form a cultural complex with at least some distinguishing features from other regions. What makes culture regional is its contrast with the whole, or with other units of the whole. Although there are many influences that contribute to the reduction of regional cultures and the promulgation of a national or continental culture (e.g., television, urbanization, federal efforts to promote national identities) and although regional culture is somewhat difficult to isolate, it does not mean that regional culture does not exist. The history, population composition, and political economy of the region provide the cultural matrix that allows regional distinctions and identities to occur.[4] Therefore, while Halifax and Vancouver have much in common as port cities, or while Toronto and Montreal are both metropolitan centers of influence, they are each part of a regional culture that makes them unique in important respects.

The regional culture explanation is somewhat difficult to define scientifically, and appears to be something experienced more intuitively. Regional culture is likely to have its greatest effect when it finds its expression in personal identity (which is our next point).

ATTITUDINAL DIFFERENCES

If regional cultural differences persist, then these differences should be reflected in the attitudes of individuals. For example, it has been documented that regional differences in attitudes towards foreign investment, the maintenance of ties with England, moral issues, or civil liberties do exist.[5] Numerous studies have also suggested that Canadians are more likely to first identify with their region, rather than the nation. One survey showed that 66% of Prince Edward Islanders, 67% of New Brunswickers, and 60% of Nova Scotians felt they shared an outlook and way of life as Maritimers that distinguished them from other Canadians.[6] Furthermore, provincial support for the francization policies of the Parti Quebecois in Quebec has usually been taken as evidence that francophone Quebecers have a prior loyalty to their region on at least some issues, which supercedes their commitment to all national objectives. After a study of communication and transportation patterns, Bell and Tepperman suggest that ignorance about what happens in other regions helps promote the phenomenon of multiple regions within the country.[7] There is some question about whether regional identities and attitudes are necessarily exclusive from, or in direct competition with, national identities and attitudes (i.e., might it be possible for national and regional loyalties to coexist?)[8] There is, however, little argument over the fact that regional identities have a powerful impact in developing regional differences in personal attitudes and viewpoints. Using the dynamic model of regionalism, not only will people feel strong attachments and sentiments to their own region, but they will apply these sentiments to their evaluation of other regions in the national system.

Devaluing other regional cultures on the basis of the presumed superiority of one's own regional culture is an attitude known as *ethnocentrism*; but the negative attitude, or feeling of distance and detachment that is the consequence of unbalanced interregional interaction, is known as *alienation*.

The most typical products of regional cultures in Canada are the attitudes that produce stereotypical evaluations of other regions. National issues (e.g., bilingualism, freight rates) provoke regional responses in which persons inhabiting a region might feel they must remain united in the face of challenges from other regions. Some regions maintain cultural or economic superiority to others, at the same time as inhabitants of other regions feel dominated or exploited. Regional attachments are then paralleled by perceptions and attitudes about other regions with whom relationships are usually unequal. It is the nature of this inequality that usually heightens the *regionalization of attitudes*.

Regional differences in identity and attitudes are not adequate explanations in themselves: differences are usually rooted in historic perceptions of what it means to be an "insider" in relation to other regions in which one feels an "outsider." At its deepest level, regional identity is rooted in the economy of a region, and this helps shape attitudes about other regions.

DEVELOPMENT IMBALANCES

One of the most dramatic causes of regionalism in Canada has been the unevenness of economic development in different parts of the society. For example, the original industrial strength of the Maritime region was displaced by greater industrial centralization in Central Canada, and the Atlantic provinces consequently went into a decline from which they have never recovered.[9] Conversely, Ontario and Quebec developed an industrial strength that gained new momentum in the post-World War II era; 75% of the leading Canadian corporations and 85% of the major financial institutions established their head offices in Toronto or Montreal.[10] Using the protective tariff to guarantee a Canadian market for their products, there was little need to develop industries elsewhere, and the rest of Canada became a market hinterland to Central Canadian industries. Freight rate squabbles and animosity regarding mortgages held by central Canadian financial institutions frequently became symbolic of hinterland resistance to regional dominance.

While Ontario and Quebec have been the centres of economic development, it is clear that the focus of this activity was the metropolitan galaxies of Toronto and Montreal. Both cities spawned an elaborate suburban system and drew supporting cities into their orbit. For example, whereas Toronto and Hamilton were once distinct cities separated by considerable green space, they are now linked in an megalopolis with little intervening green space. This is a consequence of the growth of new interstitial cities such as Burlington, Oakville, and Mississauga.

From a national point of view, what is significant is that little economic and population growth took place outside of these two metropolitan areas. Vancouver, as a Pacific port city with a coastal climate, experienced some growth, but the foci of economic development in Canada clearly centered on Toronto and Montreal. Analysts use the term *primate city* to describe a situation where a country has one or two surpassingly large cities that dominate the rest of the country, and whose development has been at such a pace that significant socio-economic and even cultural differences emerge between these cities and their supporting regions, and the rest of the nation. The overdevelopment of these metropolitan areas in comparison to the underdevelopment of other urban centres in other regions, has become an important aspect of the dominance of Central Canada over other regions. The employment opportunities available in the industrial regions has meant that persons seeking work or career advancement are forced to leave the hinterland regions and move to Ontario or Quebec. This movement contributes to further population imbalances.

Clement has argued that the overdevelopment of one region can only take place at the expense of the underdevelopment of other regions.[11] Perhaps more than any other factor, it is usually thought that

REAL PEOPLE 4.1

Tires and Regions

1980

The federal government has announced $42 million in aid, and the Nova Scotia government has promised $14 million, to Michelin Tire Company to assist them in expanding their two existing plants in Nova Scotia and to build a third one there. Grants totalling $56 million will be used to strengthen the French-owned company's operations in the one province.

"Unfair" cried the National Rubber Workers Union. "This will mean the loss of jobs in Ontario and Quebec tire plants. We'll urge our members not to buy Michelin tires."

"Unfair" cried a tire competitor. "Michelin should do this with their own money, not the taxpayers. Government subsidies for them mean we can't compete. We already closed our Calgary plant and now will close our Whitby operation."

Questions to Consider

Why do you think the government became involved? Why was the union opposed to government support of a Nova Scotia plant? Why was the competitor angry? What does this example have to do with regionalism?

the National Policy of 1879 is at the root of this regional imbalance. This federal program of protective tariffs, immigration incentives, and railway development, was particularly organized around western settlement and the provision of a captive hinterland for Central Canadian industry. Since manufacturing was concentrated in Ontario and Quebec, the hinterland regions had little to exchange except raw materials and, if these were not available, then the exchange balance became even more unequal. One study of import-export trade ratios with Ontario demonstrated that, whereas Quebec's ratio with Ontario was quite close (4:5), Alberta's (1:8) and Saskatchewan's (1:15) was unbalanced and Prince Edward Island (2:47) and Newfoundland (3:1000), were even more unbalanced in favour of Ontario.[12]

The dominance of Central Canada does not mean that all other regions are equal. On the contrary, because some regions have raw materials or resources that the industrial centre needs, they have a more favourable exchange ratio than regions that have little to exchange. Such a contrast becomes clear when comparing the traditional position of the Maritime region with the West, where oil and gas has been found in abundance. Yet it is precisely this exchange of finished goods for raw materials that ensures the continued dominance of the industrial regions. It is for this reason that the West, and particularly Alberta, attempted to use their resources as a basis for industrial development in order to participate in the employment and technological growth that could result. It is also for this reason that Newfoundland attempted to use the development of its own offshore oil as an employment opportunity for Newfoundlanders first, rather than for any other Canadians who might apply. All of these developments, and others which are likely to follow, symbolize efforts to rearrange the old imbalances which have been such a major part of regional inequalities.

Development imbalances are caused by the regional nature of capital control. The concentration of capital in Central Canada ensures that industrial development is strongest in that region. Industrial development in other regions can only take place by shifting economic development from this region, and a variety of forces resist this dispersion. Much of the regionalism characteristic of Canadian society is rooted in the conflicts generated by differences in levels of industrialization.

ELITE CONTROL

The economic disparities between regions do not just happen by themselves. They are the product of the use of capital and power to effect a particular pattern of development. In Chapter 3, it was noted that the research of Porter and Clement demonstrated that the economic elite of Canada were primarily resident in Ontario and Quebec. The corporate power that developed in these two Central Canadian provinces meant that weaker corporations in other parts of Canada were either bought out to reduce the competition or were subject to price wars which were usually won by Central Canadian corporations.[13] Such consolidation meant that capital, control, and power became regionally concentrated and centralized. But by focusing on elite control, it becomes clear that it is not so much geo-political units like Ontario or Quebec which maintain a regional dominance over the rest of Canada; rather, such dominance is the result of activities of the capitalist class, which resides primarily in the two primate cities of Toronto and Montreal.[14] Their desire to expand markets, maintain production efficiency, and thereby maximize profits, leaves little room for concern over regional disparities.

Because of their power and interrelatedness with other elites, the economic elite are able to lobby for federal and provincial policies that support their interests. For example, a protective tariff is essentially an economic mechanism that would not exist without legislative decree. Therefore, a proposed tariff that supports a Central Canadian industry requires that the capitalist class demonstrate to the political elite why such legislation is in the national interest, and not just their personal interest. Labour unions and their elite, and the voting public in Central Canada are then drawn in to support such a policy, because it protects both the jobs and the capital of supporting services and industries. The problem is that capital investment and control is regionally concentrated rather than dispersed, and hinterland regions seldom share directly in the benefits of such national policies. Instead, the regionalization of capital and political control is more likely to lead to discussions in these outlying regions about the cost of Confederation. Such discussions often centre around the higher price of manufactured goods charged by protected, monopolistic industries located far from their captive markets.

The traditional strength of the capitalist class in Ontario and Quebec does not mean that there is no economic elite in other regions. In fact, each region has its own local elite who may benefit from the regionalization of Canadian society as agents for the central elite. The local elite may even occasionally try to challenge the capitalist class in other regions. The regional elite's attempts to marshall the powers of the region through the political apparatus of a province have been called *province building*.[15] The goal of province building is to use the legislative power of the province to provide tax incentives, grants, or policy challenges aimed at other regions that will assist in providing a more favourable environment for capital formation and industrial development in a particular region. Regions then may compete against each other, as happened in 1980 when Alberta unsuccessfully attempted to wrestle some economic activity away from Ontario and Quebec. Clearly, then, within a national state, regional units struggle against each other for development, and it is the economic and political elite in each region who are frequently at the centre of the heightened competition and struggle between regions. Because federal elections are usually won or lost in Ontario and Quebec (where the most parliamentary seats are), the elite who dominate this region are the elite who control national policy.

If the dominance of Central Canada is supported by a symmetry between this regional elite and the federal elite, then effective challenges to this regional dominance require an alternate legislative vehicle. Thus, capitalist classes in the regions that seek expansion will form alliances with their local provincial governments to challenge the dominance of the national-central Canadian bourgeoisie. For this reason, regionalism has become equated with provincialism because the local economic and political elite use the province to challenge federal control, and to promote local development. Federal-provincial hostilities and confrontations reflect the interests of the regional elite, and long-standing popular sentiment may even be manipulated in order to create regional solidarity.[16] In recent years, some politicians have successfully won provincial elections precisely through accentuating regional-national cleavages.

In short, regionalism is intimately related to internal power, and struggles for power, within a national society. Elites *internal* to a region and elites *external* to a region play a significant role in charting the nature of regional economies and regional relationships.

NORTH-SOUTH LINKAGES

Another explanation of regionalism is based on Canada's intimate relationship with the United States. Natural alliances and mutual interests are viewed as emerging from geographical proximity of Canadian and American regions. Stevenson has argued that regionalism in Canada must be seen in its continental context, as Confederation and the National Policy sought to obliterate the cross-border regional relationships that had existed long before 1867.[17] He noted that some opponents of Confederation in the Maritimes based their opposition on the fact that they felt closer attachments to the New England states, and feared the dominance of Central Canada. Similarly, some people in the southwest peninsula of Ontario felt that they had very strong ties with residents of New York and Michigan.

If these north-south linkages were displaced by Confederation, Stevenson demonstrates that they have been revived as a consequence of the decline of European ties, and the shift of economic power and people away from the American Northeast and Central Canada, to the West and (in the case of the U.S.) to the South. Neighbouring provinces and states have begun to look to each other in an effort to find solutions to mutual problems (e.g., energy, environment) through cooperation.[18] Each Canadian region then develops its own pattern of interrelationships with an allied American region and this affiliation is based on economic development, travel, and even cable TV and professional sports. Energy agreements (e.g., Columbia River Treaty, Quebec-New York power grid), industrial development (e.g., the automobile industry which links Ontario and Michigan), religious ties (e.g., Mormons of Utah and Alberta), and sports (e.g., hockey and baseball divisions) are all based on north-south links, and each can detract from or compete with national ties.

The accessibility of Canada to American capital can also be considered as a cause of regionalism. In the first place, American investment in Canada has a strong regional dimension in that many American subsidiaries in British Columbia have headquarters in California, Alberta subsidiaries are tied to southwestern multinationals, subsidiaries in Ontario are based in Michigan, Illinois, or New York, and American subsidiaries in Quebec tend to be headquartered in either New York or New Jersey. The fact that the traditional centre of industrial strength in the United States has been the Northeast, and that this area was adjacent to Ontario and Quebec meant that subsidiaries were located close to home offices. Consequently, other regions were neglected by these multi-nationals and uneven economic development resulted.[19]

The second way in which American investment impinges on regionalism is that the regional elite may also be corporate leaders (compradors) of foreign firms. Their corporate position forces them to accept the status quo and, particularly when it comes to resources and manufacturing, they support existing policies, which may foster regional disparities, because it suits corporate goals.

In this sense, American investment did not cause regionalism so much as it exacerbated and sustained regional imbalances that already existed. Regions with a manufacturing industry competed strongly to retain their leadership, and were successful in attracting American industries. Regions with little manufacturing, but a strong resource base, also attracted American capital — but only for the extraction of resources. Thus, U.S. investment in Canada retained regional patterns already established and, furthermore, brought Canadian regions into closer contact with similar American regions. If it is manufacturing that drew together Toronto, Cleveland, and Detroit, it is energy that joins Calgary, Denver, and Dallas.

Because this foreign investment is so important to the regional economy, the host region will be far more sympathetic to foreign investment than other regions might be. Ontarians may ridicule the American multi-national oil companies of Alberta, but Westerners have often been less than sympathetic about support for more expensive vehicles and appliances produced by American subsidiaries in Ontario. Thus, north-south linkages help accentuate regional disparities and hostilities.

POLITICAL STRUCTURE

Regionalism might also be explained as a consequence of the Canadian political system itself. The principle of "representation by population" provides for greater political representation for areas with a larger population. Consequently, population imbalances within the nation (e.g., two-thirds of the population live in Ontario and Quebec) create an awesome concentration of power — the votes of persons in regions other than Ontario and Quebec are seldom vital to the outcome of an election. When elections are essentially decided in those two provinces, residents of other regions feel disenfranchised. If those in Quebec and Ontario cast their vote with the party that is elected, there is the feeling that the government will cater to the majority in Central Canada. When residents in less populous areas elect a Member of Parliament whose party forms the opposition, they realize that their representative has no input into the formulation of the ruling party's policy. In either case, many regions feel the federal government has little sympathy or obligation to address their needs.

Furthermore, the strong party discipline required of the parliamentary system gives little opportunity for the expression of regional interests.[20] When this is combined with perceptions that the major national parties are controlled by Central Canadian interests, a sense of futility emerges in the hinterland regions. Occasionally, this sense of futility erupts into anger, and a "protest party" (or a "third party") with a strong regional basis may emerge on the national scene to challenge the major parties. These protest parties have been particularly successful in the West, where their ideologies have contained a strong anti-central Canadian sentiment. There is, therefore, as yet no federal vehicle (such as a regionally apportioned Senate) to enable regions to encounter one another on an equal footing.

Regions frequently have turned to their provincial governments as the "real" defenders of their interests. Federal-provincial conferences become the forum where all provinces have an input as equals, and seek to negotiate with the federal government as though its interests and those of the provinces are inherently opposed. Governments then confront other governments as large and powerful institutions, each with their own professional personnel, each concerned about survival, and each struggling to establish or retain jurisdictional competence over their territory. Cairns has called this form of regionalism *governmentalized societies*.[21] The relationship between inter-governmental conflict and elite control becomes clearer as peripheral political and economic elites become frustrated with their hinterland position. Through a policy of *economic provincialism*, priority is given to development within a particular region.[22] An example of this policy would be Newfoundland's argument in 1981 that, in any jobs created by an offshore oil boom, Newfoundlanders rather than any other Canadians should have employment priority. Regional confrontations are produced by the attempts of hinterland regions to challenge the status quo. Thus, the more regions seek equality through industrial development, the more they struggle and compete over scarce commodities, and this struggle strengthens the regional conflict.[23] It is for this reason that regionalism is, at least partially, politically propagated.

Any explanation for the persistence of regionalism cannot rest on a single factor; regionalism is a complex phenomenon and we have only sketched the more dominant contributing factors. Our discussion can now shift to illustrations of how these factors have operated in specific regional situations. Three regions have been selected for a closer analysis. The Prairies and the new West will provide the first case study; then, we will turn to the Atlantic region and, finally, to the North. All three areas have had relatively high visibility and recognition as peripheral regions to Central Canada. They make a significant comparative study, however, because their geographic and economic contexts support different social worlds.

THE CASE OF QUEBEC

Before we move on to our specific regional analysis, however, we should note that no discussion of regionalism in Canada would be complete without a rather lengthy analysis of Quebec. In fact, it could reasonably be argued that the salience of regionalism in the society as a whole is at least partially a consequence of the regional solidarity of Quebec. This solidarity is based upon a linguisitc and ethnic commonality grounded in an historical group percpetion. This commonality, in combination with territorial dominance and political control in the province, has led some francophone Quebecers to argue that Quebec is not just a region of Canada, but a distinguishable nation. As long as Quebec remains a part of Canadian society, its socio-cultural attributes make it perhaps the most distinctive region of all. Most Quebecers share a language and an ethnic heritage which are quite different from those of most other Canadians.

Since the act of Confederation, Quebec has been rather successful in negotiating special considerations with the federal government that accommodate its own cultural needs. This fact has not gone unnoticed by other regions in Canada who have periodically demanded special concessions for their own regional aspirations. In this way, the example of Quebec has been instrumental in heightening regional desires for more localized control and more equitable economic policies, and in using the province as the bargaining mechanism to obtain desired ends. Thus, from at least one perspective, Quebec has helped contribute to the regionalization of Canadian society. Other regions may lack an ethnic basis for their regional community, but the large economic gap between their region and Central Canada has accentuated their regional grievances.

A more detailed discussion of Quebec will be left for the next chapter even though many of the same regional dynamics discussed here apply. The importance of Quebec as a significant region in Canada, however, needs to be acknowledged at the outset, and the decision to omit it at this point in no way should be construed as underestimating Quebec's critical position as a powerful and distinctive region of Canada.

Region Study I:
The Prairie West and the New West

No one who has driven from Winnipeg to Calgary can forget the wide open spaces marked only by grain elevators, jutting up into the sky to remind one that indeed, far up ahead, another town is situated. Bounded by the tundra of the territories to the north, the Prairies are intimately tied to the Great Plains of the Dakotas and Kansas to the south, where grain farming remains a staple crop. It is in this geographic area that a regional culture has emerged that reflects a people's social and economic adaptation to a particular environment.

Separated from Central Canada by the Canadian Shield, the West had no natural ties with the East. Similarly, the Rockies prevented a natural continuity with the coastal communities of British Columbia to the west. If the space between Vancouver and Toronto was to be claimed and held as Canadian territory, then deliberate steps would have to be taken to integrate the Prairie region and, thereby, prevent British Columbia from being totally isolated. The program established by the federal government to accomplish these objectives was known as the *National Policy*.[24] The policy had three main features: the settlement of the Prairie region through encouragement of immigration and use of the *Homestead Act*, which provided land for settlement at an extremely low price; the establishment of an east-west transportation system, the Canadian Pacific Railroad, to link Vancouver with Toronto, thereby facilitating the movement of persons and goods needed by the Prairie community and reversing the more natural north-south ties; and the legislation of a protective tariff to ensure a market for Central Canadian manufactured goods. In this way, the National Policy succeeded in settling, claiming, and integrating the Prairie region into the Canadian fabric.

The society that grew up in this regional territory was an extension of Central Canada, and yet also separated from it. The burgeoning and aspiring industrial economy of the "centre" was easily distinguished from the single industry agricultural economy of the Prairies, and a metropolis-hinterland relationship developed. While it is clear that both regions needed each other, the tariff, by inhibiting the purchase of cheap machinery or goods produced in the United States, created a regional resentment that led Prairie people to view their interregional Canadian relationship as one of exploitation. Almost from the beginning, then, a regional attitude of alienation developed among persons resident on the Prairies.[25] That attitude was the consequence of a political economy of dependency.

Regional discontent became widespread because it touched everyone. Mortgages were held by Central Canadian banks; appliances, farm implements, and automobiles were manufactured in the "east"; canned goods came from Ontario. Virtually everything was imported into the region, and the region had little to exchange except grain which was primarily sold on international, rather than national, markets. The instability of these international prices was caused by uncertainties in crop production insect infestations, and drought. The unbalanced import-export situation made Prairie residents realize that they had become captive to national policies. This realization was heightened during the Depression, as frustrated and economically beleaguered Prairie farmers struggled to pay their Central Canadian creditors.

The "J-curve theory" suggests that social unrest is most likely to occur when rising expectations are frustrated, and conditions become worse rather than better.[26] The new settlers on the Prairies were prepared for hard work because, ultimately, they expected prosperity but these expectations were frustrated by climatic, market, and general economic conditions over which they had little control — control was exercised by a dominant Central Canada. The Prairies then produced a series of reform movements such as the Non-Partisan League, United Farmers of Alberta, Social Credit, and the Cooperative Commonwealth Federation, that were based to a large extent on the hostilities felt towards Central Canada and monopoly capital.[27]

Western alienation, then, has a long history, and spans the Prairie provinces. Sometimes it is expressed in the perception of a regional conspiracy against the West. Most frequently however, alienation focuses on elite control from Central Canada, whether it be of large corporations, banks, or political parties. Gibbins speaks of this attitude as a *regional ideology* because it is a socially shared set of beliefs with a recognized history and constituency, all based on estrangement from the Canadian heartland.[28]

The Prairies was the last large area to be settled in Canada in which land was still available for agriculture — most of this settlement occurring from 1870 to 1920. The source of immigration, and pattern of settlement, helped make the Prairies unique. For one thing, the federal government encouraged large numbers of Europeans to settle in the West. Many of these settlers came directly from Europe and organized their relocation in a bloc settlement. Other immigrants came as individuals from Ontario, the United States, or England, and settled next to people with whom they had little in common. The end result was that the Prairies became an interesting, multi-ethnic, agricultural community without parallel in rural Canada.[29] For this reason, many Prairie residents were later offended by the proposed federal policy on bilingualism and biculturalism.

TRANSITION FROM THE "OLD WEST" TO THE "NEW WEST"

The depression years were difficult as the newly settled population struggled to survive, but the post-war experience totally changed the face of the Prairie population, as agriculture went through a significant consolidation. From 1941-1966, the number of farms on the Prairies fell by one-third, the average farm increased in size by 80%, farm land was used more intensively (cow herds increased by 72%), and the number of farmers and farm labourers decreased substantially.[30] People moved to Prairie cities, and then frequently to Toronto or Vancouver for the employment available in these booming cities. Thus the changes that took place between the 1940's and 1960's meant that it was no longer possible to speak of the people of the Prairies as primarily an agrarian population.

As the agrarian population became overwhelmed by an urban population, the economy of the region shifted from agriculture to service, retailing, administration, and a small amount of manufacturing.[31] Perhaps most significant was the discovery of oil at Leduc in 1948, which inaugurated the modern era of energy production in Alberta. The discovery of oil and gas at various locations in Alberta led to the development of an active petroleum industry, again with strong linkages to the American South. Thus, the north-south ties, which were natural with agriculture, were supplemented by energy relationships. Calgary became the administrative centre for this development and, due to the fact that the provincial government was considered the owner of these resources, the province demonstrated a new-found prosperity from the rents and royalties accruing from energy development. For this and a variety of other reasons, Alberta developed an economic edge over the other Prairie provinces.

The discovery of gas in British Columbia, and both conventional oil and heavy oil discoveries in Saskatchewan, has contributed to a "New West." Whereas wheat farming had created a commonality between the three Prairie provinces of Manitoba, Saskatchewan and Alberta in the early years, these later years have seen the energy-producing provinces of British Columbia, Alberta, and Saskatchewan develop a commonality. But, just as grains were a staple extracted from Prairie soil and shipped and processed elsewhere, so energy became a staple extracted in the West and marketed in the industrial centres of Canada and the United States. In either case, the raw material was taken out of the region and the West essentially remained a hinterland. This inspired a new wave of western protest in 1980-81 and a desire to change that hinterland condition.[32]

To governments perpetually short of revenue, income from energy provided a significant economic advantage that threatened to change the whole balance of power.[33] The Alberta Heritage Trust Fund, for example, made the Alberta government a major creditor and investor within Canadian society; but, more than that, this money was a means to foster the economic development of the provinces. Instead of being a resource-rich hinterland where the staple was to be transported to industrial markets elsewhere, governments that possessed and controlled such resources sought to use them as the basis for greater regional development. As energy became an even more valuable commodity through the 1970's (as OPEC countries threatened the industrial countries with cutbacks and price increases), it became increasingly clear that the supply and price of energy *could* give the Western region enormous advantages.

The item most symbolic of the hinterland position of the West through the years has been "discriminatory" freight rates, frequently referred to as the "Crow rates." As a consequence of the Crow's Nest Pass Agreement of 1897, the federal government approved the movement of grain by railroad at rates below cost in order to assist farmers to get their product to market.[34] The fact that this low rate only applied to grain, however, discouraged the shipment of other products processed in the West. Furthermore, a higher rate prevailed for shipping manufactured goods into the West, and Westerners were constrained to buy these products as a consequence of the protective tariff. While the Crow rate was beneficial to farmers in one way, it created higher prices for durable goods. As the population in the West became less agrarian and more urban, the new urban middle class Westerner tended to favor the abolition of the Crow rate because industrial development in the West would provide new opportunities for employment and upward mobility. The tensions and disagreements produced by the death of the Crow rate in 1983 reflected the concern among Westerners that they maintain their solid agricultural base while participating in new prospects for industrialization.

It was the expanding middle and upper classes of urban professionals, entrepreneurs, and provincial civil servants, particularly in Alberta, that began to look to the province to help diversify and strengthen the local economy.[35] Simultaneously with the rise of a new regional bourgeoisie, small Canadian energy companies emerged in the West to take advantage of the boom. The availability of jobs in the West, combined with an industrial slow-down in Ontario and Quebec, resulted in heavy shifts of population to the West in the late 1970's and early 1980's. These events had a widespread societal significance because they indicated a dramatic alteration of the traditional metropolis-hinterland relationship. The regional elite and the ascendant regional middle class formed a coalition that sought to use the provincial government as the vehicle to protect regional interests.

A Western separatist movement burst on the scene in the early 1980's as a direct consequence of the new expectations by Westerners for regional economic development.[36] The February election of 1980 was decided in the "East" before many Westerners even voted, and this, coupled with the fact that only two members of the governing party (Liberals) were elected in the entire West, reawakened the old sense of disenfranchisement among Westerners. The federal-provincial confrontations over energy revenues, the National Energy Policy, and the proposed new Constitution all combined to suggest to Westerners that federal assertiveness in the face of Western aspirations was really another expression of Central Canadian control.

In any event, important forces had been set in motion that might have contributed to a change in traditional Central Canadian-Western relationships. Yet the principle enunciated earlier — that the growth of one region usually must take place at the expense of another — helps to explain why there was resistance to any significant shift in regional development. To the extent that the West might continue to attempt to diversify, and thereby strengthen, its economy, it is likely to engender continuing regional conflict.

Region Study II: The Atlantic Region

In our examination of the West, we have seen how agriculture and energy have provided the stimuli for regional identities and established socio-economic structures and traditions. Shifting focus to the eastern end of the country, we note that fishing serves here as the backbone of regional identity. As Prairie residents are "people of the land," Atlantic residents are "people of the sea." The ocean has inspired ship-building and overseas transportation which have facilitated regular contact with international trading partners. The ocean, too, has offered seafood as part of the regular diet, and mist and fog as part of the climate.

The relationship of this region to the sea has led to its designation as the "Maritimes." It is significant to note, however, that just as British Columbia has a somewhat different history and settlement experience from the Prairies in the West, so Newfoundland at the eastern extremities of Canada possesses its own unique identity and heritage quite apart from the provinces of Nova Scotia, New Brunswick, and Prince Edward Island. While the body of water (Cabot Straits) separating Newfoundland from these provinces symbolizes significant distinctions in geography, culture and politics, it is possible nevertheless to speak of this cluster of provinces as one Atlantic region, for there is much in their socio-economic condition that they hold in common.

The fishing village image of the region is unfortunate in one respect, because it is based on a worn stereotype. In the first place, a declining proportion of the population is engaged in commercial fishing; the majority of the population is urban. Second, the image is essentially pre-industrial in nature, and implies that the region has never embraced the process of industrialization. In point of fact, the region did have a thriving industrial base at one time and then lost it through a process of inter-regional transfer.

The long stretches of Atlantic coastline characteristic of the region have meant close contact with ocean-going vessels. This contact has resulted in regular interaction with Europe (particularly Britain) and the New England States. Early settlers came from Britain and France (Acadiens). Later, with the arrival of the Loyalists from the United States, the period from 1815-1860 became known as a time of considerable prosperity: the shipping industry grew rapidly, the merchant marine expanded to rank fourth in the world, and banks and insurance companies were established to finance and protect the capitalist expansion. Rawlyk and Brown refer to the eve of Confederation as the "Golden Age" in Atlantic Canada, when the prospects for an industrial future were bright indeed.[37] The Atlantic region was not oriented towards the interior of the continent, but to trading links with the eastern U.S. seaboard and Britain. Nova Scotia, in particular, developed industries around iron, steel, textiles (including cotton mills), rope factories, glass works, and sugar refineries.

The prospect of participating in Confederation was met with mixed feelings. On the one hand, there was the "beachhead" possibility of the Atlantic region serving as the key trading centre between the interior provinces and Europe. There were also potential markets for local products in the Canadian interior. On the other hand, there was a legacy of fear surrounding Central Canadian ambitions and politics. The breakdown of reciprocity negotiations with the U.S., however, and the failure of railway development (the Intercolonial Railway was not completed until after Confederation), together with a sense of the inevitable, led to provincial decisions to join Confederation (except Newfoundland which joined much later, in 1949).

Some regret has always remained in the region. Nova Scotia, in particular, spawned an anti-Confederate movement in the 1860's and secession was considered in the 1880's.[38] Perhaps most notable was the post-World War I Maritime Rights Movement, which was essentially a regional protest against the inequities of Confederation. What were the long-term effects of Confederation for the region?

Perhaps the most dominant feature of post-Confederation years was that the anticipated industrial expansion of the region never materialized and, in fact, recession took place. Part of the reason for this decline was a decline in the overseas staples trade (e.g., fish and lumber), but an additional problem was that the region was unable to compete with industries in Central Canada. While the Intercolonial Railway initially provided access to Western markets for Maritime industries, a change in the freight rate structure (which had originally made it cheaper to ship goods to the West than to the East) took away the advantage from Maritime industries and these industries were never able to recover.[39] Thirdly, the lack of both capital and markets forced many Maritime industries to sell out to Central Canadian interests. This fostered a continual process of consolidation and centralization of industry in Central Canada.[40] Fourth, federal policy became preoccupied with the problems of the West, and this put the Atlantic region in competition for federal attention. The addition of the Western provinces to Confederation meant that the strength of the Maritime provinces in political decision-making diminished considerably.

The end result of this process was the industrial decline of the Maritimes. The Maritimes Rights Movement (1919-1927) was a protest against the declining status of the region, which was an effect of the growing dominance of Central Canadian metropoles and the rise of Western competition.[41] The growing weakness of one region was clearly related to the increasing strength of another region, as the National Policy produced net benefits to Central Canada at the expense of other regions, such as the Prairies.[42] The Prairies, however, had no industry, while Maritimes industries had, at one time, thrived. As the Maritimes grew weaker therefore, a process of deindustrialization occurred. Symbolic of this reversal was the significant emigration of population between 1900-1930. Most of these people went to the industrial centres of New England.[43] A pattern of regional exploitation was established whereby Central Canada marketed its consumer goods in the Maritimes but, in turn, did little to provide a strong economic base for the region. The Maritimes then reverted to exporting staples such as coal, potatoes, wood and wood products, apples, and fish, and returned to a position of economic dependency on Central Canadian metropoles.

The relatively late entrance of Newfoundland into Confederation was not without considerable debate and controversy. The primary settlements on the eastern shores of the island reinforced pro-British ties and a transatlantic orientation that included Europe and South America. Yet considerable uncertainties existed in building an economy on variable foreign markets which Newfoundlanders could not control.[44] Dependence on volatile markets, such as Spain and Brazil, produced economic vulnerability. One of the greatest dilemmas in Newfoundland was that a very high birth rate, and a declining fishery, produced significant unemployment. While some industrialization was attempted initially by local governments, emphasis soon shifted to mining and pulp and paper, both developed largely by capital external to the region. The demand by the people for better services (e.g., schools, water systems, etc.), and the heavy expense involved in providing those services to a dispersed population, prompted government to sponsor resettlement programs. These produced greater urbanization, but did not increase employment opportunities.[45] While local patriotism, British links, and economic dependency made the union with Canada unattractive to some Newfoundlanders, the potential for modernization and federally supported development led in the referendum of 1948, to a 52.4% decision in favour of joining Confederation.

It is clear from the discussion above that the Atlantic region has not fared well within Canadian society, at least in terms of economic indicators.[46] Rawlyk refers to the feelings engendered as "a paranoid style of regionalism," sustained by a conspiracy theory focused on Central Canada.[47] In an attempt to reconcile economic disparities, the federal approach has been to use transfer payments, or equalization grants (unemployment insurance and grants for hospitals, roads and universities) to ensure a higher standard of living for the region. Some incentives have also been provided to private enterprise (e.g., Bricklin, Michelin Tire) to create employment, but these efforts have been marginally successful at best. Most significant to other centres of economic growth in Canada, the Atlantic region has provided a large reverse labour pool of short-term and long-term migrants to other regions where labour is needed.[48]

In an attempt to change this peripheral condition, it was not surprising that the energy resources of the Maritimes were viewed as presenting new opportunities for regional development. The growth of an expanding middle class, comprising well-educated provincial civil servants whose loyalties and interests were intimately tied to the region, produced a chorus of voluble advocates for expansion of provincial development of the energy industry. Even though oil was yet another staple for export, it did mean some prospects for new job opportunities and economic growth. The struggle for ownership and control of offshore drilling between the federal and provincial governments was fought with the goal of reducing, at least partially, the level of regional dependency and achieving greater self-sufficiency. While dependency has not been eliminated, local governments appear determined to turn the growth potential of their energy resources to regional economic advantage.[49]

Region Study III: The North

Most of the Canadian population lives in the southern sector of the provinces and for these persons, the North may simply refer to the upper provincial regions, where summer cottages, fishing, and hunting abound. For our immediate purpose, however, "the North" will refer to a distinct area north of 60° latitude, without provincial status. This area is known as the Territories and is composed of the Yukon and the Northwest Territories. Images of this region are of tundra, permafrost, short summer nights, ice and snow.

The sparse population and remote location of the North has meant that the region traditionally has been of minor importance to the Canadian economy. Even after the area was claimed as part of Canada, the government maintained a laissez-faire approach to the development of the region, leaving the major initiatives to the fur traders (Hudson's Bay Company) and the church (Anglican and Roman Catholic).[50] The vast area and the relatively inhospitable climate meant that both the traditional economy (fishing, hunting and trapping) and the small settlements of semi-nomadic people were far removed from direct southern Canadian influences.

Southern Canadians have been attracted repeatedly to the North by resources which, though difficult to obtain, offered the promise of quick wealth. Early examples of the activity surrounding this attraction can be observed in the Yukon Gold Rush of 1898 and, later, the mining boom around Yellowknife in the 1930's. As well as gold, there was oil and considerable activity was generated by the discovery of oil at Norman Wells in 1921, on the North slopes of Alaska in 1968, as well as by the more recent exploration at several land points throughout the Territories and offshore in the Beaufort Seas. Other mineral developments which have attracted interest because of their industrial uses are tungsten, silver, lead, and copper.[51]

Much of this resource based activity has occurred in a "boom or bust" cycle. What has produced these fluctuations? In the first place, these economic developments have taken place with southern capital put forward by large southern corporations employing a transient southern workforce who moved into the North only for the duration of a project. In the second place, resource extraction has depended on external markets, where gains or slippage in price could either heighten, or entirely close down, the extraction process. Problems of transportation, accessibility, and high labour costs meant that high retail prices were necessary to maintain operation. Conversely, drops in the prices of resources led to the abandonment of expensive extraction procedures. Thirdly, native workers, usually hired for temporary or seasonal terms, were poorly integrated into the operation. Not only did the wage economy change expectations among native workers, but it also began to bring into conflict socio-economic elements within the structure of traditional native economy. At the very least, the flurry of activity in the boom phase contrasted greatly with the bleakness of shut-down, and this contributed to instability in native society. Finally, because most of the wages and profits were taken out of the region, the resource activity had little lasting impact on the development of the region — a classic colonial situation.

What development took place in the North, then, was clearly related to the industrial needs of the South in the post-World War II era. It should be noted also that the North represented a strategic political territory for defense in the Cold War between the United States and the Soviet Union.[52] The establishment of a series of radar lines such as the DEW Line and Pine Tree Chain Line, as well as the construction of the Alaska Highway, all represented a growing number of southern intrusions into a previously unimportant territory. In sum, the needs of regions and countries external to the North contributed to the area's increasing importance within Canadian society. This developmental pressure is clearly changing the face of the North — both environmentally and socially.

No other region of Canada is tied as directly to federal controls as the North. Lacking status as provinces, all natural resources in the Territories (and the resultant royalties) are under the control of Ottawa. The Federal Government appoints a Commissioner for each Territory. In the case of the Northwest Territories, the Commissioner lived in Ottawa until 1967, at which point white civil servants were transferred to Yellowknife to administer the Territory. In addition the Federal Government exerts political control through the Department of Indian and Northern Affairs (DINA), serves as a major employer and is also the primary source of funds for health and welfare. Because nurses and teachers, as well as wildlife and resource officers, are all hired by the government, the number of civil servants in the North is three times the national average.[53] Additionally, transfer payments, in the form of welfare and unemployment assistance, illustrate further dependency on federal funds and institutions. It is this economic and political dependency that has perpetuated the coexistence of both wage and traditional native economies.

Amidst this colonial reality, a political awareness has begun to emerge among indigenous peoples, reflecting a desire for more direct control and power over the affairs of the North. Symptomatic of the desire to effectively exert control has been the recent efforts to obtain provincial status for the Territories, and even to create new political units (like the proposed Nunavut province in the eastern Arctic, suggested by the Inuit Tapirisat of Canada). Such status would effectively remove the federal government from direct control over the region.

REAL PEOPLE 4.2

Morning Musings . . . So Far Away

Cambridge Bay in the Arctic Circle

"I lay in my bed struggling to wake up. CBC Yellowknife gave the weather for all the major points in my world. Fort Simpson, Inuvik, Hay River, Resolute. The music was stirring and helped me wake up. The news came on. I heard about the problems in Ottawa, the concerns of apple growers in Nova Scotia and the automobile makers in Ontario. Last night I watched WGN TV from Chicago via satellite. There is something exciting about that world in the south. But me — I'm a Northerner, and its a long way from where I am at. I went south to take some courses but now I'm back helping my own people. Hunting and fishing is our life. But we live in modern settlements. I think I'll change the dial. CBC Inuvik carries programs in our native language. That helps bring our people together."

Questions to Consider

What does this example illustrate about the enduring nature of regional sentiments? What role do you think the CBC has in integrating the regions of Canadian society? How might satellites affect life in the Canadian North? How might satellites affect Canadian society in general?

Secondly, the growing indigenous rebellion against external control is evident in the emergence of vocal native groups striving to create greater political awareness among their people, and seeking to obtain more effective political representation to negotiate with the outside. Groups such as the Indian Brotherhood of the Northwest Territories, the Council of Yukon Indians, the Inuit Tapirisat, the Federation of Natives North of Sixty, and the Committee for Original Peoples' Entitlement, are all committed to enhancing the position of native peoples in the North in relation to white southern Canadians.

The third way in which this political awareness has been expressed has been in the demand for the settlement of land claims. The Dene Declaration signed at Fort Simpson in 1975 makes it clear that indigenous peoples want land, not government handouts of money. Control of land means real control of whether development will occur, the pace of that development, and some resultant control over the impact of the changes proposed. Built from the assumption that the white man was an invader, the settlement of land claims becomes coextensive with the right to self-determination. It is not surprising then that the proposal for gas pipelines through the region became symbolic of the fight by native peoples in the region for protection of and control over their own destiny.[54]

Contrary to the experience of the Atlantic region where emigration has been an important element of territorial demographies, there has been little movement of native peoples from the North towards employment opportunities in the South.[55] The transience in the North is largely created by white workers who view their northern work assignment as temporary. The fact that 75% of the communities with more than 50 inhabitants do not have a consistent economic base has produced considerable debate as to whether there should be southern development of the North, or any development at all.[56] The response among native Northerners has essentially been that development should be under their control and should utilize their labour. Much like the provinces in the Western and Atlantic regions, Northerners have increasingly come to the conclusion that decisions about resources should benefit their own region first, rather than so obviously treat the region as a hinterland with needs secondary to those of southern metropoles.[57] It is in this sense that resources, regionalism, and underdevelopment contribute to a complex saga that evokes comparisons with those regions of Canada discussed above.

Regionalism Revisited

While the history and economy of each of these regions is quite different, and the conditions of social life are quite varied, there are some aspects which denote a common existence. First, prosperity in each region depends greatly on staple extraction and resource development, whether it be grain, coal, fish, fur, oil, or minerals. Second, these primary industries are export-oriented, and little if any secondary industry has developed in the hinterland region. Third, the existence of qualitative differences between these regions fails to mask the fact that they support the industrial heartland of Canada. Fourth, each region has its own list of grievances focusing on control from outside the region. The most critical complaint links transportation policies (freight rates, shipping costs) to uneven development. Fifth, a new class of regional elites and middle class boosters are seeking greater regional control over development and change within the area. While regional protest movements are not new, conflict will probably become an even greater issue in the struggle for the redistribution of power.

In Chapter 1 it was pointed out that when regional differences are politicized to articulate regional concerns, regionalism has developed. The social bonding between people that is necessary before regionalism becomes a political factor, requires participation in movements expressing regional collective interests. Historically, most of the regionalist movements have been based on protest. *Protest regionalism* is a sociopolitical reaction triggered by erosion of position, and is aimed at either reversal of the decline or protection against further decline.[58] Such slippage involved both the Maritimes Rights Movement and the United Farmers Movement in the West. More recently, regionalist activity has been oriented towards new opportunities for growth. *Entrepreneurial* or *expansionist regionalism* describes the actions that result from the desire to generate or take advantage of new opportunities to benefit a region and its inhabitants. It is not surprising that the energy shortage has made oil and gas the basis for new hopes and expectations of regional growth and development.

As noted in Chapter 3, the federal government is aware of the issues presented by regionalism, and has taken steps to ameliorate some of the economic discrepancies with various forms of transfer payments. Few of these steps, however, have touched the need for more far-reaching change. Even if political and economic disparities could be reduced, there are numerous other arguments to suggest that the vastness of the country will ensure that regionalism will endure as a fact of life in Canadian society.

Further Exploration

1. Discuss regional stereotypes thought to be representative of your region. Explain why they exist, and assess their accuracy.
2. When does a regional difference become a regional disparity? What mechanisms have been tried over the years to reduce regional disparities? Why have these succeeded or failed?
3. In your view, why is regionalism such an oft-discussed aspect of Canadian society? Is it a figment of the imagination of the media, or is it real?

Selected Readings

David Bell and Lorne Tepperman, *The Roots of Disunity: A Look at Canadian Political Culture* (Toronto: McClelland and Stewart, 1979).

David M. Cameron, ed., *Regionalism and Supranationalism* (Montreal: Institute for Research on Public Policy, 1981).

Ralph Matthews, *The Creation of Regional Dependency* (Toronto: University of Toronto Press, 1983).

Landmark Canadian Document III

Document: *Northern Frontier, Northern Homeland: The Report Of The Mackenzie Valley Pipeline Inquiry: Volume One and Two* by Mr. Justice Thomas R. Berger. Ottawa: Minister of Supply and Services, 1977.

Issue: The proposals by Arctic Gas and Foothills Pipeline to build a gas pipeline through the Yukon and Northwest Territories prompted the need for an assessment of the impact of such a development on the existing population and physical environment.

Quotation: "The North is a region of conflicting goals, preferences and aspirations. The conflict focuses on the pipeline. The pipeline represents the advance of the industrial system to the Arctic. . . The impact of a pipeline will bear especially on the native people." (p. viii).

Context: The Federal Government anticipated that the construction of a gas pipeline would eventually lead to the construction of an oil pipeline adjacent to the first line. Concern was expressed for the impact that construction activity and environmental alterations would have on the ecosystem. Furthermore, how would the native populations and their distinctive way of life be affected?

The need for the shipment of gas and oil southward was a direct response to the demands of the industrial system. Arctic Gas was a consortium of American and Canadian companies that wanted to transport gas from Prudhoe Bay in Alaska, as well as gas from the Mackenzie Delta in Canada, to southern Canada and the United States to maintain the high technology industrial operations there. Foothills Pipeline, a Canadian company, had the same objective regarding Canadian gas. The point was that the Northern territory would be considerably altered, not because of needs within the area but as a response to southern industrial demands. Thus while southern Canadians and Americans viewed the North as a frontier to be exploited and developed, the native peoples of the North viewed this area as their homeland to be preserved and sought to maintain their way of life. The question then focused on whether the industrial needs of external societies infringed on native communities.

Procedure: Under the direction of Mr. Justice Berger, formal hearings were held in Yellowknife in 1975, and 300 experts testified regarding the nature of Northern conditions and the social and environmental effects of the proposed pipeline. 32,353 pages of testimony were taken in 204 volumes. In addition, hearings were held in 35 communities throughout the Western Arctic and the Mackenzie Valley in 1975-76, and 1,000 presentations were made representing the views of the native people.

The Report: The Report (as its title suggests) clearly distinguished between the needs of urban industrialization, economic development, and business interests on the one hand, and the native peoples whose natural habitat served as the basis for a cohesive and meaningful culture and social structure. Consequently, Berger rejected a coastal Yukon pipeline on the basis that it would disturb the ecosystem of caribou and waterfowl, and he preferred a southern Yukon Alaska highway route. He accepted a Mackenzie Valley route as an energy corridor, but suggested a delay of ten years in order for a series of precautionary measures to be set in place and land claims to be settled.

In addition to fears of oil spills diminishing albedo (reflective capacity of ice), and effects on wildlife, the Report focused on the socio-economic impact of the pipeline on the native people. It was projected that the employment provided by construction would be temporary at best (most of the skilled labour would be brought in from the south anyway), and harm to their own native economy of hunting, fishing, and trapping would only create more unemployment. Thus the incidence of violence, alcoholism, crime, and welfare dependence would increase. Berger felt that it was not so much that the native people wanted to recover a dying way of life, but that they wanted a greater measure of control, self-determination, or choice about their own future based on their own ideals and aspirations instead of having these changes imposed on them by others.

Assessment: The hearings had a positive effect in bringing the people of the North together to resist external encroachments. The negative experience of Indians with the James Bay Project just prior to this issue, showed native people the necessity to work together to defend their cause. As a response to fears of southern interference, they developed the idea of the Dene nation (a people with a common worldview and historical experience) to demand native self-determination in what is known as the Dene Declaration.

As a consequence of the public reaction aroused, the MacKenzie Valley pipeline was abandoned as an energy corridor for the immediate future. But it has been suggested that the Report was particularly useful because it gave Southerners a clearer idea of the feelings and perspectives of Northerners. Much of the discussions on impact effects were largely hypothetical, and we know little of what the actual effects would really have been.

To what extent did the Report play on native fears rather than make systematic analysis? Did the Report take into consideration differences in viewpoints maintained by native people themselves? Is the Report predicated on an overly simplistic dichotomy between the traditional native economy and an industrial economy? These are some of the questions that have been raised about the Report. However, as a consequence of the Report, gas and oil producing companies have found other means (e.g. tankers) and routes (Alaska Highway) to get their products to market and Mackenzie Valley is not currently a live option.

Further Reading: For an assessment of the Report in relation to the work of social scientists specializing in the North, read Richard F. Salisbury's brief review "The Berger Report — But Is It Social Science?" in *Social Sciences In Canada*, 5:3(1977) 14-15. For an interesting comparison with the James Bay Hydroelectric Project, read B. Richardson, *Strangers Devour The Land: The Cree Hunters Of The James Bay Area Versus Premier Bourassa And The James Bay Development Corporation.* Toronto: Macmillan, 1975.

ENDNOTES

[1]This statement is consistent with Matthew's view that regions are not natural but created. Ralph Matthews, *The Creation of Regional Dependency* (Toronto: University of Toronto Press, 1983).

[2]Odum and his colleagues devote specific attention to economic factors such as regional differences in income, occupation, and other indicators of standard of living. John Shelton Reed, "Sociology and Regional Studies in the United States." *Ethnic and Racial Studies* 3(1980):40-51.

[3]John Shelton Reed discusses a number of reasons why regional sociology in the United States declined. "Whatever Became of Regional Sociology?", in his *One South: An Ethnic Approach to Regional Culture* (Baton Rouge: LSU Press, 1981), 33-44.

[4]Richard Simeon and David J. Eklins suggest that unique historical and sociological factors may be important contextual elements that create cultural differences between provinces. "Provincial Political Cultures in Canada," in D.J. Elkins and Richard Simeon, eds., *Small Worlds: Provinces and Parties in Canadian Political Life* (Toronto: Methuen, 1980). Ralph Matthews argues that regionalism is the sum product of economic, social organizational, and political factors. "The Significance and Explanation of Regional Divisions in Canada: Toward a Canadian Sociology." *Journal of Canadian Studies* 15(1980):51.

[5]Richard Simeon and Donald E. Blake, "Regional Preferences: Citizens' Views of Public Policy," in Elkins and Simeon, eds., *Small Worlds: Provinces and Parties in Canadian Political Life*, p. 100.

[6]Cited in Roger Gibbins' *Regionalism: Territorial Politics in Canada and the United States*, (Toronto: Butterworths, 1982), p. 179.

[7]David Bell and Lorne Tepperman, *The Roots of Disunity: A Look at Canadian Political Culture* (Toronto: McClelland and Stewart, 1979), pp. 154-157.

[8]See, for example, David Elkins, "The Sense of Place," in David J. Elkins and Richard Simeon, eds., *Small Worlds: Provinces and Parties in Canadian Political Life* (Toronto: Methuen, 1980), pp. 21-23; and Roger Gibbins, *Regionalism: Territorial Politics in Canada and the United States*, p. 178.

[9]T.W. Acheson, "The Maritimes and Empire Canada," in David J. Bercuson, ed., *Canada and the Burden of Unity* (Toronto: Macmillan, 1977), pp. 87-114.

[10]Carl Cuneo, "A Class Perspective on Regionalism," in Daniel Glenday, Hubert Guindon, and Allan Turowetz, eds., *Modernization and the Canadian State* (Toronto: Macmillan, 1978), p. 188.

[11]Wallace Clement, "A Political Economy of Regionalism in Canada," in Glenday, Guidon, and Turowetz, *Modernization and the Canadian State*, p. 100.

[12]Kenneth Campbell, "Regional Disparity and Interregional Exchange Imbalance," in Glenday, Guidon, and Turowetz, *Modernization and the Canadian State*, p. 120. For other evidence of regional disparities, see D.F.G. Sitwell and N.R.M. Seifried, *The Regional Structure Of The Canadian Economy* (Toronto: Methuen, 1984).

[13]This explains why the argument that a region lacks development because it lacks entrepreneurs must be qualified by the power of greater corporate strength. For a discussion of this point, cf. Matthews, *The Creation of Regional Dependency* (Toronto: University of Toronto Press, 1983), pp. 46-47.

[14]Wallace Clement, in Glenday, Guidon and Turowetz, eds., *Modernization and the Canadian State.* p. 94.

[15]Cf. Larry Pratt, "The State and Province-Building: Alberta's Development Strategy," in Leo Panitch, *The Canadian State: Political Economy and Political Power* (Toronto: University of Toronto Press, 1977), pp. 133-162.

[16]This is essentially the point of Roger Gibbins, who argues that regionalism might be a much more salient idea to provincial elites than to their electorates. *Regionalism: Territorial Politics in Canada and the United States* (Toronto: Butterworths, 1982), p. 176.

[17]Garth Stevenson, "Canadian Regionalism in Continental Perspective," *Journal of Canadian Studies* 15(1980):16-28.

[18]Trans-border relations between the New England states and Maritime provinces are illustrated in R.H. Leach, R.B. Riley, and Thomas Levy, "State-Province Relations Across the Canadian Border," *State Government* 48(1975):150-155. Cf. also R.H. Leach, Don Walker, and Thomas Levy, "Province-State Trans-Border Relations: A Preliminary Assessment," *Canadian Public Administration* 16(1973):469-482.

[19]Cf. Bell and Tepperman, *The Roots of Disunity: A Look at Canadian Political Culture,* p. 146.

[20]For discussions of the political basis of regionalism, cf. Roger Gibbins, *Regionalism: Territorial Politics in Canada and the United States.*

[21]Alan C. Cairns, "The Governments and Societies of Canadian Federalism," *Canadian Journal of Political Science* 10(1977):707.

[22]Larry Pratt, "The State and Province Building: Alberta's Development Strategy," p. 157.

[23]Richard Simeon and Donald E. Blake, "Regional Preferences: Citizens' Views of Public Policy," in Elkins and Simeon, *Small Worlds: Provinces and Parties in Canadian Political Life,* pp. 101-102.

[24]For an excellent summary discussion of the National Policy and its implications in one volume, see the *Journal of Canadian Studies* 14:3(1979).

[25]George F.G. Stanley, "The Western Canadian Mystique," in David P. Gagan, ed., *Prairie Perspectives* (Toronto: Holt, Rinehart and Winston, 1970), pp. 6-27.

[26]James C. Davies, "Toward a Theory of Revolution," *American Sociological Review* 27(1962):5-19.

[27]J.F. Conway makes an interesting argument that these movements were essentially a class challenge for reform of the capitalist system by the agrarian petit-bourgeoisie. The fact that the Progressives also reached into Ontario illustrates that this protest had more of a social class, rather than regional basis, he suggests. "The Prairie Populist Resistance to the National Policy: Some Reconsiderations," *Journal of Canadian Studies* 14:3(1979):77-91. For an excellent review of the problems of the West in Confederation, see also his *The West: The History of a Region in Confederation,* (Toronto: James Lorimer, 1983).

Some of the key book-length studies on these movements include
W.L. Morton, *The Progressive Party in Canada* (Toronto: University of Toronto
Press, 1957); S.M. Lipset, *Agrarian Socialism: The Cooperative Commonwealth
Federation in Saskatchewan* (New York: Doubleday, 1968); C.B. Macpherson,
Democracy in Alberta: Social Credit and the Party System (Toronto: University of
Toronto Press, 1953); John A. Irving, *The Social Credit Movement in Alberta*
(Toronto: University of Toronto Press, 1959).

[28]Roger Gibbins, *Prairie Politics and Society: Regionalism in Decline*
(Scarborough: Butterworths, 1980), pp. 167-169.

[29]Howard Palmer, ed., *The Settlement of the West* (Calgary: The University of
Calgary, 1977) as well as the books of C.A. Dawson. For an account of the social
organization and evolution of the Prairie community system, see Carle C.
Zimmerman and Garry W. Moneo, *The Prairie Community System* (Agricultural
Economics Research Council of Canada, 1970).

[30]John Stahl, "Prairie Agriculture: A Prognosis," in David P. Gagan, ed.,
Prairie Perspectives, p. 66.

[31]Gibbins argues that the breakdown of the dominance of the rural
agricultural economy has reduced the distinctiveness of the region and brought it
into increasing competition with other urban industrial areas of Canada. *Prairie
Politics and Society: Regionalism in Decline.*

[32]Cf., for example, John Barr and Owen Anderson, eds., *The Unfinished
Revolt* (Toronto: McClelland and Stewart, 1971).

[33]For an assessment of the actual possibility of such a shift in power, see a
symposium entitled "Power Shift West: Myth Or Reality?" in *Canadian Journal
of Sociology* 6:(1981):165-183.

[34]For an assessment of the freight rates issue, cf. David Harvey, *Christmas
Turkey Or Prairie Vulture? An Economic Analysis Of The Crow's Nest Pass Grain
Rates* (Montreal: Institute Of Research For Public Policy, 1980), and Howard
Darling, *The Politics Of Freight Rates* (Toronto: McClelland and Stewart, 1980).

[35]John Richards and Larry Pratt, *Prairie Capitalism: Power and Influence in the
New West* (Toronto: McClelland and Stewart, 1979).

[36]Larry Pratt and Garth Stevenson, eds., *Western Separatism: The Myths,
Realities and Dangers* (Edmonton: Hurtig, 1981).

[37]G.A. Rawlyk and Doug Brown, "The Historical Framework of the
Maritimes and Confederation," in G.A. Rawlyk, *The Atlantic Provinces and the
Problems of Confederation* (Breakwater, 1979), p. 4.

[38]Colin D. Howell, "Nova Scotia's Protest Tradition and the Search for a
Meaningful Federalism," in David J. Bercuson, ed., *Canada and the Burden of
Unity* (Toronto: Macmillan, 1977), pp. 169-191.

[39]Ernest R. Forbes, "Misguided Symmetry: The Destruction of Regional
Transportation Policy for the Maritimes," in David J. Bercuson, ed., *Canada and
the Burden of Unity*, (Toronto: Macmillan, 1977), pp. 60-86. It should be pointed
out that as a response to the recommendations of the Duncan Commission, The
Maritime Freight Rates Act was passed by the Federal Government in 1927 to
restore some of the previous freight advantages to the region, but these rates
lacked the previous flexibility and failed to have the desired result.

[40]T.W. Acheson, "The Maritimes and Empire Canada," in David J. Bercuson, ed., *Canada and the Burden of Unity*, p. 93.

[41]Ernest R. Forbes, *The Maritime Rights Movement, 1919-1927: A Study in Canadian Regionalism*, (Montreal: McGill-Queen's University Press, 1979).

[42]Ernest R. Forbes explores aspects of the common hinterland condition of the Maritimes and the Prairies and discusses the factors that have prevented them from forming a coalition as allies. "Never The Twain Did Meet. Prairie-Maritime Relations 1910-1927," *Canadian Historical Review* 59(1978):19-37.

[43]Rawlyk and Brown estimate that 300,000 people left the region during this period with three-quarters migrating to the United States. "This Historical Frame-work of the Maritimes and Confederation," in Rawlyk, *The Atlantic Provinces and the Problems of Confederation*, p. 33.

[44]Cf. G.A. Rawlyk, "The Historical Framework of Newfoundland and Confederation," in *The Atlantic Provinces and the Problems of Confederation*, pp. 48-81; and James Hiller and Peter Neary, *Newfoundland in the Nineteenth and Twentieth Centuries: Essays in Interpretation* (Toronto: University of Toronto Press, 1980).

[45]In 1961, there were 815 communities of less than 300 inhabitants in Newfoundland and this was reduced to 545 communities in 1971. Ralph Matthews discusses the resettlement program, its objectives, and consequences in *The Creation of Regional Dependency*, Chapter 9. For an interesting study of small communities that resisted resettlement, see his *There's No Better Place Than Here: Social Change in Three Newfoundland Communities* (Toronto: Peter Martin, 1976).

[46]For an interesting lay expression of the frustrations of Maritime under-development, cf. Paul MacEwan, *Confederation and the Maritimes* (Windsor, N.S.: Lancelot Press, 1976). David Alexander also suggests that Atlantic Canada could have a stronger role in Confederation in his *Atlantic Canada and Confederation* (Toronto: University of Toronto Press, 1983).

[47]George Rawlyk, "The Maritimes and the Canadian Community" in Mason Wade, *Regionalism in the Canadian Community 1867-1967* (Toronto: University of Toronto Press, 1969), p. 102.

[48]Robert J. Brym and R. James Sacouman argue that the capitalist system itself through competition, concentration and the desire for cheap labour and raw materials has produced underdevelopment in Atlantic Canada. The disparity in the region between large external capitalists and producers at subsistence and wage labour levels (e.g. miners and fishermen) results in capital drain, a subsistence economy, and chronic unemployment. *Underdevelopment and Social Movements in Atlantic Canada* (Toronto: New Hogtown Press, 1979).

[49]Cf. Douglas House who describes the dilemma of oil as both a threat and an opportunity. "Big Oil and Small Communities in Coastal Labrador: The Local Dynamics of Dependency," *Canadian Review of Sociology and Anthropology* 18(1981):433-452.

[50]K.J. Rea, *The Political Economy of the Canadian North* (Toronto: University of Toronto Press, 1968), p. 345 ff.

[51]For a good discussion of the role of minerals in the economy of the North, see Rea, *The Political Economy of the Canadian North*, Chapter 4.

[52]E.J. Dosman, ed., *The Arctic In Question* (Toronto: Oxford University Press, 1976).

[53]Gurston Dacks, *A Choice of Futures: Politics in the Canadian North* (Toronto: Methuen, 1981), p. 18.

[54]For some opinions on the impact of pipelines on the north, cf. Donald Peacock, *People, Peregrines, and Arctic Pipelines* (Vancouver: J.J. Douglas, 1977), Earle Gray, *Super Pipe: The Arctic Pipeline* (Toronto: Griffin House, 1979), and James Woodford, *The Violated Vision: The Rape of Canada's North* (Toronto: McClelland and Stewart, 1972).

[55]Robert M. Bone, "Population Change in the Northwest Territories and Some Geopolitical Consequences," *Journal of Canadian Studies* 16(1981):01.

[56]Louis-Edmond Hamelin, *Canadian Nordicity* (Montreal: Harvest House, 1979), p. 220. See also Colin Alexander, *Angry Society* (Yellowknife: Yellowknife Publishing Co., 1976) for the views of a Euro-Canadian Northerner who rejects the concept of no development but prefers it to take place under the auspice of northerners.

[57]Some issues are whether Northerners should be given priority in hiring or training for employment and whether full-time positions should be restricted to Northerners. For a good discussion of all the issues related to Northern control of development, see Robert F. Keith, *Northern Development and Technology Assessment System* (Ottawa: Science Council of Canada Background Study 34, 1976).

[58]The distinction between protest regionalism and expansionist regionalism is made by Raymond Breton, "Regionalism In Canada" in David M. Cameron, ed., *Regionalism and Supranationalism* (Montreal: Institute for Research on Public Policy, 1981), pp. 64-67.

5 The Issue of Ethnicity

Canapress Photo Service

"The process of becoming Canadian in outlook has gone far in the Canadian-born children of immigrants. It will go on to completion in their children, or at least their children's children. . . At the same time community conflicts and institutional disturbances tend to retard it [assimilation] and render doubtful the seeming advantages of a sudden precipitation of new peoples into a great variety of contacts with those who differ so widely from themselves. It is for this reason that assimilation . . . is such a disturbing matter for all concerned."

— Carl A. Dawson, the first sociologist in Canada, and the founder of the only Department of Sociology in Canada for many years (at McGill University), in his classic *Pioneering in the Prairie Provinces: The Social Side of The Settlement Process* (1940), p. 38.

THE SETTLEMENT OF CANADA by persons of diverse origins has automatically heightened the importance of ethnicity within the society. Since immigration has been a prevalent factor in the construction of Canadian society, the official federal policy of multiculturalism has in recent years encouraged residents to remember, rediscover or celebrate their ethnic origins.

Ethnicity is an amalgam of factors relating to place of birth, mother tongue, and customs and traditions maintained by individuals or their ancestors.[1] In the Canadian experience, ethnicity is usually rooted in the societal culture of another nation-state, and thus has a significant foreign component. Ethnicity may also be used to represent a blend of foreign and domestic components, such as the hyphenated-Canadian (e.g., Japanese-Canadian, Italian-Canadian, etc.). When ethnicity is acknowledged as an important aspect of one's self-concept, it becomes one's *ethnic identity*. From a macro perspective, ethnic identities give Canadian society a unique character, but may also retard the development of a holistic, societal consciousness.

The importance of ethnicity as an historical fact in Canadian society cannot be denied, and it is of particular importance to determine the implications of ethnicity for contemporary society.

Ethnic Origin and Ethnic Identity

It was established in Chapter 1 that immigration from numerous sources has been an important component of growth in Canadian society. For this reason, the decennial census has always asked questions that would indicate ethnic backgrounds of the population through a category known as *ethnic origin*. Prior to the 1981 census, ethnic origin was determined through the father, but in 1981 ethnic origin was broadened to include the ethnic or cultural group to which the respondent or respondent's ancestors belonged on first coming to this continent. Note that the respondent can choose what best represents his or her ethnic origin (whether it is technically correct may be another matter), and that it is assumed that the respondent's ethnicity is something other than Canadian. Also, for the first time in 1981, respondents could state that they were of multiple origins, if they chose to do so (which most did not). As a result of these changes, the data gathered in 1981 differs from the data gathered prior to that year. For this reason the data on ethnic origins is presented in two tables.

Table 5.1 provides an historical view of the ethnic origin of the Canadian population. The Table also indicates the declining strength of those of British origin, and the rather stable proportion of those of French origin in the total population. The most remarkable gains have been among Southern and Eastern Europeans and Asians. Table 5.2

TABLE 5.1 **Ethnic Origin of the Canadian Population in Percentages for Select Years at Fifty Year Intervals 1871, 1921, 1971**

	1871	1921	1971
British	60.55	55.41	44.60
French	31.07	27.91	28.70
Dutch	.85	1.34	2.00
German	5.82	3.35	6.10
Italian	.03	.76	3.40
Jewish	*	1.44	1.40
Polish	*	.61	1.50
Russian	.02	1.14	.30
Scandinavian	.05	1.90	1.80
Ukrainian	*	1.21	2.70
Other European	.11	2.44	3.90
Asiatic	*	.75	1.30
Indian and Eskimo	.66	1.29	1.40
Others and not stated	.84	.45	1.00

Note: * indicates data incomplete due to small numbers

Source: Computed from 1971 Census of Canada, Statistics Canada, Catalogue 92-723, Table 1.

shows the 1981 data, and reflects the reality of a much greater ethnic diversity in contemporary Canadian society than was found in 1871 when Canada was much more of a duality of French and English. While Asians, Africans, South and Central Americans, and Southern and East Europeans were virtually absent in 1871, they now make up a significant proportion of the population.

Perhaps language may serve as a better indication of the importance of ethnicity as a factor in Canadian society. The census distinguishes between *mother tongue* (i.e., the first language learned in childhood and still understood), and the language used at home.[2] The data indicates that only 13% of the population have a mother tongue other than English or French, and about 6.5% of the population still use as their home language, a language other than English or French. What is clear from this data is that longevity of residence in Canada mutes the effect of ethnicity, at least to the extent that language represents an impor-

TABLE 5.2 **Ethnic Origin of the Canadian Population in Percentages, 1981**

Country or Area of Origin		Examples
British	40.2	
French	26.7	
West European	1.9	Belgian, Dutch
North European	1.4	Finn, Danish, Norwegian, Icelandic
Central European	6.9	Austrian, German, Slovak, Polish
East European	2.7	Rumanian, Russian, Ukrainian
South European	5.4	Italian, Portuguese, Croatian, Yugoslav
Jewish	1.1	
Asian and African	3.5	Uganda, India, Chinese, Nigeria
North and South American	2.2	Chile, West Indies, Inuit
Multiple Origin	7.6	
Unclassified	.4	

Source: Compiled and computed from Statistics Canada, Catalogue 92-911, Table 1.

tant bearer of culture. In this respect, ethnic origin by itself does not indicate the degree of attachment which a person may feel toward his or her ethnic group.

While it seems clear that the residents of Canada are of diverse origin, that fact in itself may be unimportant in the long-term given the propensity of immigrants to adjust to Canadian realities over the generations. If most immigrants eventually learn English or French and even use it as the dominant language at home, then this probably serves to reduce the influence which ethnic origin may have. Ethnic origin may also be so confused by intermarriage that it ceases to be a meaningful concept. It is clear therefore, that length of residence in Canada over several generations may reduce the importance of ethnicity in both a cultural sense, and in relation to personal identity. Ethnic background or ancestry, then, may not tell us much about the saliency of ethnicity in a society. It is probably more useful to determine ethnic identity, or the sense in which one views oneself in terms of that ethnicity.

But even ethnic identity does not provide a clear picture. For example, one study found that 80% of anglophones thought of themselves as simply "Canadian" rather than in other ethnic terms.[3] Among those with ancestors from neither England or France, 60% claimed to be simply "Canadian." However, among those of French ancestry, about one-half thought of themselves as French-Canadian, and 23% thought of themselves as Quebecois. In general, persons preferring an ethnic identity other than Canadian were more likely to be a first or second generation resident in Canada, or living in a geographic territory with a high concentration of persons from the same ethnic background, or had married within their ethnic group, or had learned a language other than English as a child.

Is ethnicity exaggerated as an issue in Canadian society? Is it a fleeting phenomenon that will disappear in succeeding generations as more persons regardless of ethnic descent are born in Canada? Indeed, has ethnicity already become irrelevant to the majority of Canadians? Or, to put the question differently, why is ethnicity given such importance in any discussion of Canadian society? Has the policy of multiculturalism fooled us into thinking that ethnicity is more importnat than it really is?

Factors Sustaining the Importance of Ethnicity

There are a number of reasons why ethnicity is far more important in Canadian society than may be readily apparent from the statistical data. The five reasons described in this section combine elements of history, government policy, intergroup struggles, and the social psychology of group belonging.

THE LEGACY OF EARLY EUROPEAN SETTLEMENT

The initial settlement of the Atlantic Region and the St. Lawrence lowlands by the French was challenged first by the Treaty of Utrecht in 1713 and then by the Conquest in 1759 on the Plains of Abraham. In both cases, an established and vigorous community of French settlers were taken under direct control by the British. By the time of Confederation it had become clear that while Canada was composed of two founding groups (the French and the English), the English had the upper hand in determining the structure of the new society.

John Porter has coined the term *charter group* to refer to the ethnic group that first settles a previously unoccupied territory and who then controls which other groups can come in.[4] While it is true that Porter's definition ignores the existence of native peoples already resident in the territory, the idea that a charter group is itself a foreign people who merely happen to be the first of a diverse stream of immigrants to enter the country makes the concept a useful one. It must be remembered however, that French and British charter groups were not of equal strength: the British were the *higher* charter group and the French the *lower*. Ultimate control of the immigration process favoured the British because the political apparatus was in their hands. One effect of this power role was to enforce among native groups, as well as ethnic groups permitted entry from other nations, an awareness of subordinate status and power. Thus, beginning in the colonial era, a power relationship emerged not only between the two charter groups, but between these and all other groups. These ethnic power relationships continue to have an effect on Canadian society.

Several features of Canadian society flow from this legacy. First, the organizational framework of the new society was based on British institutions and traditions — a fact which other ethnic groups would not always appreciate. Second, the British allowed francophones to retain some control over events in Quebec, and this is why Confederation is sometimes viewed as a pact between these two founding groups. Clearly the French and English have developed different interpretations of this ethnic power relationship, but it is this very relationship which is at the root of the famed *duality* of Canadian society. This fact was to become an important justification for the linguistic arguments that Canada ought to have two official languages. In general, the relationship gave the French more or less equal status, and, above all, elevated that group above other ethnic groups. While the implications of these perceptions are still not clear in the minds of many Canadians, the evolution of the French-English duality issue, and the struggle to arrive at a common understanding of that duality, help maintain ethnicity as an important issue in Canadian society.

A third consequence of this duality is that the divisiveness and conflicting loyalties between the two charter groups sets a pattern for other ethnic groups who seek to retain their own ethnic loyalties. Since the British and French were in conflict themselves, the society had a greater built-in tolerance for the perpetuation of ethnic identities.

TERRITORIALITY

In Chapter 1 it was argued that territoriality is necessary to establish a sense of society. When an ethnic group resides in a particular area, that group is more likely to maintain its identity as a subgroup of the national society. If members of all ethnic groups were evenly dispersed throughout the country, ethnicity would not be so important; but because this is not the case, ethnicity remains a critical variable in Canada.[5]

Quebec is a province with an overwhelming concentration of persons of French descent who still speak French. Quebec francophones have used the political structure of the province as a vehicle to maintain their ethnic identity, and this has undoubtedly been the most important factor sustaining ethnicity as a factor in Canadian society. Supported by Quebec's ethnic claims, francophone communities in other parts of Canada (e.g., St. Boniface, Manitoba, northern New Brunswick), have asserted their own ethnic claims. Francophone attempts to ensure ethnic vitality in Quebec have inspired anglophone minorites in that province to assert their rights as well. It appears, therefore, that territorial concentrations of ethnic groups create variable *majority-minority group relationships*. Because the mere existence of a minority suggests subordinate status or lack of power, conflict between the majority group and the minority group becomes a particular possibility when a group that is a majority in one territory is a minority in another territory. Thus while persons of French descent are a minority in Canada or Ontario, they are a majority in Quebec where anglophones are a minority. This territorial variation in majority-minority group status sustains ethnicity as an important factor in Canadian society.

Other ethnic groups also exhibit some territorial concentration. Historically many rural areas were settled by persons of a similar ethnic group (e.g., Germans in the Kitchener-Waterloo area of Ontario or Ukrainians in the aspen belt of northern Saskatchewan). Ethnic segregation has also been discovered in large urban areas. Generally speaking, the larger the urban area, the higher the segregation with Western and Northern Europeans the least segregated, East Europeans somewhat segregated, and South Europeans and Asians most segregated.[6] This fact heightens the visibility of ethnicity in urban areas, and serves as a reminder that ethnic differences are an important feature of the society.

IMMIGRATION POLICY

A third reason for the continuing significance of ethnicity in Canada can be found in the waves of immigration that have been so characteristic of the society. While the source of immigration was completely open in the early years, there was a 2:1 ratio of British to French in the total population at the time of Confederation, and these two ethnic groups made up 90% of the population. Other ethnic groups were small and usually consisted of other Northern Europeans. In the succeeding years (and in particular with the policies of Clifford Sifton, Minister of the Interior in the last decade of the nineteenth century), the desire to populate the West and fill labour needs led to the immigration of large numbers of other Europeans including Ukrainians, Germans, and Scandinavians. This immigration lasted until the onset of the Depression. After the Second World War, immigration from Europe began again, though it was not until the 1960's that large numbers came from Southern Europe (particularly Italy and Portugal). The migration source in the 1970's shifted again, and encompassed peoples from the West Indies and Asia.

Immigration to Canada was not random, but rather expressed government policy about the suitability of the migrating group. In essence, this meant that immigration was particularly encouraged from Great Britain, with some preference also given to other Northern European countries.[7] These other European groups were encouraged to settle less preferable land in the northwest, or to fill blue collar industrial needs. In this way, the British charter group maintained its control over the development of the society. More importantly, however, these repeated waves of immigration reinvigorated ethnic groups already resident in Canada, and reminded them of their own ethnicity.

In 1967, a point system was introduced as a way of evaluating the merits of a potential immigrant. This system reduced the source discrimination of previous immigration policy.[8] In conjunction with the new *Immigration Act* in 1978, the result has been to encourage more non-European migration, particularly among non-Caucasians. Perceptions of responsibilities for the economic and political refugees of Third World countries have raised controversies that are at the heart of the question of what ethnic groups are preferred in a multicultural society. Residents of the society have not only been reminded of their own ethnicity, but of differences between themselves and the new immigrants. In other words, repeated waves of immigration have made the matter of ethnicity a livelier issue in Canada than it would be in a society where immigration had ceased or was minimal.

IN-GROUP SOLIDARITY
Ethnic identity is more easily consolidated when ethnicity is translated into participation in an ethnic organization. In an unfamiliar social world, the individual can find in the minority group an alternate society with norms, customs, and values which are more congenial.

The importance of ethnic organizations in sustaining ethnic loyalties varies with the ethnic group. Raymond Breton has coined the term *institutional completeness* to refer to the degree to which ethnic communities provide a structure of organizations which provide most of the services required by their members.[9] Ethnic periodicals, welfare organizations, medical care, retail outlets, and churches provide a wide range of the services needed by the ethnic group member. The more institutionally complete an ethnic group is (i.e., the more that services are available to the ethnic group member within the ethnic group), the greater the likelihood that social interaction with the rest of the society will be limited. Breton found that relatively high institutional completeness was registered by Greek, German, Hungarian, Italian, Lithuanian, Polish, and Ukrainian groups, while low institutional completeness was indicated by Austrian, Belgian, Spanish, and Swedish ethnic groups.

The greater the difference between the ethnic group and the predominant culture in an area, the greater the likelihood that the ethnic group will be more institutionally complete. The theory of *social distance* indicates that cultural differences can serve to distinguish ethnic groups even when different groups are living in close physical proximity. A British immigrant is not nearly as socially distant from the dominant culture in Anglo-Canada as an Italian or an Asian Indian; hence the ethnic group is of less importance to the Briton.

Numerous studies have demonstrated that many ethnic groups have developed mechanisms to tie their own people together. We have seen that the English elite developed institutions and mechanisms to maintain its own ethnic superiority. As we shall see, the French have been very successful in ensuring their own relative institutional completeness. The Italians in Toronto have created grocery stores, newspapers, television shows, churches, social clubs, and social/medical assistance groups, all of which provide solidarity for Italians who are the second largest ethnic group in Toronto.[10] The Jewish community in Canada has likewise established its own institutions (to a large extent centred around the synagogue), to provide assistance to new immigrants and to support Jews and Jewish causes in other countries. These institutions also serve to sustain Jewish identities in Canada.[11] The Greek community in Montreal has approximately sixty organizations which serve a variety of needs among people of this ethnic background.[12] Pakistani Muslims, who previously formed an "incipient" community, have now been able — as a consequence of the infusion of immigrants in recent years — to provide a wide range of structures to accommodate their kinfolk.[13]

To some extent, these ethnic associations may be transitional ties which help immigrants to adjust to their host society. In-group solidarity will, however, remain important for some people because of intense ethnic loyalties, or because of a perceived social distance between themselves and the dominant ethnic groups in their area. Ethnic organizations, moreover, can contribute to the *politicization of ethnicity*; ie., the articulation of ethnic group interests to the wider society.[14] Thus, we are made aware of ethnic concerns and differences, through organizations which have as their mandate the advancement of ethnic interests.

VISIBLE MINORITIES

The concept of ethnicity has been used throughout this chapter in a manner which might imply that ethnicity includes race. Race and ethnicity are clearly not the same thing, though they may be related. A *racial group* is physically identifiable, and an *ethnic group* is culturally identifiable. It is possible to be of the same race but be culturally different (e.g., Caucasians may be either British or French), just as it is possible to be of the same culture but racially different (e.g., Americans may be either white or black). Racial differences frequently set in motion a complex of cultural differences because of the visibility of race. People who are of the same race, but of different ethnic backgrounds may have to work harder to sustain their cultural differences when they live together in the same society. In this discussion, ethnicity includes race, and will refer to any group whose culture sets them apart. Non-Caucasian groups in Canada can be referred to as *visible minorities*.

Race is a highly visible distinction among persons. It is something that no amount of cultural adaptation can completely eradicate. Colour of skin identifies people to each other, and leads to the development of stereotypes or generalizations about persons of different skin colour. Both prejudice as an attitude and discrimination as behaviour resulting from that attitude, may occur when people associate race with cultural attributes with which they are unfamiliar, and to which they feel superior. Indeed, research has demonstrated that non-European origin groups, most of whom are not Caucasian, have been the most likely to experience problems with social acceptance and job discrimination in Canada.[15]

Non-white immigration to Canada was initially related to the importation (after 1834) of blacks as slaves or escaped slaves from the United States to Ontario and Nova Scotia.[16] On the West coast, Chinese were brought into British Columbia to work on the Canadian Pacific Railway through the 1880's, and some Japanese and East Indians also came to Canada during that period. Each of these Asian groups encountered a generally hostile reaction from most members of the host society. Two unfortunate incidents of Canadian history were the head tax of $500 imposed on Chinese immigrants to discourage their entry into Canada, and the forced relocation of Japanese into camps in the interior of British Columbia during the Second World War. Through the years, federal policy has always been basically racist, and non-white immigration was discouraged until the point system reduced the obvious discrimination.

It is clear that the blacks in Nova Scotia, and the Japanese and Chinese in British Columbia have now been in Canada for many years and several generations.[17] They have more recently been joined, however, by immigrants from the West Indies, Haiti, Viet Nam, Hong Kong, India, Pakistan, Uganda, and many other countries. Each of these immigrants has brought with them their cultural and racial identities. For example, blacks from Haiti bring with them their French language, while blacks from the West Indies typically use English, and their culture reflects their many years of British cultural influence. Rather than finding cohesion with others of their racial group, these visible minorities all maintain important cultural/ethnic differences. Thus, is ethnicity retained as an important issue in Canadian society. The relatively easy identification of visible minorities reminds Canadians of the ethnic diversity of their society. It is also important to note that visible minorities include native groups. Their role will be examined later in this chapter.

The five factors discussed above are not meant to be exhaustive, but are meant to demonstrate why ethnicity has been, and will continue to be, a vital issue in Canadian society for some time to come. While the structure and substance of ethnic diversity has changed over time, and while new generations of children born in Canada develop different feelings and expressions regarding their ethnic background, the continuation of immigration in conjunction with recent government policies encouraging the maintenance of ethnic traditions and identities has supported ethnicity as an important underlying variable in the population. Barring any further significant immigration, it might be expected that some aspects of ethnic differentiation will disappear, while other aspects will be politicized and perhaps new coalitions formed. It might also be expected that tolerance and mutual understanding will remain an important objective.

Group Conflict

The co-existence of many ethnic groups is only important if ethnicity is a significant basis for group formation among members of the society. To those minorities for whom ethnic identities are important, the threat of absorption or subordination by stronger groups is a constant fear. Group conflict is not only a mechanism of self-defense, but also of group advocacy which strengthens and reaffirms the boundary and identity of the group.[18] Thus, for example, it is through conflict that Canadian native peoples remind each other, as well as the white Canadians, of their differences, and it is also through conflict that the French develop group cohesiveness in the face of differences from the English.

Ethnicity does not always engender conflict, for the mere presence of minority groups does not in itself mean that inter-group conflict will result. Furthermore, characteristics such as race or language that differentiate persons in a highly visible manner from the dominant society, are not sufficient to provoke group conflict. The minority group normally accepts its subordinate status quite passively unless two factors are present: a feeling of deprivation and a sense of group awareness.

Relative deprivation is the disadvantage a group feels when comparing its own status or opportunities with those of another group. Whether one feels deprived or not is a relative matter since it obviously depends on the standard of comparison. For example, as long as francophone Quebecers compared themselves with other French Quebecers there was little conflict, but as soon as they began comparing themselves with anglophone Quebecers, they felt they were deprived and sought measures by which inequalities could be overcome.

Group awareness is the feeling of unity which is felt by persons who share similar characteristics. This awareness also clarifies the distinctions between the group and other people. Not only do group members become aware of qualities held in common among themselves, but of the cohesiveness and power of the group as a unit. When group members no longer see themselves as friends but as comrades with objectives which contrast to non-group members in similar ways, militancy is injected into intergroup relations. For example, Canadian native peoples were for many years just a loose aggregation of people with similar characteristics. When they developed a sense of group awareness, however, perceptions of collective power ensued, as did opportunities to advocate ideas to the wider society. Groups such as the Union of Ontario Indians, or the Manitoba Indian Brotherhood, have an important role to play in unifying native peoples by making them aware of their common identity, and representing them to the wider society.

If an ethnic group possesses little sense of relative deprivation and little group awareness, conflict will not be expressed even though the ingredients for such conflict may implicitly exist. The Inuit provide an example of a group in whom a sense of deprivation and group awareness is only just emerging.[19] Because the majority group is becoming both the standard for comparison and the opposition with which one must negotiate concessions, overt conflict is escalating.

This discussion provides a framework for the presentation of two forms of ethnic group conflict which dominate in Canadian society: the conflict between the French and English and the conflict between native and white people.

Quebec and the French-English Conflict

A phrase that is typically used to describe Canadian society is that of
"two solitudes" or "two nations warring within one bosom." The
reality of two ethnic groups with different ideas about the shape of
Canadian coexistence has been maintained to a large extent through
considerable territorial segregation. Nowhere is this clearer than in the
comparison of the two provinces in Canada which have the largest
population: Ontario and Quebec. In Ontario 52.6% of the population
is of British ethnic origin and 7.7% is of French descent. Quebec on the
other hand, has a population which is 80.2% French and 7.7% English.
Ironically, each province has the same percentage of the other province's majority group as a minority. Quebec is also 88.2% Catholic
whereas Ontario is only 35.6% Catholic. When it comes to the language
most frequently used at home, 86% use English and 3.9% use French in
Ontario, but in Quebec 82.5% use French and 12.7% use English.
These figures explain why there are deep-seated conflicts between these
two neighbouring provinces. Evidence presented in Chapter 1 suggests
that these differences also extend to Quebec's uniqueness in relation to
other provinces.

THE EVOLUTION OF QUEBEC SOCIETY

In contrast to many of the early settlements in the United States, the
early French settlements were not populated by dissenters, but by
people who wanted to retain ties to France through church, state and
commerce. Thus the key persons in these settlements were initially
administrators, missionaries, traders, and explorers. Moniere has
argued that, even after the Conquest by the British in 1759, there was a
vitality to the francophone community that was only suppressed by the
defeat of the Patriots in the 1837-38 Rebellion.[20] This rebellion was the
first movement for independence among francophones in Quebec.

What did the British conquest imply for Quebec society? First of all,
it caused resentments and antagonisms towards the British that were
submerged, but not obliterated, in the ensuing years. This event and all
that it came to symbolize, has been referred to as a *primordial event*
because it made an indelible mark on the French-Canadian people, and
produced a minority complex which they have recently struggled to
overcome.[21] The second effect of the Conquest was the *social decapitation* of Quebec. The previous French leadership was replaced by British
leadership, particularly in political administration and in mercantile
commercialism. The third effect is based on "*the beacon of light*" theme,
in which the French community insulated itself against alien British
influence by organizing the agricultural habitant family around the
small-town parish. Parish priests emerged as the leaders of this society,

buttressing a French identity by promoting both Catholicism and the French language in the midst of a more widespread identification with Protestantism and the English language.

The British were content not to interfere with French culture because British ambitions for Canada revolved primarily around economic development. In exchange for their subordination to British political and economic control, the French were allowed control over their own culture which focused at that time on parish and school life. The *Quebec Act* of 1774 restored French civil law, and placed education under the control of the Catholic church. The will to survive as a French cultural entity led to agrarian isolationism which was reflected in a defensive and conservative Quebec government. Led by doctrinally conservative priests (many of whom had fled France in disagreement with the liberalizing effects of the French Revolution), and supported by an extremely high fertility rate, the French-Canadian community succeeded in preserving its cohesiveness and strength.[22] In fact, the community grew to the point of overpopulation and this caused great numbers of francophones to migrate to the New England States as employment from industrialization became available there.

Anglophone dominance went unquestioned as long as Quebec remained rural and agrarian. By the early decades of the twentieth century, however, significant changes had occurred. These included greater urbanization, and the growth of an emergent industrial complex centred around textiles. Cheap hydro-electric power and capitalist demands for natural resources contributed to a significant movement away from agriculture as the material basis of population. Accompanying these changes was a decline in the birth rate, and a desire for education that was oriented toward active participation in the technological society. In sum, increasing urbanization, secularization (i.e., less traditional church control), and industrialization, brought the French community in more direct contact with the anglophone elite and capitalist structures.[23] This contact, which increased as the century progressed, became the source of a sense of group awareness, and a sense of relative deprivation among francophone Quebecers.

The defeat of the provincial Union Nationale party in 1960 by Liberals, is usually viewed as symbolic of a changing worldview in Quebec. This change was known as the *Quiet Revolution*. Urbanization had two class-related effects. The first was the growth of a working class of industrial workers who developed critical views of anglophone capitalist exploitation.[24] The second was the growth of a new middle class of white collar workers in the public sector (and to some extent also in the private sector), who saw their ambitions for upward social mobility blocked by anglophone dominance and control.[25] Learning English, and discarding French accents, were typically viewed as necessary for success in the anglophone system, though such changes could not alter the fact that anglophones were both the owners of capital, and the real decision-makers in Quebec. As a result of this entrenched anglophone dominance, the emerging francophone middle class sought changes in French-English relations, as well as a restructuring of traditional Quebec society.

The first thrust of the Quiet Revolution was devoted to *rattrapage* ("catching up"), in order to bring Quebec into the stream of modern western economic development. The creation of a provincial Ministry of Education in 1964 replaced the church control of education with a new emphasis on technological and industrial skills such as engineering and accounting. One result of this change was that university enrollments grew at an unprecedented rate. As a means to foster economic development in Quebec, francophone-owned enterprises such as the steel corporation (SIDBEC), were given financial aid. In addition, as an effort to provide employment opportunities within a francophone mileu of an important Quebec resource, Quebec Hydro was nationalized in 1962. These were some of the means used by the government of Quebec which were designed not only to encourage Quebec participation in industrial development, but also to strengthen francophone control over Quebec's destiny. These measures were adopted in the hope that Quebecois might become *maître chez nous* ("masters in our own house"). Using a *structural theory of exclusion*, it has been argued that the Quebecois sought to challenge the English establishment, and remove all barriers that restricted their own opportunities in Quebec.[26]

During the 1970's, the process of *l'epanouissement* ("flowering") of Quebec continued with a heavy reliance on the government of Quebec as a mechanism of change.[27] During this decade, measures were taken which not only affected the economy, but also the culture in which the language issue dominated. Disappointed that French-Canadian participation in the direction of the economy had not proceeded far enough, and convinced that language was pivotal to the preservation of francophone identity, the government began to consider laws that would change the working language of anglophone enterprises in Quebec, and the language of education among immigrant children. The flowering of the new Quebec identity climaxed with the replacement of the "French-Canadian" label with that of "Quebecois," but with the election of the avowedly separatist Parti Quebecois in 1976. Prior to this election the non-francophone population was more or less left alone amidst widespread Quebecois euphoria. After 1976, however, the Quebec government began to intervene more directly in the anglophone community of Quebec. Bill 101 was passed in 1977 to ensure that French was not only the official language of Quebec but that it would be, with few exceptions, the language of instruction and work.

Second Session
Thirty-first Legislature
Assemblée Nationale Du Québec

BILL 101
CHARTER OF THE FRENCH LANGUAGE

Assented to 26 August 1977
Selected Excerpts

This bill is to replace the Official Languages Act passed in 1974, and declares in Section 1 that French is the official language of Quebec.

In Chapter II, the Act recognizes certain language rights, namely:

— the right of every person to have the civil administration, semi-public agencies, and business firms communicate with him/her in French, and to speak French in deliberative assembly;

— the right of workers to carry on their activities in French;

— the right of consumers to be informed and served in French;

— the right of persons eligible for instruction to receive that instruction in French;

In Chapter III, the Act declares French to be the language of the legislature and the courts.

In Chapter IV, the Act makes French the language of civil administration.

In Chapter V, the Act requires the public utility firms, the professional corporations, and the members of the professional corporations, to ensure that their services are available in the official language, and to use the official language in their texts and documents intended for the public, and in their communications with the public administration, and with artificial persons.

In Chapter VI, the Act requires employers to draw up their written communications to their employees, and their offers of employment or promotion, in the official language.

Chapter VII deals with the language of commerce or business. The inscriptions on a product, or on its wrappings, or on a leaflet, brochure, or card supplied with it, will be required to be in French. The same rule will apply to catalogues, brochures and folders, toys and games, contracts predetermined by one party, job-application forms, order forms, invoices, receipts and quittances, signs, and posters, and firm names.

French alone will be permitted on signs and posters and in firm names, with certain exceptions.

The chapter provides for certain cases where one language other than French will be allowed.

In Chapter VIII, the Act prescribes that the instruction given in the kindergarten classes, and in the elementary and secondary schools must be in French.

School bodies not already giving instruction in English will not be required to introduce it.

To obtain a secondary school leaving certificate, it will be necessary to have a speaking and writing knowledge of French.

Nothing in the proposed Act will prevent the use of an Amerindi language in providing instruction to the Amerinds.

Titles II, III, IV, and V establish an Office de la Langue Francais to oversee the application of the Act and certify francization, and establishes a commission to ascertain contraventions of the Act. Penalties are also established.

With a goal of *sovereignty association* (or political independence accompanied by economic association with the rest of Canada), the Quebec government issued in 1979 its White Paper entitled *Quebec-Canada: A New Deal*.[28] It was this document which prepared the way for the promised referendum concerning Quebec independence. Held on May 20, 1980, the referendum rejected the separatist position of the Parti Quebecois, although the party itself was re-elected in 1981.

In sum, since 1960, the Quebec state abandoned its traditional position of defensive nationalism, and instead adopted a philosophy of advocacy and intervention on behalf of its constituent French majority. The provincial government became a means of collective advancement, and frequently its policies were a challenge to the federal government. Refusal to sign the new federal constitution (1982) symbolized Quebec's fusion of historical and contemporary group consciousness.[29] At the same time, the lack of acute public fervour for further inter-group conflict and other radical political objectives, has led some to describe the 80's in Quebec as *la morosité* or "disenchantment". Perhaps gains have been achieved which, to many Quebecois, make further action unnecessary.[30]

QUEBEC REFERENDUM
May 20, 1980

"The government of Quebec has made public its proposal to negotiate a new agreement with the rest of Canada, based on the equality of nations.

This agreement would enable Quebec to acquire the exclusive power to make its laws, administer its taxes and establish relations abroad — in other words, sovereignty — and at the same time, to maintain with Canada an economic association including a common currency.

Any change in political status resulting from these negotiations will be submitted to the people through a referendum.

On these terms, do you agree to give the government of Quebec a mandate to negotiate the proposed agreement between Quebec and Canada?"

	Result
Oui Yes	40.44%
Non No	59.56%

Voter turnout — 85.61% of those eligible to vote

UNDERSTANDING THE NEW SPIRIT IN QUEBEC

In most developing societies, modernization has meant the blurring of cultural distinctions as the impact of foreign influence led to massive changes within the traditional society. Somewhat paradoxically, Quebec has experienced both social changes and economic development at the same time that cultural distinctions have been sharpened. Instead of yielding to the pressures of anglo-conformity, Quebec has accentuated its cultural uniqueness. What underlying forces made this development possible? How can we understand this surge of nationalist spirit? While this is a very complex matter which resists simple explanations, five interpretations can be offered.

The most obvious explanation is the *historical resistance to colonialism*, which was heightened by the more direct contact with anglophones resulting from industrialization and urbanization. Industrialization only accentuated the issue of anglophone (whether Canadian or American) control, and provoked a collective spirit of resistance to that control. This explanation does not provide, however, an understanding as to who led the resistance. Moniere has referred to the double class structure which existed in Quebec, and which was based on nationality.[31] The emergence of an *active francophone bourgeoisie* who found the ideology of the Quiet Revolution and sovereignty association congenial with their own interests, provides a second explanation for the rise of the new spirit in Quebec. A stronger state which protected Quebec from alien influences meant not only cultural nationalism, but also economic nationalism. The Quebec bourgeoisie supported the nationalist movement because it in effect challenged the competing Canadian bourgeoisie.[32]

Quebec nationalism was not only thought to be in the interests of the francophone elite, but also in the interests of the new middle class of young, university educated, and upwardly mobile persons who were angered by obstacles to mobility within Quebec. Thus, the *rise of the new middle class* provides a third explanation for the new Quebec spirit.[33] Confident in their own abilities, and frustrated by the blockage and control in anglophone corporations, these francophones found government, government corporations, and government agencies to be growth industries in the economic development of Quebec. Here they could not only find employment but also exert some policy control. Thus, the new middle class strongly supported and participated in provincial intervention. Indeed, research has shown that, among Quebecers embracing the new identity as "Quebecois," those preferring this to the old French-Canadian label were likely to be younger and possess higher levels of education.[34]

The fourth and fifth explanations suggest that Quebec underwent social change that may have been too rapid. The swiftness of social change, including the destruction of the old order, produced uncertainties in making the transition to the new order. Some people sought to reassert traditional values, while others had new ideas about the direction in which things should move. One solution to confusion was to *direct internal aggression against outsiders.*[35] The need to unite against external threats provided the basis for much collective action which would not have been possible in other circumstances. The changes within Quebec reflected an intense *desire to forge a new identity.*[36] Caught between the old culture and the culture of modernization, Quebecers sought a new image, a new self-concept, and a new collective identity. Finding their new image in the designation "Quebecois," they strove to replace the old identity by uniting ethnicity and polity in an assertion of nationalist sentiment.

LANGUAGE AND GROUP SURVIVAL

One of the factors heightening nationalist feeling in Quebec has been the perception of francophone cultural survival as a critical issue. Immigration provided one threat to francophones, because most immigrants learned English and became part of the anglophone majority, thus upsetting the balance of power both in the country as a whole and in Quebec. The other perceived threat experienced by francophones residing in parts of Canada outside Quebec was the difficulty in maintaining their language and culture.

Francophones Outside Quebec. Francophones, with some exceptions, were dispersed throughout anglophone communities, and found it difficult, therefore, to maintain their mother tongue. Because francophone migrants to English-Canada were concerned more with adaptation and adjustment to their new environment than with cultural survival, they became *invisible minorities*.[37] Furthermore, over the generations, children of francophones found it virtually impossible to maintain their mother tongue. The French language was much more likely to survive where residential segregation supported a reasonable amount of institutional completeness among the francophone population. Areas such as St. Boniface, Manitoba, and rural areas adjacent to the Quebec borders in New Brunswick and Ontario, supported French-speaking communities. Generally, however, the greater the distance from Quebec, the greater the extent of language loss.[38]

Bilingualism. The federal policy of bilingualism was meant to reaffirm to francophones, located in Quebec and elsewhere, that they were not second class citizens. As a founding partner of Confederation, francophones were to possess the same rights and privileges as anglophones. The policy declared the federal government's commitment to make its services accessible to both anglophones and francophones throughout Canada. The new nationalist spirit in Quebec spilled over to francophones groups elsewhere so that they became bolder in demanding their rights to bilingualism (particularly in education). At the same time however, the tightening of the boundaries of nation and state (as expressed in the new identification of the Quebecois), created distance between francophones inside and francophones outside of Quebec. The end result was, as Guindon expresses it, that the policy of bilingualism became politically irrelevant to Quebec, and a political irritation to anglophones outside of Quebec.[39] Many anglophones became defensive about their own language, and viewed bilingualism as a threat. Others found it difficult to accept a policy of federal bilingualism so long as the government of Quebec established a converse policy of French unilingualism in that province.

The emerging pattern of French-English relations seems to support the idea, proposed by Richard Joy, that two languages of unequal strength cannot coexist in intimate contact. Calling this the *bilingual belt thesis*, Joy points out that linguistic segregation in Canada is proceeding in such a way that linguistic minorities are disappearing.[40] Just as French is being overwhelmed as a living language outside Quebec, so English is being overwhelmed by the strength of French in Quebec. Bill 101, for example, is just another in a series of developments that have made anglophones less comfortable in Quebec. The bilingual belt, where French and English coexist, can only be found, according to Joy, in a narrow strip along the Quebec border. This area includes the Eastern Townships of Quebec, the Ottawa Valley, Northern Ontario, and the City of Montreal. The effect of Bill 101, moreover, may actually have been to shrink this bilingual belt. In sum, Canada seems to have moved towards *territorial unilingualism* with bilingual federal institutions at the core.[41]

A more positive form of bilingualism is taking place in the educational system, where children are learning both official languages. The most striking gains have occurred among anglophone elementary school children. French is increasingly being taught in elementary schools, and French immersion schools are also in greater demand.[42] English has been taught at the secondary school level among francophones in Quebec for some time. Now there is exposure at the elementary level as well. Familiarity with the second language is surely promoted by this approach. At this time, however, this familiarity should not be equated with widespread working bilingualism, in which both languages can be used by persons at any given time in everyday life.[43]

Anglophones In Quebec.   The issue of language and group survival had, as its initial focus, the survival of francophones outside Quebec. More recently, however, Bill 101 has raised the question of the survival of anglophones inside Quebec. When French became the official language of Quebec and English lost its official status, the anglophone community felt its own existence threatened. The militant reaction of anglophones has at times exacerbated the antagonism already felt by francophones toward anglophones, and strengthened Quebec nationalist objectives.[44] Bill 101 employed language as an economic and political tool in such a way as to transform ethnic nationalism into territorial nationalism.[45] The heightening of the Quebecois identity placed all Quebec anglophones in a dilemma which accentuated their minority group status.

The massive concentration of Quebec anglophones (75%) in the metropolitan Montreal area, and in some rural settlements in the Eastern Townships and Ottawa Valley, in conjunction with the fact that only one in three of these anglophones is bilingual, suggests that the anglophone population maintained its identity through close ties with English-America; e.g., Ontario, New York.[46] Quebec anglophones have, until recently, lacked leadership, organization, and a sense of community. This, coupled with large-scale anglophone emigration, has caused Quebec anglophones to seek out the protection of the federal courts.

Developments in Quebec since 1960 have clearly affected the nature of Canadian society, and have restructured French-English relations. These relationships coexist in dynamic tension. Many aspects have yet to be resolved. In recent years, however, another restructuring of ethnic relations has occurred among Canada's aboriginal peoples, and it is this restructuring upon which we now focus our attention.

Native-White Conflict

Native contact with Europeans first came through dealings with explorers, traders, and trappers, who needed the assistance of native peoples in the New Land. The increasing immigration of Europeans adopting agriculture as a livelihood, however, posed problems to the native way of life due to differences in attitude toward land ownership, commercial uses of plants and domestication of animals. With their superior technology and sheer numbers, white people used either brute force, or the threat of force, to remove native people from the path of European settlement. In this way, the Euro-Canadian domination of native peoples in Canada began.[47]

The *Indian Act* of 1876 made native peoples, in essence, wards of the Federal Government, placing them on tracts of land called reserves. More importantly, the *Indian Act* defined explicitly who may be considered "Indians." This definition divided native people into those with treaty status, and those with no status at all. Until recently, persons were considered status Indians (and therefore entitled to receive whatever benefits were forthcoming from that status) only if their fathers were considered Indians, regardless of their mothers' status.[48] The marriage, or informal sexual association, of large numbers of whites with Indian women resulted in offspring that formed a marginal group of native people with no status at all. These persons are called either non-status Indians or Metis. Historically *Metis* are the children of the union of European (mostly French and Scottish) men and Indian women. Metis, usually found in Western Canada and the Northwest Territories, are traditionally Catholic and French-speaking.[49] While there are approximately 300,000 status Indians in Canada, there are considerably more non-status Indians and Metis (approximately 750,000). Realizing that their rights had been ignored when western lands were transferred from the jurisdiction of fur trading companies to the Canadian government, the Metis formed a provincial government which attempted to negotiate a new accord with Canada. In 1885, the Metis, led by Louis Riel, staged a rebellion. The rebellion ended with the defeat of the Metis, and Riel was found guilty of treason and hanged.[50] Most Metis today subsist on marginal farmland in the northern part of the western provinces and in the Northwest Territories. The history of their mistreatment has recently inspired renewed protests for the redress of Metis grievances.

Found above the tree line in the Arctic region are another category of native peoples, known as *Inuit*. Consisting of about 18,000 people, many of whom live in small isolated settlements, the Inuit have no status under the *Indian Act* but have been acknowledged by the federal government as having some kind of claim in their territory.

These four groups (status Indian, non-status Indian, Metis and Inuit) form the native people of Canada who make up only a small minority of the Canadian population (just over 2%). Together with other aboriginal peoples living within nation-states throughout the globe, they form what has been called the fourth world.[51] In recent years they have been caught up not only in concerns over land rights, but the entire issue of self-determination. Two issues have served as the focus for heightening conflict with white society. One was the Berger Inquiry into the proposed MacKenzie Valley Pipeline, and the other was the struggle in 1982 for the entrenchment of rights in the repatriated Constitution. In both cases, native peoples' views were sought and opportunity became available for the articulation of native positions on matters affecting them.

It is interesting to note that only in recent years have native people organized themselves in a deliberate effort to defend their rights and assert control over their own fate. In doing so, a sense of group aware-ness has emerged as a result of their struggle to reverse exploitation and control by Euro-Canadians. With this awareness, moreover, a sense of solidarity and heightened group pride has developed as liaisons have been established with other native people. The Inuit, for example, have attempted to maintain measured social separation from whites in order to retain their identity and their collective rights.[52] The Inuit in the eastern Arctic have recently demonstrated a determination to establish their own political jurisdiction called Nunavut. In the western Arctic, the Inuit and Indians united to form the Dene, and in 1975 proclaimed the Dene Declaration in an attempt to assert both aboriginal and politi-cal rights.[53] In both of these cases, the concept of nation as ethnic collectivity is linked to that of geographic territory in order to circum-vent the perceived negative affects of Euro-Canadian colonization.

The long history of government dealings with native people makes it clear that the ultimate goal of government has been to assimilate native peoples into the white majority. To the extent that this has been a deliberate policy and undertaken without the consent and participation of native peoples, the policy can be considered racist.[54] In response to this policy, native people have banded together, creating organizations to increase the visibility of native concerns, lobby the government and affect its policy in Ottawa.[55] Status Indians formed the National Indian Brotherhood which became the Assembly of First Nations in 1982. The Metis have joined with non-status Indians to form the Native Council of Canada, and Inuit have formed the Inuit Tapirisat of Canada. In 1970, the government agreed to provide funding to these organizations in order to assist them in representing their people.

The demand for natural resources in the white industrial community has frequently placed new pressures on native lands, and this has required a higher native profile on issues affecting them. For example, the James Bay Project and several other hydroelectric projects proposed by provincial governments in the northern part of their provinces, have enormous affects on native social organizations and economics. While in some instances it appears that native groups are resisting these developments altogether, in other instances the desire is to assert native control over the pace and substance of development.

Rather than thinking in the individualistic terms common among other Canadians, native people think of their community as a collectivity. This is not to suggest that native people are unified in most matters, for one of their perennial problems has been fragmentation into groups with different interests and alternate views over what directions native peoples should take. Nevertheless, native people have attempted to use group pressure to effect a change in their position within Canadian society while seeking to maintain their own identity. Thus, native groups have remained at the margins of Canadian society as a "cluster of satellites" bridged to each other by a common relationship to the federal government.[56]

The Meaning of Multiculturalism

Much of the dynamic of Canadian society has its origin in ethnic differences among the population. As the response to the Royal Commission On Bilingualism And Biculturalism broadened to include residents of Canada who were neither English or French, it became clear that it would no longer be prudent for government policy to ignore the wide range of other ethnic groups represented in the country. Consequently, in 1971, the Federal Government declared a policy of *bilingual-*

ism within a multicultural framework. The official status given to ethnic differences by this policy has allowed ethnicity to be evaluated much more positively in the public mind than before.

Multiculturalism, then, precludes assimilation of ethnic groups, for to assimilate is to lose those characteristics which differentiate individual identity from group identity. In Canada, assimilation has meant anglo-conformity; i.e., that ethnic groups feel pressured to conform to the anglo-majority. While anglo-conformity may have been the objective in Canada in the past, multiculturalism represents a new approach.

Multiculturalism is also thought to contrast with *amalgamation* in which each ethnic group contributes something, but loses its identity as the people of a state find a totally new identity. This is the melting pot thesis which supposedly contrasts Canada with the United States. In contrast to a melting pot, Canada is said to be a pluralist society. Pluralism occurs where cultural differences coexist in an atmosphere of mutual toleration. This Clairmont and Wiens have called "The Canadian Way."[57]

Since many of the early immigrants to Canada settled in rural areas of the country, they were able to retain some of their ethnic identity. At the same time, however, it must be recognized that (at least until the Second World War), there were very strong pressures on ethnic groups to Canadianize, and discrimination towards non-Anglo-Saxons was strong.[58] *Nativism* prevailed as opposition grew toward any group that posed a threat (real or imagined) to Canadian life. The greater prosperity of the post-war years, however, caused a relaxation of inter-ethnic attitudes. In addition, the backlash against the Bilingualism and Biculturalism Commission by non-charter ethnic groups, and the model of a proud ethnic identity established by francophones in Quebec, both contributed to the recognition of the need to more fully appreciate the role of ethnic cultures in Canadian society as a whole.

The policy of multiculturalism seems to imply that people are encouraged to maintain their own ethnic cultures in Canada. In reality, that scenario is virtually impossible. Not only will these cultures be modified through the process of relocation, but they will also be difficult to sustain at all. With the exception of francophones in Quebec who have their own school system, media supports, and regulations controlling economic and cultural environment, other ethnic groups in Canada are bombarded with media influences, school materials and the workworld of anglophone culture. One study found that ethnic cultures experience enormous struggles in maintaining their languages beyond the first generation.[59] Can a complete culture survive without full institutional supports and a language which sustains it? How is it possible to have two official languages and a plurality of cultures all with equal value?

REAL PEOPLE 5

The Meaning of Ethnicity

The show was over. It had been a rather spectacular demonstration of Hungarian folk dance. The costuming and the choreography, and the vibrant faces of the young performers was really impressive.

I watched them sing the words of those folk songs in their native tongue. I could see their parents in the wings beaming with pride. They were first generation immigrants from Hungary who still had fond memories of their homeland. Now they were passing those traditions on to their children.

"Great show!" I said to several of the youth after the performance. "You've got a great heritage and you represent it well. By the way, do you all speak Hungarian at home?"

"Once in a while" or "occasionally," several suggested.

"Not me," exclaimed a tall male. "I'm not even Hungarian. I'm the only one in the group who isn't Hungarian."

Somewhat surprised, I countered, "But why did you join the group?"

"It's neat to part of some tradition," he retorted.

Questions to Consider

What do you think being Hungarian means to the young people? Why might being part of an ethnic tradition be considered "neat" — even if it is not your own? In what sense might emphasizing an ethnic tradition be a risk?

In the first place, not all cultures are of "equal" value except in the ideal sense of equality. In reality, pressures towards either anglo-conformity or franco-conformity are still strong. In the second place, the fostering of certain aspects of culture should not be confused with the preservation of a complete culture. In the third place, multicultural-ism aims to effect people psychologically by giving them confidence in their own identity, and seeks to create a "respect for others and a willingness to share ideas, attitudes and assumptions."[60] The preservation of ethnic folkdances, cuisine and other arts does not equate to preservation of culture. Instead, it has been argued that these cultural fragments give minority group members the illusion of preserving their ethnic identity while at the same time ensuring anglo-conformity.[61]

Roberts and Clifton refer to this form of ethnicity as *symbolic ethnicity* because it represents a nostalgic allegiance to a culture which is not part of everyday behaviour.[62] Through it, people can retain a link with their heritage while still participating fully in the benefits of mainstream Canadian society. Somewhat less cynical, Breton calls this phenomenon *partialized ethnicity* or *fragmented ethnicity*.[63] He argues not that a culture must be maintained in isolation to survive, but that some segments of an individual's life (e.g., occupation) may be de-ethnicized, while other aspects (e.g., kinship and friendship) may remain within the confines of ethnic expectations. Isajiw has noted that there is a further reason why aspects of ethnic culture may be important. Technological culture seems to heighten the need for identity, and later generations may become involved in "ethnic rediscoveries," selecting a few items from their cultural ancestries and maintaining them in their private lives.[64]

If multiculturalism has such a fragmented meaning in reality, then it is clear why groups intent on preserving their entire culture do not want to be viewed as just another ethnic group. Support for multiculturalism has certainly not been as strong in Quebec, and various native groups have also opposed attempts to view their demands as the requests of ethnic groups.[65] For both francophones and native peoples then, group belonging represents instrumental action to defend minority interests.[66] Furthermore, the experience of the United States demonstrates that, even there, ethnicity persists in spite of the melting pot ideology. Thus, although there is reason to support a cynical view of multiculturalism as a political tool or a psycho-social adaptive device, there is also reason to think that ethnicity will continue to be an important part of individual and collective identities for at least a portion of the population. How ethnicity will be expressed in the future and to what extent it will be used as a basis for cleavages in Canadian society remains to be seen.

Further Exploration

1. Why do some people want to "shed" their ethnicity while other people eagerly maintain it? Why do people several generations removed from immigration want to rediscover their ethnic background?

2. What factors strengthen ethnic identity? What factors reduce the salience of ethnic identity in Canadian society today?

3. What do you think multiculturalism really means? Should governments fund ethnic associations?

4. In Canada, there is frequent reference to "the French problem" or "the native problem." Instead, why might it be called "the English problem" or "the white problem?"

Selected Readings

Anderson, Alan B. and James S. Frideres, *Ethnicity In Canada: Theoretical Perspectives* (Toronto: Butterworths, 1981).

Frideres, James S., *Native People In Canada: Contemporary Conflicts*, Second Edition (Scarborough: Prentice Hall, 1983).

McRoberts, Kenneth and Dale Posgate, *Quebec: Social Change And Political Crisis*, Revised Edition, (Toronto: McClelland and Stewart, 1980).

Landmark Canadian Document IV

Document: *Report Of the Royal Commission On Bilingualism And Biculturalism:* Volumes I-VI. Ottawa: Queen's Printer, 1967.

Issue: Discontent among francophones about the continued vitality of their language and culture within Canada raised questions about the nature of existing French-English relationships. It was hoped that discussions and systematic deliberations would result in appropriate reforms to help francophones feel more a part of Canada.

Quotation: "The chief protagonists, whether they are entirely conscious of it or not, are French-speaking Quebec and English-speaking Canada. And it seems to us to be no longer the traditional conflict between a majority and a minority. It is rather a conflict between two majorities: That which is a majority in all Canada, and that which is a majority in the entity of Quebec." (p. 135, *A Preliminary Report*).

Context: An uneasy national stability had existed for years in Canada based on the dominance of the English-speaking majority. The early 1960's brought challenges to this view of Canada by francophones (particularly in Quebec) who objected to this uni-dimensional perception. Francophones were particularly sensitive to inequalities in the work world, where managerial positions were usually always held by anglophones, in the federal civil service where linguistic biases assumed English unilingualism, and in cultural matters where the preservation and defence of French-

Canadian culture was threatened by anglo urban industrial culture. Furthermore, the possibility of separatism as a solution to these long-standing problems had already been expressed.

Sensitive to these demands, the federal government proposed the concept of Canada as a bilingual and bicultural society, and set up this Commission to clarify the nature of the problems that existed and to seek solutions to bring about greater harmony.

Procedure: The Commission consisted of ten persons under the co-chairmanship of A. Davidson Duntan and André Laurendeau. Hearings began in the fall of 1963 and continued through 1964. Voluntary associations, occupational groups, and individuals presented briefs to the Commission. Twenty-three informal regional meetings were held in which 11,800 persons participated. Since linguistic education was a provincial matter, meetings were also held with provincial premiers and their delegations. In 1965, fourteen formal hearings were held where the Committee did not just listen to what people had to say (as in the informal hearings), but took the opportunity to seek clarification and engage in precise questioning.

The Report: The hearings of the Commission led its members to believe that Canada was not just in the midst of conflict or tension but of crisis, and that far-reaching changes must be instituted to retain the two language groups within the same state. Countries like Belgium and Switzerland were cited as examples where innovation successfully accommodated more than one ethnic group.

Distinguishing between individual bilingualism (a rare equal command of two languages) and institutional or state bilingualism (where principal public and private institutions provide services in both languages), the Commission recommended that French and English both be declared official languages in all aspects of the federal government. Provinces possessing an official language minority of at least 10% were also to declare French and English as official languages, and areas within provinces where an official language minority predominated were to be accorded the rights of a "bilingual district." Education in both English and French languages were to be available throughout the country and parents were to have the right to choose the language of education for their children.

The Commission recommended that francophones be given equal opportunity in the work world of the civil service and the private sector. This meant that French language working units were to be established, that services and communications should be provided in both languages, that management level appointments should be balanced between anglophones and francophones, and that language training ought to be available for employees to develop skills in both official languages.

Assessment: Perhaps more than any other Royal Commission, the work of this Commission fundamentally restructured Canadian culture. As a consequence of their work, two languages are available on the box of your favorite breakfast cereal, while you listen to instructions prior to take-off on your next flight, and when you read signs at a National Park. These changes and others like them were the result of the Official Languages Act passed in 1969. An Office Of The Commissioner Of Official Languages was also established to annually monitor the progress towards the goal of equal status for both French and English.

But it was precisely this notion of equality of the two languages that generated considerable controversy. Since the terms of reference of the Commission was not to inquire into the feasibility of a policy of bilingualism and biculturalism, but to recommend steps to ensure that Canada became "an equal partnership between the two founding races," a policy bias or assumption underlay much of the Committee's work. Consequently, much of the rhetoric generated in the hearings was largely a fundamental debate with the terms of reference and the policy that it represented.

One by-product of the policy underpinnings of the Commission was the emergence of opposition from persons of other ethnic backgrounds, whose outcries of discrimination eventually led to the deletion of biculturalism and the statement of the official federal policy of multiculturalism. While Ottawa was envisioned as a model meeting point between French and English, it became clear that the West in particular possessed a plurality of ethnic groups who also sought recognition and acceptance.

For social scientists, one of the highlights of the work of the Commission was the recognition of the need for research to clarify the role of language and culture in Canadian society. In an attempt to generate factual and up-to-date information on French-English relations, more than 150 research projects were completed (listed in Vol. I, 201-212), most of which were done by university-based specialists. A wealth of data and discussions on everything from national opinion surveys, to French-English differences in work habits, to comparisons with other multi-ethnic countries provides important background and reference materials.

Further Reading: The multi-volume Report of the Commission is a valuable if cumbersome piece to read. A one-volume abridged edition by Hugh R. Innis, *Bilingualism And Biculturalism* (Toronto: McClelland and Stewart, 1973) presents the highlights of the original report.

ENDNOTES

[1] This paragraph alludes to the subjective and objective aspects of ethnicity which, in their complexity, make the concept of ethnicity very difficult to define simply. For a discussion of the issues involved, cf. Wsevolod W. Isajiw, "Definitions Of Ethnicity," *Ethnicity* 1(1974): 111-124.

[2] The data cited here were computed from Statistics Canada, 1981 Census of Canada, Catalogue #92-902, Table 1, and 92-911, Table 4.

[3] Frances E. Aboud, "Ethnic Self-Identity," in Robert C. Gardner and Rudolf Kalin, eds., *A Canadian Social Psychology Of Ethnic Relations* (Toronto: Methuen, 1981), pp. 43-44.

[4] John Porter, *The Vertical Mosaic*, p. 60.

[5] Leo Driedger, "Ethnic Identity In The Canadian Mosaic" in his *The Canadian Ethnic Mosaic* (Toronto: McClelland and Stewart, 1978), pp. 10-16.

[6] T.R. Balakrishnan, "Changing Patterns Of Ethnic Residential Segregation In The Metropolitan Areas Of Canada," *Canadian Review Of Sociology And Anthropology* 19(1982): 92-110.

[7] Jean Burnet, "The Social And Historical Context Of Ethnic Relations", in Robert C. Gardner and Rudolf Kalin, *A Canadian Social Psychology Of Ethnic Relations*, p. 28.

[8] Anthony H. Richmond, "Canadian Immigration: Recent Developments And Future Prospects," in Leo Driedger, ed., *The Canadian Ethnic Mosaic*, pp. 105-123.

[9] Raymond Breton, "Institutional Completeness Of Ethnic Communities And The Personal Relations Of Immigrants," *American Journal Of Sociology* 70(1964): 193-205.

[10] Clifford J. Jansen, "Community Organization Of Italians In Toronto" in Leo Driedger, ed., *The Canadian Ethnic Mosaic*, pp. 310-326.

[11]William Shaffir, "Jewish Immigration To Canada," in Jean Leonard Elliott, ed., *Two Nations, Many Cultures: Ethnic Groups In Canada* (Scarborough: Prentice-Hall, 1979), pp. 280-289.

[12]Efie Gavaki, "Urban Villagers: The Greek Community In Montreal," in Jean Leonard Elliott, ed., *Two Nations, Many Cultures: Ethnic Groups In Canada* 2nd. Ed., (Scarborough: Prentice Hall, 1983), pp. 123-147.

[13]Regula B. Qureshi and Saleem M.M. Qureshi, "Pakistani Canada: The Making Of A Muslim Community," in Earle H. Waugh et. al., eds., *The Muslim Community In North America* (Edmonton: University of Alberta Press, 1983), pp. 127-148.

[14]The relationship between ethnicity and power is discussed in Jorgen Dahlie and Tissa Fernando, eds., *Ethnicity, Power and Politics In Canada* (Toronto: Methuen, 1981).

[15]Raymond Breton, "West Indian, Chinese And European Ethnic Groups In Toronto: Perceptions Of Problems And Resources," in Elliott, *Two Nations, Many Cultures: Ethnic Groups In Canada*, 2nd, ed. pp. 425-443. For case studies of several visible minorities, cf. K. Victor Ujimoto and Gordon Hirabayashi, *Visible Minorities And Multiculturalism: Asians In Canada* (Toronto: Butterworths, 1980).

[16]For a short history of non-white immigration into Canada, see Subhas Ramcharan, *Racism: Nonwhites In Canada* (Toronto: Butterworths, 1982), pp. 12-18.

[17]See Donald H. Clairmont and Dennis W. Magill, *Africville: The Life and Death Of A Canadian Black Community* (Toronto: McClelland and Stewart, 1974); Frances Henry, *Forgotten Canadians: The Blacks Of Nova Scotia* (Don Mills: Longman, 1973); Morris Davis and Joseph F. Krauter, *The Other Canadians: Profiles Of Six Minorities* (Toronto: Methuen, 1978); also Peter S. Li and B. Singh Bolaria, eds., *Racial Minorities In Multicultural Canada* (Toronto: Garamond Press, 1983).

[18]Lewis Coser, *The Functions Of Social Conflict* (Glencoe: Free Press, 1956), p. 38.

[19]Inuit Tapirisat Of Canada, *Political Development In Nunavut* (Ottawa, 1979). See also a discussion of the implications of Euro-Canadian labelling on native people, Graham Watson, "The Reification Of Ethnicity And Its Political Consequences In The North," *Canadian Review Of Sociology And Anthropology* 18(1981): 453-469.

[20]Denis Moniere, *Ideologies In Quebec: The Historical Development* (Toronto: University of Toronto Press, 1981), p. 288. See also Francois-Pierre Gingras and Neil Nevitte, "The Evolution Of Quebec Nationalism", in Alain G. Gagnon, ed., *Quebec: State And Society* (Toronto: Methuen, 1984), pp. 3-4.

[21]The three concepts developed here (primordial event, social decapitation, and beacon of light) can be found in numerous places, but one good reference is Richard Jones, *Community In Crisis: French-Canadian Nationalism In Perspective* (Toronto: McClelland and Stewart, 1972).

[22]Kenneth McRoberts and Dale Posgate, *Quebec: Social Change And Political Crisis*, Rev. ed. (Toronto: McClelland and Stewart, 1980), p. 30.

[23]For a review of the social changes occuring in Quebec and their implications, see Raymond Breton, "The Socio-Political Dynamics Of The October Events," in Dale C. Thomson, ed., *Quebec Society And Politics: Views From The Inside* (Toronto: McClelland and Stewart, 1973), pp. 213-238, and William D. Coleman, *The Independence Movement In Quebec 1945-1980* (Toronto: University of Toronto Press, 1984).

[24]Sheilagh Hodgins Milner and Henry Milner, *The Decolonization of Quebec* (Toronto: McClelland and Stewart, 1973), Chapter 10.

[25]For the classic statement on this phenomenon, see Hubert Guindon, "Social Unrest, Social Class and Quebec's Bureaucratic Revolution," *Queen's Quarterly* 7(1964): 150-162.

[26]Raymond Murphy, "Teachers And The Evolving Structural Context Of Economic And Political Attitudes In Quebec Society," *Canadian Review Of Sociology And Anthropology* 18(1981): 157-182.

[27]For a good discussion on the role of the state in the new Quebec, see Henry Milner, *Politics In The New Quebec* (Toronto: McClelland and Stewart, 1978), Chapter 3.

[28]McRoberts and Posgate, Chapter 10 presents a good discussion on the meanings and objectives of sovereignty association and the strategies involved.

[29]Stanley B. Ryerson, "Disputed Claims: Quebec/Canada" in Alain G. Gagnon, ed., *Quebec: State And Society*, pp. 59-67.

[30]Reginald Whitaker presents an argument demonstrating that the referendum may have settled matters and reduced the need for further action, "The Quebec Cauldron: A Recent Account", in Gagnon, *Quebec: State and Society*, pp. 88-91.

[31]Moniere, *Ideologies In Quebec*, p. 287.

[32]Pierre Fournier, *The Quebec Establishment*, 2nd Rev. ed. (Montreal: Black Rose, 1976), pp. 204-205.

[33]Marc Renaud, "Quebec New Middle Class In Search Of Social Hegemony," in Gagnon, ed., *Quebec: State And Society*, pp. 150-195.

[34]Bernard Blishen, "Perceptions Of National Identity," *Canadian Review Of Sociology And Anthropology* 15(1978): 128-132.

[35]Daniel W. Rossides, *Society As A Fundamental Process: An Introduction To Sociology* (Toronto: McGraw Hill, 1968).

[36]Charles Taylor, "Nationalism And The Political Intelligentsia," *Queen's Quarterly* 72(1965): 150-168.

[37]The concept of invisible ethnic minorities and its application to francophones in Toronto is developed in Thomas R. Maxwell, "The Invisible French: The French In Metropolitan Toronto" in Elliott, *Two Nations, Many Cultures*, pp. 114-122. The insecurities felt by francophone groups in an English environment are described in Sheila McLeod Arnopoulos, *Voices From French Ontario* (Montreal: McGill-Queen's University Press, 1982). The role of intermarriage in the anglicization of French minorities is discussed in Charles Castonguay, "Intermarriage And Language Shift In Canada, 1971 and 1976," *Canadian Journal Of Sociology* 7(1982): 263-277.

[38]Ronald Wardhaugh, *Language And Nationhood: The Canadian Experience* (Vancouver: New Star, 1983), p. 107.

[39]Hubert Guindon, "The Modernization Of Quebec And The Legitimacy Of The Canadian State," *Canadian Review Of Sociology And Anthropology* 15(1978): 227-245.

[40]Richard Joy, *Languages In Conflict: The Canadian Experience* (Toronto: McClelland and Stewart, 1972).

[41]For a good review of this trend, see Roderic P. Beaujot, "The Decline Of Official Language Minorities In Quebec And English Canada," *Canadian Journal Of Sociology* 7(1982): 367-389.

[42]*Annual Report 1981, Commissioner Of Official Languages* (Ottawa: Government of Canada), pp. 194-195.

[43]Ronald Wardhaugh, *Language And Nationhood*, pp. 54-55.

[44]Sheila McLeod Annopoulos and Dominique Clift, *The English Fact In Quebec* (Montreal: McGill-Queen's University Press, 1980), p. 125.

[45]Raymond Breton, "The Production And Allocation Of Symbolic Resources: An Analysis Of The Linguistic And Ethnocultural Fields In Canada," *Canadian Review Of Sociology And Anthropology* 21(1984): 123-144.

[46]Gary Caldwell and Eric Waddell, *The English Of Quebec: From Majority To Minority Status* (Quebec: Institut Quebecois De Recherche Sur La Culture, 1982), pp. 27-71.

[47]Victor Valentine distinguishes between the "accommodation" typical of the pre-Confederation period between native peoples and whites, and the "domination" typical of the post-Confederation era. "Native Peoples And Canadian Society: A Profile Of Issues And Trends," in R. Breton, J.G. Reitz, and V.F. Valentine, *Cultural Boundaries And The Cohesion Of Canada* (Montreal: Institute For Research On Public Policy, 1980), pp. 71-78.

[48]Sally M. Weaver, "The Status Of Indian Women," in Jean L. Elliot, *Two Nations: Many Cultures*, 2nd. ed. pp. 56-79.

[49]D. Bruce Sealey and Antoine S. Lussier, *The Metis: Canada's Forgotten People* (Winnipeg: Pemmican Publications, 1975); and also their *The Other Natives: The-Les Metis* (Winnipeg: Manitoba Metis Federation Press, 1978).

[50]G.F.G. Stanley, *The Birth Of Western Canada: A History Of The Riel Rebellion* (Toronto: University of Toronto Press, 1978).

[51]George Manuel and Michael Posluns, *The Fourth World: An Indian Reality* (New York: Free Press, 1974).

[52]See John S. and Carolyn J. Matthiasson, "A People Apart: The Ethnicization Of The Inuit Of The Eastern Canadian Arctic," in Leo Driedger, *The Canadian Ethnic Mosaic*, p. 235. For an analysis of the role of out-group conflict in uniting native people, cf. James Frideres, "Indian Identity And Social Conflict," in the same volume, pp. 217-234.

[53]Mel Watkins, *Dene Nation: The Colony Within* (Toronto: University of Toronto Press, 1977).

[54]James S. Frideres, *Native People In Canada: Contemporary Conflict*, 2nd. ed. (Scarborough: Prentice Hall, 1983), pp. 2-6.

[55]For a good account of how the federal government attempts to "administer" Indian affairs and the political role the National Indian Brotherhood, see J. Rick Ponting and Roger Gibbins, *Out Of Irrelevance: A Socio-Political Introduction To Indian Affairs In Canada* (Toronto: Butterworths, 1980). Indian-government relationships are also discussed in Leroy Little Bear, Menno Boldt and J. Anthony Long, eds., *Pathways To Self-Determination: Canadian Indians And The Canadian State* (Toronto: University of Toronto Press, 1984).

[56]Victor Valentine, "Native Peoples And Canadian Society", p. 117.

[57]D.H. Clairmont and F.C. Wien, "Race Relations In Canada", in Jay E. Goldstein and Rita Bienvenue, eds., *Ethnicity And Ethnic Relations In Canada* (Toronto: Butterworths, 1980), pp. 313-315.

[58]Howard Palmer, "Reluctant Hosts: Anglo-Canadian Views Of Multiculturalism In The Twentieth Century," in *Conference Report, Second Canadian Conference On Multiculturalism* (Ottawa: Government of Canada, 1976), pp. 81-118. See also his *Patterns Of Prejudice: A History Of Nativism In Alberta* (Toronto: McClelland and Stewart, 1982).

[59]Jeffrey G. Reitz, *The Survival Of Ethnic Groups* (Toronto: McGraw Hill Ryerson, 1980).

[60]Jean Burnet, "Multiculturalism 10 Years Later", in Jean L. Elliott, ed., *Two Nations: Many Cultures*, 2nd. ed. p. 239.

[61]David R. Hughes and Evelyn Kallen, *The Anatomy Of Racism: Canadian Dimensions* (Montreal: Harvest House, 1974), pp. 190-191.

[62]Lance W. Roberts and Rodney A. Clifton, "Explaining The Ideology Of Canadian Multiculturalism," *Canadian Public Policy* 8(1982): 88-94.

[63]Raymond Breton, "The Structure Of Relationships Between Ethnic Collectivities" in Driedger, ed., *The Canadian Ethnic Mosaic*, pp. 60-61.

[64]Wsevolod W. Isajiw, "Olga In Wonderland: Ethnicity In A Technological Society," in Dreidger, ed., *The Canadian Ethnic Mosaic*, pp. 29-39.

[65]John W. Berry, Rudolf Kalin and Donald M. Taylor, *Multiculturalism And Ethnic Attitudes In Canada* (Ottawa: Government of Canada, 1977).

[66]Evelyn Kallen, *Ethnicity And Human Rights In Canada* (Toronto Gage, 1982), Chapter 8.

6 The Question of Uniqueness

H.H. Hiller

"In addition to the things which could be done anywhere to add to the knowledge of human societies, what are the features of Canadian life to which the "more-so" principle might apply — those things which are highlighted somewhat in Canadian life, and from which one might learn something more about some aspect of human society than one would elsewhere."

— Everett C. Hughes, an American analyst of social change in Quebec (1940's), suggesting a distinctive thrust for Canadian researchers.

NO STUDY OF A NATIONAL SOCIETY would be complete without comparing it to other societies. This is necessary because ethnocentric attitudes easily develop due to lack of knowledge of other societies, and therefore it is assumed that the character of Canadian society is quite unique. But is this assumption of the uniqueness of Canadian society correct? In actual fact, comparisons with other societies suggest that while no two societies are identical, there are parallels between phenomenon which shape Canadian society and those in other societies. Through an examination of some of these features, similarities and differences to other societies become obvious, and our horizons are broadened beyond our own limited experiences.

No attempt is made in this chapter to exhaustively detail the many ways in which Canadian society contrasts with other societies. In fact, some of the contrasts will remain implicit or weakly developed because social scientists have not engaged in much comparative work as such work is both difficult and complex.[1] Yet it is possible to identify some of the characteristic features of Canadian society, to look for parallels in other societies, and to outline some of their significance and meaning in that social context. While we can conclude that Canada is unique in many ways, most of the issues which shape Canadian society can also be found in certain other societies. Consequently, the comparative analysis proposed here, while not definitive, should help us place this Canadian society in a global context.

The question of uniqueness will be addressed through focusing on the following societal characteristics: population density, population distribution, and population redistribution; historical origins; immigration and ethnicity; regionalism and nationalist movements; and language and culture. While we could examine societies which are strikingly different from Canadian society, most of the comparisons will be drawn from societies which have a level of development similar to Canada's, and with which Canada has had historic ties. These societies include the United States, Australia, the United Kingdom, and selected countries in Europe.

Demographic Comparisons

POPULATION DENSITY: THE GLOBAL CONTEXT

Two fundamental aspects of Canadian society which suggest its uniqueness are its large land surface, and its relatively small population.

Canada has the second largest land surface in the world. The Soviet Union's land surface is more than double the size of Canada's, whereas China and the United States are slightly smaller than Canada (see Table 6.1). Brazil is approximately 85% the size of Canada, and Australia has three-quarters of the land surface of Canada. These six countries have the largest land surfaces of all countries in the world.

TABLE 6.1 **Population Size, Land Area, and Density for Selected Countries, 1982**

Country	Population	Surface Area (KM²)	Density
Canada	24,098,473	9,976,139	2
Soviet Union	262,436,227	22,402,200	12
China	1,031,882,511	9,596,961	106
United States	226,545,805	9,372,614	25
Brazil	118,674,604	8,511,965	15
Australia	14,574,488	7,686,848	2
India	685,184,692	3,287,590	216
Argentina	27,947,446	2,766,889	10
Greenland	49,630	2,175,600	0
Mexico	67,395,826	1,972,547	37
Iran	33,708,744	1,648,000	24
Nigeria	55,670,055	923,768	89
France	54,257,300	547,026	99
West Germany	60,650,599	248,577	248
United Kingdom	55,671,000	244,046	229
North Korea	25,120,174	220,277	264
Phillipines	48,098,460	300,000	169
Japan	117,060,396	372,313	314

Source: Compiled from United Nations Demographic Yearbook, 1982, Table 3, pp. 134-140.

Population size however, tells us a different story. China's population is largest by far, followed by the population of India. While Canada has the second largest land surface in the world, comparatively, it has a very small population. Industrialized countries like France, West Germany, and the United Kingdom have more than double Canada's total population located within 5% or less of Canada's total land area. Mexico has almost three times Canada's population in a territory only one-fifth as large. Japan has less than 4% of the territory Canada has, but a population almost five times as large. India's territory is one-third the size of Canada's even though it has a population more then 28 times larger.

The best measure of these national differences is expressed in the population density per square kilometer. Canada has the most in common with Australia, where a smaller population and smaller land size yields a density of 2 persons per square kilometer, which is the same as Canada. Russia, Brazil, and Argentina also have rather low densities in spite of large land surfaces, which suggest that these countries have significant portions of their territory which are uninhabited due to an inhospitable climate or terrain. It is interesting to note that even though North Korea, Iran, and the Phillipines have populations which are virtually the same, 1½ times larger, and double that of Canada (respectively), their considerably smaller land surfaces results in these countries having a population density which is much higher than Canada's.

Whatever Canada has in common with most other countries of similar territorial size, it lacks in population. China and the United States are close to Canada in total land area, but their population densities are much higher. So the evidence makes it clear that Canada is somewhat distinctive in terms of both its land size and population density. Canada is not the only country which has a low population density, but only Greenland has a population density which is lower than Canada's. Again, Canada most closely resembles Australia, which has one of the world's larger territories (though smaller than Canada's), and a population about three-fifths the size.

POPULATION DISTRIBUTION: AUSTRALIA

A relatively small population residing on a large land surface is not the only similarity between Canada and Australia. Figure 6.1 reveals that the population of Australia is unevenly dispersed throughout the territory. Just as Canada has its Golden Triangle of high population concentration in southern Ontario and southern Quebec, so Australia has its own population concentration in the southeast corner of Australia south of a line from Adelaide to Sydney. Well over one-half of the total population of Australia lives in this relatively small geographic area. The remaining population concentrations are also found in coastal locations along the east coast, and the southwest coast (the area of Perth), with only a small scattered population in inland locations.

One of the consequences of this uneven population distribution is that 61% of the total population of Australia is found in two states, Victoria and New South Wales (compare with Ontario and Quebec whose percentage of Canada's total population is very similar). Victoria and New South Wales are also the two states where the two largest cities are located (Table 6.2), namely Sydney at 3.3 million, and Melbourne at 2.8 million people.[2] The dominance of these two cities is rather similar to the dominant position of Toronto and Montreal in Canada. Brisbane, with 1.1 million residents is a second order metropolitan centre similar to Vancouver. In addition there are several smaller urban areas with a population under 1 million, such as Adelaide and Perth, which are capitals of the states of South Australia and Western Australia respec-

FIGURE 6.1   **Ecumene of Australia**

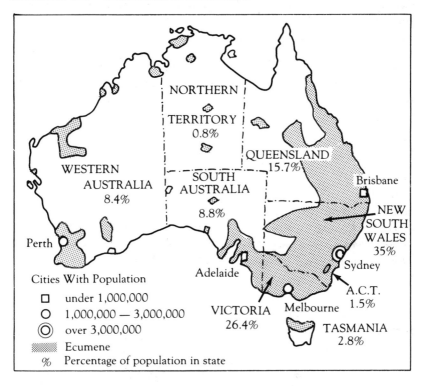

tively. These urban concentrations of population make Australia a
highly urbanized country in spite of its vast land mass. Fully 69.6% of
the population of Australia live in cities of over 100,000 people, and all
of these cities are located along the coast, except for Canberra which is
slightly inland.

Uneven population distribution also means that while some states
dominate largely because of their large urban metropolitan populations,
other states lag behind largely because their urban centres are smaller,
and the rural areas are not conducive to high density agriculture. There
are vast grain farms, and some ranching is undertaken in some of the
outback areas, but these populations are not only dispersed, but distinctly different from the more urban people of southeast Australia.
Western Australia in particular has felt a significant sense of isolation
and, with its 8.7% share of the population, has occasionally produced
independence movements that have sought to achieve greater control
over their region in the face of the perceived dominance of east Australia.[3] Canada has no parallel to the ACT (Australian Capital Territory)

TABLE 6.2   **Percentage Total Population and Percentage Metropolitan Population For Australia, by State or Territory, 1983**

	% Total Population	% Population In Cities Over 100,000
New South Wales	35.1	75.5
Victoria	26.5	74.6
South Australia	8.8	72.2
Western Australia	8.7	70.7
Queensland	15.7	52.4
Tasmania	2.9	40.0
Northern Territory	.8	—
Australian Capital Territory	1.5	—

Source: *Australian Yearbook 1983* (Canberra: Australian Bureau of Statistics), p. 122.

which includes the urban centre of Canberra as a small territory similar to the District of Columbia in the United States. On the other hand, the lower level of metropolitan urbanization in Tasmania (Table 6.2) is perhaps somewhat like that of the Atlantic provinces in Canada, and the weakly populated Northern Territory (.8% of the total population) has some parallels with the Northwest Territories in Canada.

Canada has a problem with poor soil or poor growing conditions which result from the cold climate. The problem in Australia is that of aridity in some locations, and a tropical rainy climate in other areas. Consequently, just as most of the population of Canada is located at the southern extremities of the country where the climate is more moderate, so the population of Australia clusters along the more temperate south and east coast. In any event large portions of the land in both countries are virtually uninhabited. These vast hinterlands, however, have been valued for their resources in Canada, and in Australia resources have more recently been discovered in sparsely inhabited areas. These resources are used for export either to urban centres, or to other countries, and thus the economies of these regions are being drawn into the vagaries of market and price instabilities. Many of the metropolis hinterland relationships which are developing in Australia are similar to those relationships experienced in Canada.[4]

By way of further contrast, it is interesting to note that with perhaps the exception of the native or aboriginal population, the higher level of economic development in Canada and Australia produces much less of a cleavage between rural and urban peoples than is found in a country like Brazil.[5] In that country there is a great disparity between the more modern affluent sector, and the majority of poor people who are primarily rural (though some are also urban poor as well). The technology gap between the traditional society and the more modern sector produces real cleavages in Brazil because large portions of the population are excluded from participation in economic growth. We will return to this matter as it relates to native peoples; but at this point it is important to indicate that rural indigenous populations are a much more significant factor in the dispersion of the population in countries like Brazil, than they are in Australia or Canada.

POPULATION REDISTRIBUTION: THE UNITED STATES

The European settlement of North America meant that the natural internal movement of population on the continent would be from east to west. By the end of the Second World War, a pattern was clearly established which resulted in the largest population concentrations being located in the Northeastern States, and extending up into Ontario and Quebec. As the centre of industrialization, the New England States had attracted both immigrants and internal migrants to their growing cities. Other industrial cities in the North such as Detroit, Cleveland, and Chicago attracted white rural populations, who had been pushed off the land by the mechanization of agriculture, and Southern black people, who began to seek employment opportunities in Northern cities. With the exception of black migration from the South, Toronto and Montreal experienced the same kind of growth from rural-urban population shifts.

While the dynamics of industrial growth meant that internal migration was clearly in the direction of the Northern cities in the United States, the gradual movement of population to the West coast (cities like Seattle, San Francisco, Los Angeles) was also occurring. The geographic centre of the population had been steadily moving westward from Maryland in 1790, to Indiana by 1900, to Illinois in 1960, and still further westward past St. Louis, Missouri by 1980.[6] Most of this shift was due to an internal redistribution of the population, rather than an influx of new residents. By the 1970's, it became clear that the Northeastern region was losing its growth dynamic; its share of the national population declined from 26% in 1950 to 21% by 1982. On the other hand, the Western region had increased its share of the population from 13% to 19%, and the South grew from 31% to 34% over the same period.[7] Over a longer period from 1920-1980, the Northeast had grown by 69% whereas the West and South had grown by 378% and 127% respectively. Essentially the population seemed to be moving from areas of high density such as the Northeast (301 persons per square mile), to areas of low density such as the West (24 persons per square mile), and the South (86 persons per square mile).

A similar long term movement to the West has also been occurring in Canada, particularly in British Columbia, and to some extent Alberta. It might be argued that Canadians have also been caught up in a general continental population shift to the American South and Southwest, whether as temporary or semi-permanent migrants. What makes Canada different, however, is that the redistribution of population within the country has not as yet had any significant effect on the redistribution of power. One exception to this statement might be the early shift away from the Atlantic region to Central Canada, noted in Chapter 4.

One argument treats the redistribution of population in the United States as a symptom of the redistribution of economic and political power in that country.[8] The people of the Southern Rim (that area south of a line drawn from the Carolinas to California) have risen to challenge the Eastern economic establishment through agribusiness, defense production, advanced technology, oil and gas production, real estate, construction, tourism and leisure. Many cities have experienced remarkable growth. The population of Houston, for example has increased from a paltry 385,000 residents in 1945 to 2.7 million in 1980, and this story is repeated in many other Southern Rim cities such as Ft. Lauderdale, Austin, and Phoenix. Instead of relying on secondary industries in manufacturing such as are found in the Northeast, Southern Rim communities encouraged tertiary, service industries (such as electronics) and quaternary, leisure-oriented industries. These initiatives provided new employment opportunities in the Southern Rim, and reduced the economic strength of the Northeast. Some have argued that this power shift has been exaggerated, in spite of the developments in the American South.[9] The truth, though, is that the South has penetrated the political and economic mainstream in a manner which has changed the nature of regional relationships.

In spite of the slow redistribution of the population westward in Canada, there is little evidence that any significant power shift is occurring. The rapid growth of Edmonton and Calgary in the 1970's has shown some evidence of reversing itself, as their growth was tied directly to the exploitation of oil and gas. The efforts at greater industrial diversification in Alberta (e.g., the establishment of an electronics industry) have had only marginal success at best. Similarly in British Columbia, a coastal climate and transportation base has increased Van-

...ada has tended to follow the British pattern of values based on
...aristocratic background of privilege, and a more hardened class
...cture.

...What evidence did Lipset use to build his case? He noted that in
...ada there was less equality of opportunity through the educational
...em, and he gathered evidence to suggest that lower levels of educa-
...al attainment were good indicators of reduced opportunity in Can-
...He noted that greater acceptance of government participation in the
...nomy indicated that Canada was more collectivist than the United
...es, where individualist free enterprise ideas were staunchly
...nded. Government involvement in broadcasting and transporta-
..., for example, and the traditional strength of the Roman Catholic
...Anglican church in Canada were viewed as part of a general pattern
...einforce traditional community values and to suppress excesses of
...vidualism. Lipset also noted the greater respect for law and order in
...ada, as evidenced by a lower ratio of policemen and lawyers to
...ulation, and indicated that Canada possessed a more stable tradi-
...al order. In contrast, higher crime and divorce rates in the United
...es indicated less respect for traditional order.

...Lipset's thesis has generated considerable controversy and debate.[16]
...e first place, Lipset depended on data from the 1950's, and Canada
...undergone considerable changes since that time, particularly in
...cation, and in the growth of divorce and crime rates. Secondly, it is
...stionable whether any of the data which he used really identifies
...inant societal values. For example, a case can be made that Canada
...ore (rather than less) egalitarian than the United States. Inequalities
...ween races, and greater gaps between the wealthy and poor Ameri-
...serve to support this case. In fact, the British working class heritage
...anada puts greater value on equality of living standards and income
...on competitive achievement. Third, Canada has produced numer-
...reform movements that have resulted in innovations in medical
..., creative third-party politics, and institutional change. Social
...ocratic ideas, such as these listed above, have been tolerated to a
...h greater extent in Canada than in the United States.

...While the Lipset thesis is clearly fraught with problems, no com-
...ensive alternative comparisons have been developed. The counter-
...lutionary experiences of Canadian society have clearly molded a
...rent society on the northern half of the continent. It could also be
...comparisons with the United States are too complex, and resist
...d generalities. But for most Canadians, such comparisons are part
...veryday life, as residents attempt to grapple with the obvious
...arities, yet remarkable (and subtle) differences between the two
...ties. Clearly, historical contrasts are meaningful for an understand-
...f the development of these two countries. Perhaps, too, differences

couver's importance and industrial viability, but little growth has
occurred outside of the lower mainland in interior cities such as
Kelowna or Penticton. In sum, if there have been some important shifts
of both population and technology away from (or in competition with)
the Northeast in the United States, there seems little evidence that any
substantial shift of power has occurred in Canada. In fact, Southern
Ontario in particular appears to have consolidated its position as the
centre of economic power.

Historical Origins: The United States

Canada shares with the United States the experience of being a colonial
outpost of European empires. Louis Hartz has proposed a *fragment
theory* which suggests that these new societies were founded as fragments
of European culture and ideology.[10] In his view, contemporary differences between societies in the New World can be traced at least partially to
the sponsoring society. While many European societies each contained
divergent ideologies like conservativism, liberalism, or socialism, the
societies of the New World tended to be constructed on only one aspect
or fragment of the European political culture. Therefore, Hartz argued,
the society of New France (French Canada) was established as a fragment of conservative feudal French society while English-America was a
much more liberal bourgeois fragment of England.

On one hand, this kind of analysis implies that English Canada and
the United States should be very similar. McRae has argued that the
conservative French fragment became entrenched with the British conquest in 1759, when the entrepreneurial spirit was removed from
Quebec, and the Catholic church took over as the guardian of traditional values and social life.[11] On the other hand, the American War of
Independence in 1776 also demonstrated the failure of the liberal
English fragment to claim the entire continent. At the same time,
however, neither Quebec nor English Canada supported the American
rebellion, and this rejection of the independence movement reasserted
Old World loyalties and ideologies in Canada, which established the
basis for essential differences between Canadian and American society.

Perhaps the most significant factor in the rejection of independence
by the northern part of the continent was the migration of the Loyalists
from the United States to Canada. These Loyalists were persons who
wanted to retain British ties. It is estimated that between 30,000 and
60,000 Loyalists arrived in Canada around the time of the American
rebellion, and prior to this Canada had only about 15,000 anglophone
residents in all.[12] Consequently, it becomes clear that in many ways,

English Canada emerged as a direct consequence of the American revolution.

Bell and Tepperman have argued that the irony of the Loyalists' position was that, while they rejected American republicanism, they remained deeply affected by their American experience. Loyalists were "anti-American Yankees," creating a "myth" about being British, and embracing a "peculiar form of coat-tails imperialism."[13] Caught between the societal worlds of the United States and Britain, Canada took up the struggle of both retaining British traditions and creating national distinctiveness in a North American environment. The context in which this took place, however, is critical. The American Revolution, and later the War of 1812 in which British forces blocked attempts by American invading forces to end British colonial rule on the continent, both served as *formative events* to delineate basic differences between the two societies.

If the United States was born of revolution, then Canada was born of counter-revolution. Revolution had meant breaking ties to the mother country, as the United States did with Britain; counter-revolution meant retaining those ties. The effect of these differences between the two societies have been illustrated in two major ways: settlement of the frontiers, and the formation of basic values.

The frontier comparisons have been made by S.D. Clark.[14] Clark felt that both societies had the common experience of settling a series of frontiers in the pursuit of staples. While there may have been similarities in the characteristic features of rugged individualism and non-traditional behaviour, the Canadian frontiers were different in that they were more stable and less disorganized because of the order created by traditional and organized authority. This traditional authority included a military police force (e.g., Northwest Mounted Police), a privileged upper class, large commercial organizations (e.g., Hudson's Bay Company), and representatives of the church (e.g., Anglican and Catholic), who provided greater social stability as outposts of empire controls. The heroes of American frontier settlement, on the other hand, were individualists who encountered the vagaries of disorder because the symbols of law and order did not precede settlement. The Davey Crockett's and Daniel Boone's, and the appointed or elected sheriff are not part of Canadian history because the institutions of empire were established in advance of settlement and created different traditions and expectations. Therefore, Canadian frontiers reflected empire controls rather than independence and experimentation, and these controls provided a very different foundation for Canadian society.

The argument about differences in basic values has been made by S.M. Lipset who concluded that Canada's counter-revolutionary tradition has made that society much more conservative and traditional than

REAL PEOPLE 6

Canadian-American Differer...

"We heard from the Canadian Consulate in Atl... going to be in Florida to visit some universities. ... our city and be on our television show. It's a br... know, lots of talk, banter and some music and ... think?"

The telephone receiver dangled on my sh... indicating that I was speechless. "Me, I'm a pro... don't sing. I don't tell jokes. You must have th...

"No — we want you," the quick retort ca... Canada Week in Florida. It's our way of honou... of Canadians who spend the winter in Florida. ... packed with Canadians. We've notified all of t... the county and they are organizing bus trips t... what do you think?

"I don't know. I'm not sure I can do anyt... know, I'm a professor — a teacher — a researc...

"That doesn't matter. You know a lot abou... teach Americans about Canada and goodness ... Anyway, the two countries are the same an... Canadians love Florida in the first place. ... think?"

Questions to Consider

What do you think are the real differences betv... Canadian society? Or are they essentially the ... does the intermingling experiences of mer... societies create a sense of similarity?

American society.[15] His thesis contrasts the tw... dichotomous variables indicating that Canada is r... particularist, and collectivity-oriented, whereas ... more egalitarian, achievement-oriented, universa... The ideology of the United States is replete w... where free enterprise, individualism, and upw... personal achievement, reign supreme. In comp...

in political structure have produced and sustained divergences. Regional or group differences (e.g., ethnic or religious) may be far more important, however, than comparisons of national origins or values. The effects, moreover, that differences in the origin of each society have had on regional and group development pose persistent and difficult questions.

Settlement, Immigration and Ethnicity: Australia

Canada and Australia were both originally British colonies, and both countries have remained members of the British Commonwealth. Just as Canada as a nation came into being by an Act of the British Parliament in 1867, so Australia was created by the *Commonwealth of Australia Constitution Act*, passed somewhat later in 1900. This British sponsorship has affected many aspects of Australian life, just as it has affected many aspects of life in Canada. In Australia however, the most basic feature stems from the primary settlement and control of Australia by persons from the British Isles.

The British did not have to compete with other European powers or settlers for control of Australia, as they had to do in Canada with the French. In Australia there was also no legacy of rebellion from British influences such as occurred in the United States, and which had such a considerable impact on Canadian society. What all three countries had in common was a dispersed native population, whose culture and constituents were deeply affected by invading colonists hoping to start a new life in the new world.[17] The population of approximately 300,000 Aborigines in Australia was severely reduced as the result of the treatment accorded them by British settlers.

White settlement began in Australia in 1788 through the British military presence, and the shipment to Australia of unwanted British convicts. Sheer distance from Europe, and the popularity of North America as an immigration destination reduced the attractiveness of Australia for European immigrants. The first major intake of free settlers was associated with the gold rush in the middle of the nineteenth century, and around one million persons entered Australia between 1852-1861. Between 1850-1900, 40% of the total population growth was due to immigration from Great Britain and Ireland. Some migration also took place from Northern Europe, but by the Second World War, Australia was still 90% British.[18] Non-Europeans had been excluded by the *Immigration Restriction Act* in 1901, and immigrant acceptability was related to perceptions of how easily an immigrant group could be assimilated into Australian society. Consequently, there was much greater ethnic uniformity in Australia than there was in North America.

The population of Australia during the Second World War was about six million people. In the next 30 years, an extremely rapid pace of growth increased the population by eight million.[19] Much of this growth was due to a high rate of immigration actively promoted by the government through travel assistance packages, particularly to British and European migrants who agreed to stay in Australia for a minimum of two years. Another source of the growth was the admission of European refugees through the sponsorship of the International Refugee Organization. The goal of migrant intake of about 1% per year during this period was established in response to a minor industrial revolution which occurred in Australia, and which created a large demand for labour. World War II had also demonstrated that the sparse population of the country provided little security in the face of a possible foreign invasion, and an alarming decline in the birth rate suggested that this problem demanded attention. The phrase "populate or perish" reflected the urgency with which Australia viewed the necessity of immigration in the immediate post-war era.

Perhaps the most significant thing about the post-war immigration policy was that the search for settlers moved beyond the British Isles to Southern and East European countries.[20] Between 1947-1974, only 40% of the large number of new arrivals came from the British Isles, and only 10% came from Northern Europe, primarily from Holland and Germany.[21] Soon however, much larger contingencies came from Southern European communities (e.g., Italy, Greece, and Cyprus), and the Eastern European countries (in particular Yugoslavia). Australia (like Canada) has recently seen a new source of immigration from Asian and African countries. The result of this immigration has been that the 90% British majority has decreased since World War II to about 77%. North Europeans have remained a constant 6-7% of the total population, whereas South and East Europeans grew from 2% to more than 12% of the population.

The relatively recent infusion of these non-British groups into Australia is important for several reasons. First, while immigrants compose only about 20% of the Australian population, the fact that over one-half of them come from non-English speaking countries, and more than one-third still regularly use a language other than English, suggest that they may have a significant cultural influence on the second generation, even though this generation will be born in Australia.[22] In fact, when immigrants and the second generation are combined, they make up about one-third of the total national population.

The second reason that this immigration is thought to be significant is that most of these migrants have settled in urban locations where they are able to establish viable ethnic communities. For example, 25% of the population of Sydney is foreign born, and when their Australian born children are included, they make up 38% of the population.[23] Whereas the pre-World War II immigration went largely to rural areas, the post-war immigration located in the largest cities, particularly Sydney, Melbourne, and Adelaide. Consequently, Melbourne has the third largest Greek population in the world behind Athens and Salonika. South and East Europeans are most likely to be found in ethnic enclaves in the inner city, whereas migrants from Holland and the British Isles are much less likely to be residentially concentrated. Furthermore, this *chain migration* from these countries usually strengthens these enclaves as immigrants sponsor the migration of friends and relatives from the homeland.

Perhaps the most critical reason that immigration remains a significant issue in Australian society is rooted in the sense of nordic superiority expressed by the British-oriented majority, who have also developed a strong sense of Australian nationalism.[24] In this context, foreigners were historically disliked, and assimilation was expected (as indicated by the label attached to immigrants as "New Australians"). When the Good Neighbour movement was established in 1950, its primary purpose was to condition Australians to accept immigration, and to assist immigrants to learn English and to assimilate as quickly as possible.[25] Such a policy was needed because immigrants came to be viewed as people with problems owing to their social and economic disadvantages, and their heightened urban visibility. Inability to speak English in the schools, and underemployment were viewed as symptomatic of the immigrant "problem." The growing viability of their ethnic enclaves, however, and their increasing ability to articulate their group needs, eventually changed these immigrant groups into ethnic pressure groups. The White Australia policy was changed by the 1970's to a multicultural model similar to Canada's.[26] In a complete reversal of the earlier approach, ethnic pluralism denoted a new desire to accommodate ethnic populations.

If Canada had not experienced the diversity of origins of immigrants who settled the West, as well as the concentration of persons of French descent in Quebec, it is probable that Canadian society would have been more similar to Australian society. While British traditions were propagated by British settlers as the dominant charter group in both Canada and Australia, they were considerably softened in Canada because of the multi-ethnic nature of the West, and the French-English duality which was at the foundations of Canadian society. In fact, the post-war shift to an official multicultural policy was a direct response to demands by francophone Quebecois, and strong representations by other European ethnic groups in the West. Since the Second World War, immigration patterns in Australia and Canada have been rather similar, although the Dutch, Yugoslavs, Maltese, and Greeks have been more prominent in Australia than in Canada.

Another significant comparison pertains to the permanence with which immigrants treat their migration to the new land. In Chapter 1 it was pointed out that the impact of immigration into Canada has been somewhat counterbalanced by emigration from Canada. Where emigration took place, residence in Canada was usually stepping stone migration to eventual settlement in the United States. Not having a strongly industrialized neighbour, Australia also lost a significant proportion of its population through *return migration* — usually to the land of origin. Immigrants from the British Isles and Northern Europe have had the highest rates of departure from Australia, usually estimated at about 20%.[27] The two year residence requirement for assisted immigrants made it difficult to know how many intended to remain in Australia in the first place, and how many viewed their stay only as a foreign travel experience. Return migration also took place in Canada, but it is doubtful whether much stepping stone migration occurred from Australia. Population loss through emigration, therefore, has been a problem common to both societies, but the reasons for these departures have been different.

The Aboriginal population in Australia is of similar proportion to native people in Canadian society, as each group represents slightly over 1% of the population. In Canada, native peoples are a distinguishable racial group, in much the same way that Aborigines, as a black-skinned people are distinguishable from the white Euro-Australians. The original white contact led to severe reductions in the Aboriginal population, though recent growth has resulted in an Aboriginal population over 100,000 with 44% living in the southern urban areas.[28] The remaining Aborigines live in more rural areas, particularly Western Australia, Southern Australia, and the Northern Territories where they make up a significant proportion of the total population. Just as native peoples form a larger share of the population in the Canadian Northern Territories than they do in the other provinces, so the Northern Territory of Australia possesses the highest percentage of aborigines at 21%.[29]

Aborigines suffered a fate similar to that of North American Indians, and were placed on Aboriginal Protectorates or reserves. The dilemma of desiring to maintain their traditional way of life while being exposed to white economic goals and urban life, has created considerable poverty and unemployment among Aborigines. In 1967, Aborigines were made a federal rather than state responsibility, and an Office For Aboriginal Affairs was established in Australia. Used primarily as a vehicle for negotiations, a white-inspired National Aboriginal Consultative Council sought to unite dispersed local tribes or clans into a single body to coordinate Aboriginal programs, and to act in an advisory capacity to the government.[30] While the granting of self-determination to Aborigines remains particularly controversial in some states, the granting of land rights has proceeded apace, and this has had great implications in the outback regions where mining and other forms of resource extraction take place. Thus, though the contexts are somewhat different, the history and plight of the indigenous peoples in both Australia and Canada appear rather similar.

Regionalism and Nationalist Movements: Scotland, Wales, and Spain

It is generally recognized that in Canada, two different conditions have produced regional political movements. One condition is *uneven economic development and disparities* that result in regional animosities or hostilities between geographic segments of the society. Examples of these movements include the Western agrarian movements and the Maritime Rights movement. The second condition is related to *ethnic solidarity*, of which the most obvious example is in Quebec. In this province, a francophone majority has evolved a national consciousness from its own heritage and traditions, which is quite distinctive from that of English Canada. While it might appear that the economic and ethnic aspects of regionalism are two different matters, the evidence suggests that nationalist (ethnic) movements are most effective when they have an economic grievance to mobilize their constituents. Put another way, regional movements with economic/political objectives are much more likely to be convincing when they have an ethnic basis. Thus, from the point of view of the state, a regional ethnic group represents a minority, while from the regional point of view, the ethnic group is a majority that ought to possess its own right to self-determination. It is from the dynamics of this debate between regional and federal objectives that societal conflict emerges.

Because industrialization and modernization are usually thought to negatively affect traditional culture, it has been assumed that ethnic minorities will eventually lose their historic distinctives, and will be drawn into the dominant social system of the majority. If this were true, we would expect Quebecers to have experienced considerable erosion of their linguistic and cultural uniqueness as they are increasingly drawn into the anglo world. Yet, surprisingly, the post-war period has seen a

FIGURE 6.2   **European Countries with Features Relevant to Canadian Society**

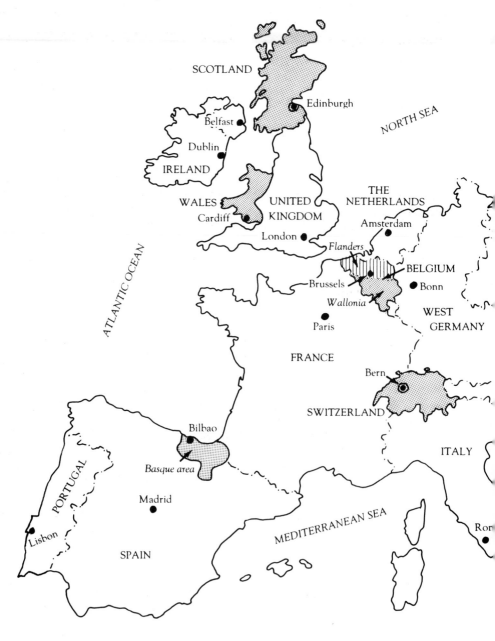

resurgence rather than a decline of ethnic identity in Quebec. What is noteworthy about this fact is that it has many parallels in other countries of the world.[31] Particularly in the 1960's, there were numerous political movements of ethnic minorities in societies where regional ethnic majorities challenged the power and policies of the federal state.

In this section, three examples of nationalist movements will be discussed: those of Scotland, Wales, and the Basques of Spain. In each case, separatist movements have emerged based on a national consciousness, but in response to varying stimuli and with varying success. Two interpretive perspectives which can be accentuated are reactive ethnicity and ethnic competition.[32] *Reactive ethnicity* suggests that ethnic solidarity emerges when a disadvantaged group rebels against a dominant authority. Ethnicity almost becomes synonymous with class consciousness because inequality intensifies the ethnic consciousness. *Ethnic competition* explains newfound ethnic solidarity by noting that groups formerly separate must now compete for the same occupations, rewards, and resources. In this case, cultural distinctives are mobilized to ensure the group obtains its share of the opportunities produced by changed conditions. Rather than treating these perspectives as in conflict with each other, there are elements of both which may be appropriate to our discussion.

SCOTLAND: MARGINALITY AND SEPARATISM

Until 1707, when the *Act of Union* with England took place, Scotland existed as an independent country. While the political state of Scotland disappeared after that time, Scottish civil society was preserved through its social institutions and traditions. Throughout most of the nineteenth century, however, when nation-states were forming in Europe, there was little Scottish nationalist feeling because of growing industrial prosperity.[33] Furthermore, because the Gaelic language was used by only a few, Scotland possessed little linguistic difference from England. At the same time, however, the Scottish Reformation had established a distinct religious difference, and Scotland also retained its own legal system. In addition, the centuries of past conflict with England had provided a pantheon of folk tales, national heroes, and martyrs, from which Scotland sustained an ethnic identity. These traditions, including a sense of history and past national greatness, were also taught in the schools. The resulting perception of uniqueness came at a time when there was a growing Scottish awareness of being marginal to the centre of British power.

By the end of World War I, unemployment had increased in Scotland as the more enterprising entrepreneurial class left for the centres of English finance and industry. Scottish people became increasingly sensitive to their peripheral status both with the British Isles, as well as in Europe. Scotland had not always had this marginal position, for in the 19th Century it was one of the first parts of England to industrialize.[34] Soon, however, the coal and iron ore deposits were depleted, unemployment in the Glasgow industrial region increased, and the Scottish economy became a branch plant economy (largely owned by the English), with frequent shutdowns as economic conditions deteriorated.

The home rule movement which began in the latter part of the nineteenth century did produce some administrative decentralization away from London. In fact, an office of the Secretary for Scotland was established in 1885 to ameliorate Scottish complaints about poor treatment, and its minister had full cabinet status. Yet the lingering animosities remained, and in 1928 the Scots National League and Scottish Home Rule Association united to form the National Party Of Scotland (SNP). In spite of high emigration of Scottish youth, skilled labour, and entrepreneurs, as well as high living costs, a low average income, and an unemployment rate double that of England, the SNP had a minimal impact.[35] In the 1950's the British government attempted to steer new industries to Scotland, and also increased public expenditures there; but these efforts had little impact. When it was announced that oil had been found offshore Scotland in 1971, control of North Sea oil exploitation became symbolic of new hopes for greater Scottish control. The SNP had also begun to shift its campaign from more broadly cultural issues to economic grievances, and the oil issue provided the anticipation of rising expectations amidst perceptions of deprivation. Thus, while in 1964 the SNP had received only 2.4% of the vote, their support increased dramatically to 30.4% in 1974.

The oil play increased Britain's interest in both maintaining control over its development in Scotland, and responding to apparent public agitation there. In 1979, a referendum was held to determine whether there should be a separate Scottish parliament, but only 32.8% voted in favour of such an idea.[36] In the same year, the SNP received only 17.3% of the vote in the national election. Two conclusions seem to be possible. First, greater local control and prosperity seemed to be favoured by a majority who did not want to go so far as to desire outright independence. Second, the threat of independence was indeed real, and had both a material and cultural basis, but the reluctance to become independent may reflect the role of the *threat* of independence as a bargaining tool to be used by a marginal region.

In some ways, ethnicity may be a less vital factor in the Scottish movement than is the attempt to seek redress from economic marginality by a depressed yet hopeful region.[37] If so, the movement is primarily economic, and has successfully mobilized its ethnic heritage towards that end. On the other hand, ethnic identity and nationalist independence may be viewed as being too extreme when the primary goal is economic survival.

The regionalist/nationalist activity in Scotland may be an example of reactive ethnicity, where ethnic differences are reinforced by geographic isolation and economic disparities. Canadian parallels with the Atlantic provinces and the West, particularly in oil and gas development, are obvious (with the exception that neither of these regions possess the ethnic solidarity to serve as a cohesive factor in external conflict). Perhaps that is one reason why independence movements in these regions have had even less success in Canada than in Scotland. Conversely, stopping short of actual independence in spite of ethnic solidarity has been a phenomenon characteristic of Quebec.

WALES: ERODED NATIONALISM

Wales was an autonomous state until the *Act of Union* in 1536 incorporated the nation into the English state. As long as the Welsh people remained rural and traditional, British rule, though resisted in some quarters, meant little to Welsh language and culture. With the onset of the industrial revolution in the nineteenth century, however, Wales underwent considerable change. By 1900, the population of Wales had increased five-fold, and by 1911 two-thirds of the population was urban.[38] Urbanization and industrialization, in conjunction with the political integration of Wales into British national parties, and a comparative geographical proximity to the British industrial complex, reduced the sense of marginality in Wales in comparison to Scotland.[39] The fact that Lloyd George, a leader of the Young Wales Movement in the late nineteenth century, became British Prime Minister symbolized this fact.

In spite of having a distinct national language (Welsh), the population of Wales became increasingly anglicized. The immigration of British people into the industrial centres of South Wales reduced the useage of the Welsh language there, and the use of Welsh became restricted to the more rural areas of northwestern Wales. If Wales, as Hechter has argued, was an internal colony for British capitalist development, it must also be recognized that Wales became a secondary centre of industry (iron and steel), rather than an undeveloped region.[40] For this reason, independence issues of a cultural nature have not had a strong appeal to the working class who have been more concerned about economic issues.

The Welsh nationalist movement, Plaid Cymru, was founded in 1925, but it has had little impact on Welsh politics. Its base has traditionally been in Northwest Wales, and it has taken a gradualist nationalist approach by focusing on cultural matters such as language. While the creation of vital Welsh institutions such as the University of Wales, the Welsh Department of Education, and the Church of Wales, had the potential of supporting language as a source of ethnic differentiation, the absence of a Welsh middle class unintegrated into British structures has removed one of the common foundations of a nationalist movement.

A referendum was held in Wales in 1979, similar to the one held in Scotland, on whether to establish a Welsh national assembly. Amidst economic insecurities, the proposal was defeated by a 4 to 1 margin. Advance polls had indicated that a majority of persons of Welsh descent had wanted a Welsh parliament; however, the large number of non-Welsh residents who had migrated to Wales overwhelmed the Welsh nationalists in the vote. Indicators are that the English-speaking Welsh voters (i.e., residents of Wales who could not speak Welsh) were fearful that the nationalists would insist on Welsh being spoken in an independent Wales, and that this would put them at a distinct disadvantage.[41] In other words, the English speaking majority were reluctant to support the nationalists who formed only a 20% linguistic minority.

Wales provides an excellent illustration of how residents of a former nation-state (Wales) can hold a dual identity (i.e., British and Welsh at the same time), almost in a regional rather than nationalist manner. Yet the integration of at least South Wales into the British economy, and the influx of persons from England into Wales, has dissolved the potency of potential nationalist appeals. This example illustrates why Quebec has fought so hard on the language issue, not only to maintain the existing use of French, but also to insist that immigrants learn French. Maintenance of the French language became pivotal in the defence of Quebec uniqueness in the face of overwhelming anglophone influence. On the other hand, just as the integration of Wales into the British economy muted interest in independence, so the integration of Quebec into the Canadian economy seems to have provided limits to support for a nationalist position.

BASQUES OF SPAIN: INTENSITY AND PROSPERITY

In the northeast corner of Spain live 1.5 million Basques. The Basques live on approximately 3% of the land surface of the country. The Cantabrian mountains almost serve as a barrier to the rest of Spain, and the coastal location of the most significant Basque population provides more of an international frame of reference, rather than an inward link to Spain. Here shipyards, steel mills, and manufacturing provide the highest average per capita income of any region of Spain.

The Basques occupy an area between France and the rest of Spain. For this reason early Spanish monarchies sought the cooperation of the Basques in border defense and, in efforts to maintain their loyalty, agreed to allow the Basque provinces to retain their own legal system which provided a substantial measure of self-governance. Part of the legacy of these concessions was the concept of *collective nobility* which automatically granted noble rank to any person of Basque parentage. While this entitlement meant little in actuality, it provided a heritage of uniqueness among these people which later came to serve as part of the rationale for greater autonomy.

Basque uniqueness is also related to language and lineage. The Basque language, Euskera, is unrelated to any Indo-European language and has a character all its own. The Basque people, moreover, have the highest incidence of Rh negative blood factor of any population in the world — a biological reflection of closed social groupings.[42] When these two factors are observed in combination with geographic location and noble status, the perception of Basque character as unique is strong.

Considerable self-governance was allowed by the Spanish monarchs until the 19th Century, when attempts were made by the Spanish government to override local autonomy. The Spanish goal of greater centralization threatened the Basque community, and the Basque nationalist movement began in the 1890's. The Basque language was a primary focus of government attack and, in the period following the Spanish Civil War (1937), it became illegal to use Euskera both in public, and in the media, or to teach it in school. By the late 1960's, Euskera was allowed back in the schools, and the new constitution of 1978 made regional languages co-official with Spanish. But all of this did not occur without considerable agitation and conflict from those in the Basque nationalist movement, who by this time had renamed their land Euzkadi.

The industrial opportunities available in the Basque cities meant that in conjunction with a tax system that discouraged agriculture, the Basque population became more urban. These same opportunities also attracted non-Basques to cities like Bilbao. Now only 65% of the population of the Basque provinces are indigenous. This decline is chiefly attributable to 20-25,000 people per year who have migrated into the region since the 1950's.[43] As a consequence of this immigration, the use of Euskera has declined, and traditional Basque family life has been in a state of upheaval. Anxious to maintain their economic position, the Basque bourgeoisie have frequently compromised their ethnicity in order to build economic bridges to other countries, or to other regions of Spain. It was precisely this greater intermingling, however, which threatened the Basque identity among the working class and the middle class. In the period frm 1968-75, the frustration among some grew so strong that an organization called Basque Homeland and Freedom engaged in revolutionary insurgent activities, including kidnapping and assassination.

The legacy of feelings of persecution by the Spanish government, and a convincing but troubled ethnic identity were further exacerbated by regional grievances of inequality. It was felt that high government taxation was not being reciprocated by either government spending or the availability of services in the Basque region, and that this uneven distribution was the result of Spanish bias against the Basques. Consequently, when the Spanish government offered a referendum to the Basque region in 1979 which proposed greater autonomy in matters of language, taxation, and the judiciary, it was overwhelmingly accepted, although about 50% of the Basque population abstained from the vote.[44]

The Basque situation illustrates many of the problems associated with challenges to ethnic identity as a consequence of internal social change. For some, any change at all was threatening, while for others change was to be embraced wholly in spite of its implications for the ethnic collectivity. Quebec has certainly faced these frustrations. Quebec also has a history of considerable regional autonomy on certain matters, which it defends in the face of centralizing government pressures. What perhaps makes the Basque region unique, however, is that its own concern for self-determination is also related to being the richest region in Spain — a position which aspiring Basques are particularly zealous to guard. It is essentially a similar group of aspiring francophones that has been effective in mobilizing Quebec opinion though Quebec's economic position has not been comparatively as strong.

Language and Culture: Belgium and Switzerland

In Chapter 5, it was argued that language is an important aspect of culture. Efforts to retain linguistic distinctiveness is clearly at the heart of the maintenance of cultural distinctives. For this reason, language has been a significant issue in Quebec, and this has had national implications for the policy of bilingualism. But what are the experiences of other countries where more than one official language prevails? A short discussion of the situation in Belgium and Switzerland will provide touchstones for comparison.

BELGIUM: BILINGUALISM AND BICULTURALISM

The country of Belgium had its origin in the Belgian Revolution of 1830. The northern half of the country was populated by persons of Dutch origin in an area known as Flanders, and those of French descent populated the southern section of Belgium in an area called Walloonia. At the time of the creation of Belgium, Walloonia was the stronger section, and partly because of the influence exerted from France, French became the official national language of Belgium. French also was the cultured language of the upper class, and therefore became the language of secondary education and upward mobility throughout Belgium.

By the latter half of the nineteenth century, a significant change in the balance of power between these two regions had begun to occur.[45] A higher birth rate in Flanders led to sizeable population increases there, and a Flemish national consciousness had emerged. Challenges were raised to the exclusiveness of the French language because the Flemish desired to use Dutch in the courts, public administration, as well as in the schools. Regional bilingualism was first initiated in Flanders, and, by 1898, Flemish became an official language of the country along with French.

The emergent Flemish consciousness also evoked a Walloonian consciousness.[46] The apparent concessions to the Flemish along with the comparative weakening of the Walloonian position (two-thirds of the total population was now Flemish), made control of the large city of Brussels critical. Flemings who moved to Brussels were becoming bilingual, whereas Walloonians remained unilingual; and yet there were still clear differences between bilingual Flemings and the French speaking Walloons. The Flemish middle classes preferred language policies which ensured the survival of Dutch, yet they were also aware that urbanization meant greater use of French.

By World War II, Belgium essentially consisted of two unilingual areas: Flanders (Flemish or Dutch) and Walloonia (French). Flemings were conscious of the fact that Brussels was already considerably French, and that this French dominance of the city was increasing. Conflicts became particularly intense as the urban population moved into the predominantly Flemish suburbs, and the battle between the two groups continued. The Constitution adopted in 1970 proposed a solution that would see Belgium have three administrative units: Flanders where Dutch would be used; Walloonia where French would be used; and Brussels where there was to be parity between the two groups with some regional unilingualism in the suburbs.[47] At the federal level, a parity principle was to prevail so that the cabinet would be composed of an equal number from both linguistic groups. The Dutch agreed to parity in the cabinet in exchange for parity in Brussels where they were a minority. The language of instruction in schools was to be the language of the area, although residents of Brussels could make a free choice. Parity was also to be sought in the civil service where the Dutch were underrepresented. Two cultural councils were to be established to ensure the cultural survival of both ethnic groups.

Rather than move to a national policy of bilingualism which Canada has done, Belgium has moved to territorial unilingualism, and established mechanisms to institutionalize parity and the survival of both groups. The tendency for urbanization to lead to francization has counter-balanced the stronger demographic and economic growth of the Flemish. Thus the idea of losers and winners in ethnic interaction is considerably muted by *parity* and *territorial unilingualism*. The Canadian bilingualism policy also represented an attempt to minimize the idea of losers and winners, although it has been less successful because it has not anticipated the tendencies towards greater territorial unilingualism. The demographic differences in size of the two charter groups has also made the concept of parity less palatable in Canada.

SWITZERLAND: LINGUISTIC TERRITORIALITY

Switzerland had its beginnings as a loose alliance of Alpine valley communities banding together to defend themselves against challenges to their independence. The idea of a voluntary federation of political communities led to a constitution in 1848 which established political neutrality, and the idea of one foreign policy, one citizenship, and a customs union. On the other hand, matters of education and culture were left totally in the hands of local jurisdictions called *cantons*.[48] No attempt was to be made to secure national political unity based on descent or language, but rather on local allegiance which was to be paid directly to the canton.

The principle of cantonal autonomy was directly related to the ethnic diversity which varied with locality. About 74% of the population of Switzerland speaks German, 20% French, 4% Italian, and less than 1% Romansch.[49] Consequently Switzerland has 23 cantons of which 14 are German, 4 French, 1 Italian, 3 bilingual, and 1 trilingual. Each canton is entitled to preserve its own language and all immigrants must learn the language used in that canton. Language boundaries are guaranteed and cannot be changed although when conflict emerges, a canton may be split (as happened when the new canton of Jura was established from a part of the canton of Berne).[50] The split was accepted because it separated the French Catholic community (Jura) from the German Protestant one (Berne), and it removed the bases for much internal conflict. Each canton writes its laws and documents in its own language.

In principle, the idea of *linguistic territoriality* is a good one because it avoids conflicts by dividing space into homogeneous units. As long as the power relationships between cantonal units are more or less equalized, local guarantees of autonomy are adequate. It is however, industrial growth and expansion, and the competition between units that sometimes results from this growth, which causes the development of conflicts either between units or within units. The notion of linguistic territoriality appears to be a policy more and more acceptable to Canadians; and yet because industrialization has frequently meant anglicization, there remains considerable ambivalence about such a policy both within and outside of Quebec. Linguistic territoriality at other local levels (e.g., Ukrainians in northern Saskatchewan) might also not be preferred and might be difficult to institutionalize.

Uniqueness Re-examined

In spite of the brevity with which some of these comparisons have been made, it is clear that many other societies struggle with issues similar to those identified in Canadian society. More lengthy analyses are needed to explain the factors that produce the different effects and that result in alternate solutions.

One idea that stands out from this comparative study is the way in which power is used either to accommodate or to repel minority interests, whether in marginal regions, weakly populated areas, among poorer people, or minority language and cultures. The basic democratic principle of majority rule can legitimate policies that create considerable societal tensions when minorities become vocal and strident. While political states may be somewhat reluctant to support the devolution (dispersal) of their powers, decentralization may be a better way to accommodate local interests. Societies like Belgium and Switzerland along with others represent a more *consociational model*, where power is shared or dispersed between groups rather than centrally mandated by a majority.[51] Canada is not unique in attempting to struggle with regional and ethnic interests and uneven economic development, so it might be expected that much can be learned by examining the experience of other societies.

Further Exploration

1. How can Canada learn from experiences of other societies? Discuss and illustrate with examples.
2. Why do people outside of North America frequently visualize Canadian society and American society as essentially the same? List some of the reasons why this assumption is not true and elaborate on them.
3. What do you think is the most important explanation for the distinctiveness of Canadian society? More than one factor may be possible but for the sake of argument isolate one explanation and develop it carefully.

Selected Readings

Charles F. Doran and John N. Sigler, eds. *Canada And The United States* (Englewood Cliffs: Prentice Hall, 1985)
Charles R. Foster, ed., *Nations Without A State* (New York: Praeger, 1980).

ENDNOTES

[1] For a discussion of some of the problems involved in comparative research, see Robert M. Marsh, *Comparative Sociology* (New York: Harcourt, Brace and World, 1967), pp. 261-286.

[2] *Australia Yearbook 1983* (Canberra: Australian Bureau of Statistics, 1983), p. 122.

[3] K.A. MacKirdy, "Conflict Of Loyalties: The Problem Of Assimilating The Far Wests Into the Canadian-Australian Federations," *Canadian Historical Review* 32(1951): 337-355.

[4] L.S. Bourne and M.I Logan, "Changing Urbanization Patterns At the Margin: The Examples Of Australia And Canada," in Brian J.L. Berry, ed., *Urbanization And Counter-Urbanization* (Beverly Hills: Sage, 1976), pp. 116-118.

[5] Elisa Maria Reis and Simon Schwartzman, "Spatial Dislocation And Social Identity In Brazil," *International Social Science Journal* 30(1978): 98-115.

[6] *Statistical Abstract Of The United States, 1984*, 104th ed., (Washington D.C.; Bureau of Census; 1984), p. 7.

[7] *Statistical Abstract Of The United States, 1984*, p. 10 and p. 12.

[8] Kirkpatrick Sale, *Power Shift: The Rise Of The Southern Rim And Its Challenge To The Eastern Establishment* (New York: Random, 1975).

[9] Robert B. Cohen, "Multinational Corporations, International Finance, And The Sunbelt," in David C. Perry and Alfred J. Watkins, eds., *The Rise Of The Sunbelt Cities* (Beverly Hills, Sage, 1977) pp. 211-226.

[10]Louis Hartz, ed., *The Founding Of New Societies* (New York: Harcourt, Brace and World, 1964), Chapter 1. For a critique of Hartz, see Gad Horowitz, "Conservativism, Liberalism, And Socialism In Canada: An Interpretation," *Canadian Journal Of Economics And Political Science* 32(1966): 143-150.

[11]Kenneth McRae, "The Structure Of Canadian History," in Hartz, *The Founding Of New Societies*. See also his "Louis Hartz's Concept of the Fragment Society And Its Applications To Canada," *Etudes Canadiennes* 5(1978): 17-30.

[12]David Bell and Lorne Tepperman, *The Roots Of Disunity* (Toronto: McClelland and Stewart, 1979), p. 45.

[13]Bell and Tepperman, *The Roots of Disunity*, p. 76, 79.

[14]See in particular "The Social Development Of Canada And The American Continental System," *Culture* 5(1944): 132-143, and "Canada And Her Great Neighbor," *Canadian Review Of Sociology And Anthropology* 1(1964): 193-201.

[15]*Revolution And Counter-Revolution: Change And Persistence In Social Structures*, Rev. ed., (Garden City: Doubleday, 1971), and "Canada And The United States: A Comparative View," *Canadian Review Of Sociology And Anthropology* 1(1964): 173-185. For a broadening of his comparison to Britain and Australia, see "The Value Patterns of Democracy: A Case Study In Comparative Analysis," *American Sociological Review* 28(1963): 515-531. A recent restatement of Lipset's argument can be found in "Canada And The United States: The Cultural Dimension," in Charles F. Doran and John H. Sigler, eds., *Canada And The United States* (Englewood Cliffs: Prentice Hall, 1985).

[16]See, for example, Tom Truman, "A Critique Of Seymour M. Lipset's Article," *Canadian Journal Of Political Science* 4(1971): 513-525; Irving Louis Horowitz, "The Hemispheric Connection: A Critique And Corrective To the Entrepreneurial Thesis Of Development With Special Emphasis On The Canadian Case," *Queen's Quarterly* 80(1973): 336-337; Craig Crawford and James Curtis, "English Canadian-American Differences In Value Orientations: Survey Comparisons Bearing On Lipset's Thesis," *Studies In Comparative International Development*, 1979; and Bell and Tepperman *The Roots Of Disunity*, pp. 24-32.

[17]Pierre L. Van Den Berghe, "Australia, Canada, And The United States: Ethnic Melting Pots Or Plural Societies?," *Australia And New Zealand Journal Of Sociology* 19(1983): 238-252.

[18]See Charles A. Price, "The Immigrants," in A.F. Davies, S. Encel, and M.J. Berry, eds., *Australian Society: A Sociological Introduction* (Melbourne: Longman Cheshire, 1977), pp. 331-355; and Dennis Laurence Cuddy, *The Yanks Are Coming: American Immigration To Australia* (San Francisco: R and E Research Associates, 1977), pp. 4-5.

[19]M.L. Kovacs and A.J. Cropley, *Immigrants And Society: Alienation And Assimilation* (Sydney: McGraw Hill, 1975).

[20]First Report Of The National Population Inquiry, *Population And Australia: A Demographic Analysis And Projection*, Volume One (Canberra: Government of Australia, 1975), p. 99.

[21]Australian Council On Population And Ethnic Affairs, *Multiculturalism For All Australians* (Canberra, 1982), pp. 33-34.

[22]*Multiculturalism For All Australians*, p. 1. The emphasis on second generation effects of immigration is repeatedly found in the Australian literature whereas it is mentioned much less in the Canadian literature. This may reflect the greater concern for assimilation in Australian society.

[23]I.H. Burnley, "Geographic-Demographic Perspectives On The Ecology Of Ethnic Groups in Australian Cities," in Charles A. Price and Jean I. Martin, eds., *Australian Immigration: A Bibliography And Digest, Part I* (Canberra: Australia National University, 1976), pp. 124-149.

[24]*Immigrants And Society: Alienation And Assimilation*, Chapter 4.

[25]Jean I. Martin, *The Migrant Presence: Australian Responses 1947-1977*, (Sydney: George Allen and Unwin, 1978).

[26]See Freda Hawkins, "Multiculturalism In Two Countries: The Canadian And Australian Experience," *Journal Of Canadian Studies* 17(1982): 64-80; and Anthony H. Richmond and G. Rao, "Recent Developments In Immigration To Canada And Australia: A Comparative Analysis," *International Journal Of Comparative Sociology* 17(1976): 183-205.

[27]Cf. *The Migrant Presence: Australian Responses 1947-1977*, pp. 30-31; and *Population And Australia: A Demographic Analysis And Projection*, p. 124. The difficulties in determining intentions of people on arrival and on departure make precise figures a problem to obtain. However, emigration is clearly recognized as a significant matter in Australia.

[28]Rita Bienvenue, "Comparative Colonial Systems: The Case Of Canadian Indians And Australian Aborigines," *Australian-Canadian Studies* 1(1983): 30-43. Donald Edgar, *Introduction To Australian Society: A Sociological Perspective* (Sydney: Prentice-Hall, 1980), p. 297. For a good overview of Australian aborigines, see K. Maddock, *The Australian Aborigines: A Portrait Of Their Society* (Melbourne: Penguin, 1972).

[29]Nicholas Paterson, ed., *Aboriginal Land Rights: A Handbook* (Canberra: Australian Institute Of Aboriginal Studies, 1981), p. 2.

[30]Colin Tatz, "Aborigines: Political Options And Strategies," in R.M. Berndt, ed., *Aborigines And Change* (Canberra: Australian Institute Of Aboriginal Studies, 1977), pp. 384-401.

[31]For brief comparisons, cf. Mary Beth Montcalm, "Quebec Separatism In Comparative Perspective," in Alain G. Gagnon, ed., *Quebec: State And Society* (Toronto: Methuen, 1984), pp. 45-58; and Peter A. Gourevitch, "Quebec Separatism In Comparative Perspective," in Elliot J. Feldman and Neil Nevitte, eds., *The Future Of North America* (Cambridge: Center For International Affairs, 1979), pp. 238-252. See also Edward Tiryakian, "Quebec, Wales, And Scotland: Three Nations In Search Of A State." *International Journal Of Comparative Sociology* 21 (1982): 1-13.

[32]For a discussion of these two perspectives, cf. Charles C. Ragin, "Ethnic Political Mobilization: The Welsh Case," *American Sociological Review* 44(1979): 619-635, and Francois Nielsen, "The Flemish Movement In Belgium After World War II: A Dynamic Analysis," *American Sociological Review* 45(1980): 76-94.

[33]Tom Nairn, *The Breakup Of Britain* (London: NLB, 1977), pp. 105-106.

[34]Jack Brand, "The Rise And Fall Of Scottish Nationalism," in Charles R.

Foster, ed., *Nations Without A State* (New York: Praeger, 1980), pp. 33ff.

[35]Milton J. Esman, "Scottish Nationalism, North Sea Oil, And The British Response" in M.J. Esman, ed., *Ethnic Conflict In The Western World* (Ithaca: Cornell University Press, 1977), p. 256-258.

[36]Jack Brand, "The Rise And Fall Of Scottish Nationalism," p. 42.

[37]This is essentially the view of Jack Brand in *The National Movement In Scotland* (London: Routledge and Kegan Paul, 1978). Brand also discusses the role of Scottish folk songs as a mobilization device among young voters.

[38]John Osmond, "Wales In The 1980's," in Charles R. Foster, ed., *Nations Without A State*, p. 45.

[39]Ray Corrado, "The Welsh As A Nonstate Nation," in Judy S. Bertelsen, ed., *Nonstate Nations In International Politics* (New York: Praeger, 1977), Chap. 6.

[40]Tom Nairn, *The Breakup Of Britain*, and Michael Hechter, *Internal Colonialism: The Celtic Fringe In British National Development* (Berkeley: University of California Press, 1975).

[41]Walker Connor, "The Political Significance Of Ethnonationalism Within Western Europe," in Abdul Said and Luiz R. Simmons, *Ethnicity In An International Context* (New Brunswick, N.J.: Transaction, 1976), p. 117, and Osmond, p. 62.

[42]Davydd J. Greenwood, "Continuity In Change: Spanish Basque Ethnicity As A Historical Process," in Milton J. Esman, ed., *Ethnic Conflict In The Western World*, pp. 84-87; and Pedro G. Blasco, "Modern Nationalism In Old Nations As A Consequence Of Earlier State Building: The Case Of Basque-Spain," in Wendell Bell and Walter E. Freeman, eds., *Ethnicity And Nation Building: Comparative, International, And Historical Perspectives* (Beverly Hills: Sage, 1974).

[43]Robert P. Clark, "Euzkadi: Basque Nationalism In Spain Since The Civil War," in Charles R. Foster, ed., *Nations Without A State*, p. 77.

[44]832,000 voted for regional autonomy and only 47,000 voted against it. International matters, trade, defense, and coinage were still to be federal matters. Clark, *Ibid*, pp. 75-100.

[45]Jaroslov Krejci and Vitezslav Velimsky, *Ethnic And Political Nations In Europe* (London: Croom Helm, 1981), pp. 103-104.

[46]Reginald DeSchryver, "The Belgian Revolution And The Emergence Of Belgium's Biculturalism," in Arend Lijphart, eds., *Conflict And Coexistence In Belgium* (Berkeley: Institute of International Studies, 1980), pp. 13-33.

[47]Aristide R. Zolberg, "Splitting The Difference: Federalization Without Federalism In Belgium," in Milton J. Esman, ed., *Ethnic Conflict In The Western World*, pp. 103-142.

[48]E.K. Francis, *Interethnic Relations* (New York: Elsevier, 1976) p. 104.

[49]Kenneth D. McRae, *Switzerland: Example Of Cultural Coexistence* (Toronto: Canadian Institute of International Affairs, 1964).

[50]Kurt Mayer, "Ethnic Tensions In Switzerland: The Jura Conflict," in Charles R. Foster, ed., *Nations Without A State*, pp. 189-208.

[51]The distinction between majoritarian and consociational societies was made by Arend J. Lijphart in his preface to *Conflict And Coexistence In Belgium*.

7 The Question of Identity

Canapress Photo Service

"The Canadian social scientist cannot take the existence of this society for granted. There is nothing about the society that can be fully understood except in relation to how the society developed, how its very survival as a society, flanked as it was by the powerful republic to the south, remained problematic . . ."

"Canadian nationhood was attained, not by the making of different people into one, or by the strengthening of forces of consensus, but by fostering the differences between people within the nation and thereby securing the differences between Canadian people and American."

— S.D. Clark, the Dean of Canadian sociology, whose career began in the 1930's.

A PERSON'S IDENTITY is something which develops as that person grows older. In a similar way, the identity of a society is something that must evolve over time. In Chapter 1, it was suggested that a national identity has been in the process of formation since Canada officially became a nation in 1867, and that many problems still exist in formulating that identity. It could also be argued that the search for identity is based upon the quest for the survival of the society — a society which has been described as being in a state of perpetual crisis.

A *societal identity* is the sum of the sentiments and cultural attributes that people share as a consequence of feeling that they belong together. A Canadian identity is formed when people collectively accept the society of the Canadian state as an integral component of their personal identity. Thus an important aspect of national identity is the *internal* unity which members of a society share with each other. In addition, identity also has an *external* component that emerges through differentiating one's own society from other societies. One study found that members of Canadian society tend to become most aware of their national identity through their travels outside the country, and in interacting with foreigners, rather than by interacting with Canadians from other parts of the society.[1] The fact that internal differences appear to obstruct the creation of societal unity means that the development of a national identity may best be achieved through international interaction.

From an international perspective, the existence of Canadian society is relatively secure. Canadians sometimes lament the fact that they are identified internationally as Americans, or that foreigners are ignorant about Canadian society, but Canadians can take comfort in the fact that the Canadian state and its boundaries are internationally recognized and acknowledged. The *spillover effect* of American influence is perhaps the greatest issue of debate, and there is clearly no unanimity about the extent to which this influence is desirable or undesirable. Nevertheless, it is the divisions or conflicts *within* Canadian society that are usually viewed as the greatest obstacles to forming a national identity. Canadians are constantly reminded of the factors that divide them (language, geography, race, social class), while factors that unite have a much lower profile.

Questions about a Societal Identity

In Chapter 1, it was argued that the people residing within the political state of Canada do form a society in the loose sense of the term. The traditional reluctance of census takers to accept "Canadian" as an answer to a question about one's ethnic background suggests that people who live in Canada are viewed essentially as descendants of people who came from somewhere else, and who have a national identity that is other than Canadian. Perhaps we can expect these perceptions to change over several generations but, at least in the recent past, the identity of Canadians as a nationality (i.e., as people sharing a common ethnic identity) has been quite diffuse.

Several questions can be posed that strike at the heart of the shape and character of a societal identity. They revolve around ideas of homogeneity, insularity, legitimacy, centralization, and inequity.

HOMOGENEITY

How uniform or similar must members of the society be in order to attain national unity? Do policies like multiculturalism, which promote a plurality of ethnic identities, detract from a Canadian identity? Does the concept of two language groups within the society create two in-groups in which only a small minority with bilingual ability are able to bridge the two groups? If this linguistic or ethnic diversity is acknowledged, how evenly dispersed must these members be in order to establish a national identity?

INSULARITY

In order to develop a national consciousness, to what extent should the national borders be sealed from foreign influence? Should members of the society be discouraged from reading foreign magazines, watching foreign television, investing in foreign countries, or listening to recordings of foreign musicians? While these items may be central to our conception of individual freedom, should the government use its powers to attempt to minimize foreign influence and thereby encourage national development? The question is, how does one determine the degree of insularity necessary to encourage national development?

LEGITIMACY

In general, members of Canadian society accept the rule of their democratically elected government as legitimate and worthy of support. Yet there have been repeated challenges to national authority and objectives by interest groups that have alternate conceptions of what the society should be like. While the FLQ may have represented an extreme challenge because of its terrorist activities, other challenges have come from farmers movements in the West, native groups, and various forms of separatism in Quebec, Newfoundland, and the West. To what extent does the democratic system where majority control is in Central Canada contribute to these challenges to legitimacy? Should allowances be made to accommodate minority interest groups? If allowances are made, do they contribute to greater or lesser fragmentation of the national identity?

CENTRALIZATION

The basic issue arising from the question of legitimacy is the extent to which diversity and decentralization can be maintained without threatening national unity. In recent years, the greatest struggles within the society have been between federal and provincial governments, and regional control has become a popular objective. At what point does regional control emasculate the federal government? Do regional identities threaten the national identity? How much decentralization can be tolerated without challenging the existence of the national society?

INEQUITIES

To what extent must the inequities that exist within the society be removed in order to create a greater sense of personal identification with the national society? Must government services be available in the mother tongue of the resident in order for that person to feel that he or she belongs to the national society? If so, can all linguistic groups expect full equality of services? Must regional variations in unemployment rates be erased in order to heighten personal self-esteem and pride in being a member of the national society? Should attempts be made to reduce these inequities, even at the expense of the alienation of others in the society who prefer the advantages of the status quo?

All of these questions are central to the emergence of a national identity. Many examples could be found to illustrate the on-going struggle within Canadian society for suitable answers to these questions. Frequently, interest groups are formed in order to rally public support for particular solutions. In most instances, the conflict that ensues creates considerable tension (for example, federal attempts to impose bilingualism on Quebec or in anglophone areas). It is possible, however, that the creation of a Canadian identity comes not through peaceful agreement on all matters (which may never be possible), but through the struggles to cope with tensions within the society.

While in one sense, societal conflict may be viewed as problematic, there is another sense in which conflict can be viewed as the attempt to find unique compromises in which conflicting parties participate together in finding solutions which may serve to reshape Canadian society. Herschel Hardin has argued that there are three conflict-laden contradictions which are central to the struggle for an emerging Canadian identity.[2] They are 1) French Canada against English Canada, 2) regions against the federal centre, and 3) Canada against the United States. In each case, the goal is not to decide in favour of one side or the other, but to attempt to find some middle ground between opposing forces. It is likely that there are additional tensions or contradictions, but the struggle with these key contending themes is at the heart of the evolution and development of national identity in Canada.

How much cohesion or unity is needed to provide a focus for a Canadian societal identity? The answer to this question depends on your perspective. There are two basic alternatives: the *pan-Canadian* or *unitary* approach and the *segmentalist* approach.[3] The pan-Canadian or unitary approach contends that the society is made up of individuals who find their collective identity in their sense of belonging to the national society. Characteristics such as a non-official language spoken at home, or other regional or ethnic loyalties, are either devalued or minimized in preference to adherence to wider allegiances to the national society. In stressing the individualist basis of society, this approach accentuates the role of the nation-state in providing the necessary feeling of belonging.

The second approach (segmentalist) focuses on the smaller groups or communities which are founded upon regional, racial, linguistic, occupational, or cultural similarities. The segmentalist expects these group commitments (rather than the individual) to serve as the building blocks of Canadian society, and does not aim to dissolve these groups even when they compete with allegiances to the larger society. Anglophones, and particularly anglophones in Ontario, are more prone to prefer the pan-Canadian approach to societal unity. Francophones and some residents of hinterland regions who have other group ties are more likely to prefer the segmentalist approach to Canadian society.

There was a time when it was thought that the pan-Canadian view of Canadian society would eventually win out. As immigrants were assimilated, as the continental crush of the dominant English language overwhelmed Quebec francophones, and as hinterland regions were integrated more clearly into the national economy, it was thought that commitments to the national society would become primary. Yet ethnic associations remain vital, Quebec uniqueness remains strong, and regional loyalties and grievances foster community attachments. Consequently, commitments to the nation-state remain diluted thereby supporting a more segmentalized conception of society, and as a result, a less cohesive societal identity prevails.

Contextual Factors in Identity Formation

The preceding discussion, including material in earlier chapters, has provided considerable evidence to suggest why Canadian society has struggled to articulate a national identity. Five factors summarize the context and milieu which shape the institutions and traditions that serve as the framework for the societal unit and its evolving identity.

REAL PEOPLE 7.1

Questioning the Taken-for-Granted

Every morning before school, nine year old Stephen dutifully practiced for his Wednesday piano lesson. This week his teacher gave him a new song to practice and Stephen picked his way through the melody. It sounded strangely familiar.

"That's it," Stephen exclaimed. "God Save Our Queen. We sing that song at school assemblies."

Mom was in the kitchen, and had vaguely overheard Stephen's discovery over the noise of his brother yelling about what clothes to wear.

"Hey Mom," inquired Stephen. "Is the Queen the Queen of the whole world?"

"No Steve, she's the Queen of England."

There was a pause as he plunked out a few more notes.

"Hey Mom, England is another country isn't it?"

"Yes dear," his Mother assured him.

"We're on a different continent than England, right Mom?"

"Yup, your right."

A few more notes come from the piano.

"Then how come we sing "OUR Queen"?

"It's always been that way Steve. Now get ready for school."

Questions to Consider

Do you think symbols of the monarchy should be more or less important in Canadian society? What are the advantages or disadvantages of their use?

THE COLONIALIST LEGACY

The British sponsorship of Canadian society has produced a legacy of British influence including the parliamentary system and British law. Pictures of the British royalty continue to appear on Canadian coins, and children are taught "God Save Our Queen" in schools as an anthem of respect toward the monarchy. The position of Governor-General (the representative of the monarchy in the government) was only first filled by a Canadian in 1952 when Vincent Massey was appointed. Even though this British sponsorship has been loosened considerably through the creation of the British Commonwealth of Nations, and Britain's shift away from her former colonies to the European Common Market, a special relationship with the mother country still prevails. Members of the royal family still make regular visits to Canada, and thousands flock to see them.

In one sense, Canada sustained her unique identity through the years as a result of this alliance with Britain.[4] On the other hand, the relationship can be viewed as essentially a maternalistic one which has shadowed the society's own expressions of independence. No issue has been more symbolic of this concern than efforts to repatriate the constitution. The *British North America Act* of 1867, as an act of the British Parliament, only served as a reminder that Canadian society had never created a charter for its own existence. It was also a stark reminder to francophones of British dominance and the French colonial defeat. Consequently, the proclamation of the new *Constitution Act, 1982* on April 17, 1982, with an amending formula and a charter of rights and freedoms, had the potential of signifying a new era in the society's independent existence. There was, however, no great outpouring of nationalist sentiment, little public enthusiasm, and perhaps more importantly, Quebec did not sign the accord.[5] Thus the document that was to be the cornerstone for the new sense of society lacked the concurrence of one of its most significant segments. In spite of efforts to minimize the colonialist legacy, colonial influences remain, and expressions of societal unity are muted by internal disagreements.[6]

PROXIMITY TO THE UNITED STATES

It is paradoxical that the more like American society Canadian society becomes, the more the struggle for a distinctiveness emerges. One analyst has referred to the amalgam of feelings between the two societies as attraction, rejection, and ambivalence.[7] Canadians feel at home in the United States where they flock in great numbers, and Americans struggle to explain subtle differences between the two societies that go beyond the metric signposts in Canada.

The interaction between the two societies is indeed considerable. Fully 95% of the international visits made to Canada in 1982 were made by residents of the United States.[8] Similarly, 96% of Canadian residents returning from international destinations were returning from the United States. The intermingling of the two societies is not just for vacation purposes, but is part of a daily lifestyle for many. The proximity of the bulk of the Canadian population to the American border makes it possible for the interaction that does occur to be more frequent and for shorter periods. Of the 33.3 million Canadian residents returning from trips to the United States, 23 million (69%) left and returned on the same day, while 68% of American visitors to Canada entered and left on the same day.

The vacillation and variation in feelings towards the United States is born of the emotional issues related to a sense of powerlessness among Canadians, and the Canadian desire to receive the respect of, and independence from, Americans who take Canada for granted.[9] Gallup Poll data reveals that feelings about Canadian-American relationships evolve in waves. In the 1960's, Canadians saw the two societies as moving closer together, in the 1970's and early 1980's as drifting farther apart. More recently, in the mid-1980's Canadians see the two societies moving closer together again.[10]

The integration of Canadian and American societies is fostered by many factors. Canadians watch a large number of American television programs which are broadcast on Canadian stations, as well as on cable networks and satellites.[11] Professional hockey and baseball games expose residents of both societies to each others national anthems. Talk of free trade, and the existence of the Autopact Agreement whereby automobiles are made in both countries for export to each other, help contribute to greater integration of the two societies. Yet a dynamic prevails that prevents this integration from proceeding too far. Some of the reasons for this resistance will be discussed later in this chapter. At this point, however, it can be stated that one of the ways in which a societal identity is constructed is through repeated attempts to distinguish Canadian society from American society in spite of the significant difficulties in doing so.[12]

One other aspect of American proximity that affects Canadian society is the constant comparisons made by Canadians about the apparent feelings about national unity and sense of destiny which exist in the United States. The American War of Independence and the succeeding events in the establishment of a new society in the United States created a pantheon of national heroes, historic documents, and a charter of ideals. For this reason it has usually been argued that, in contrast, the Canadian identity has been diffuse because Canadian society has lacked this kind of revolutionary origin.[13] While a national mythology may help differentiate a society and contribute to the arousal of patriotic feelings, it may be wrong to assume that societies are impoverished if they lack this kind of origin, or the heightened collective feelings about the society which result from such an origin. In sum, members of Canadian society are frequently affected by ideals of national unity and societal identity that they observe in American society, even though these may not be appropriate ideals for Canada given the differences between the two societies.[14]

INTERNAL CLEAVAGES

Perhaps the two most important variables explaining lack of cohesion within Canadian society are language and region. Language implies not only communication barriers between people, but also cultural differences that go beyond the two largest groups — English and French. In one sense, the notion of Canada as one country but two nations, enhances the imagery of two solitudes. The existence of two different language broadcasting networks within the Canadian Broadcasting System, for example, implies far more than the use of two different languages; it signifies two different presentations of the news which are targetted to two different groups. In another sense, the idea of dualism is weakened by the diversity of ethnic backgrounds in the anglophone component of the society, where little sense of nationhood prevails in comparison to Quebec.[15] Consequently, bilingualism and multiculturalism appear to accentuate differences, rather than to promote similarities which might serve as a focus for societal identity. The attempt to build a united front among some native people (as expressed in the concept of the Dene Nation), only further accentuates dividing points in the society.[16]

Region also provides a discordant note because, as noted in Chapter 4, local loyalties may take precedence over national ones. One study of Nova Scotia adolescents found that these young people perceived greater similarities among Maritimers than between Nova Scotians and Canadians living in other regions.[17] Another study discovered that, in contrast to American students who were first immersed into the national political culture, Alberta children tended toward a provincial rather than federal political culture.[18] Uneven economic development has also caused regional feelings to coalesce around provincial governments, and this pits the sub-units of the national society against one another, or in opposition to the federal government, thereby arousing further animosities.[19]

Are these disintegrating factors of linguistic culture and regional culture the explanations for a fragmented national identity, or are they a consequence of a fundamentally weak societal identity? This question is perhaps analagous to the question of which came first — the chicken or the egg. For a society in the process of identity formation, however, it is important to note that a regional or ethnic identity may be in competition with a national identity, but they are not necessarily incompatible with a national identity held simultaneously.[20] In other words, being a Prince Edward Islander, a farmer of Scottish origin, and even a Maritimer does not necessarily exclude the broader and more distant Canadian identity. It is this leap from local to regional to national which demonstrates the considerable variation between members of the society. Indications are rather strong that in spite of the diversity of reactions, some attachment to the national society is felt by most of its members. In other words, the national society is, at least in some important ways, part of every resident's frame of reference.

SOCIAL ISSUES AND NATIONAL DEBATE

Differences of opinion have a long heritage in Canadian society. Most of these differences are based on traditional group cleavages such as ethnicity or region. Recently, issues have emerged that tend to span these traditional groups creating national debate based on new alignments, and initiating new forms of national dialogue.

One of the basic dilemmas within the society has been the extent to which material progress or a high standard of living should take preeminence over other broader principles.[21] Until the late 1960's and 1970's, the post-war rush for economic development was predominant, and in large measure this dominance still remains. Nevertheless, beginning with the Viet Nam War era, new questions were raised within the country about what kind of society its residents wanted it to become. Social issues such as native rights and gender equality, and environmental issues such as pollution, acid rain, resource depletion, and nuclear armaments have resulted in a great deal of societal debate.[22] While agreement on these issues seldom prevails, their importance is that they stimulate discussion which is oriented towards the articulation of a national position. Members of the society are exposed to a diversity of opinions on these issues, and they become more attuned to the need for the shaping of national policies which reflect a societal perspective. Put more bluntly, the issue is not so much whether resources are being depleted too rapidly, but how resource depletion will affect the national economy, which in turn affects the well-being of all. In other words, social issues create the national debates and the federal policies which heighten national consciousness. Through these issues, individuals in the society are aroused to articulate their position about what they would like their society to be.

THE EVOLUTION OF SYMBOLS OF SOCIETAL UNITY

For many years, Canada's identity as an independent entity was shaped by its position as a sponsored society. The symbols of societal unity were those of the Mother Country, such as the use of the Union Jack as the flag, and the singing of "God Save The Queen" at public gatherings. The fact that these symbols were irritating reminders to French-Canadians of colonial defeat by the British only served to increase

divisiveness rather than symbolic unity. It has only been since 1980 that
"O Canada" has had official status as the national anthem, although it
had been used for many years. Perhaps even more significant is the fact
that the anthem's bilingual version is not widely used. Furthermore, the
flag with the Maple Leaf was only adopted in 1965.[23] Thus, the crystalli-
zation of a national identity, rather than a sponsored identity, has only
been made possible through these symbols, and these symbols have
only appeared in recent years. Vestiges of the old symbol system still
remain, but the transition from personal identity to societal identity
should be greatly aided by symbols which provide a common focus for
the society as an independent entity.

The birth of new symbols in a society articulating its identity is a
painful process. These public symbols help specify the boundaries and
coherence of a society as a *people,* rather than just a collection of
individuals, and therefore the identification with these symbols by the
society is important. What happens, however, if the change of the
symbols of societal unity create so much conflict that people feel like
strangers in their own society? Raymond Breton has engaged in very
significant analysis of this problem in Canada.[24] He notes that while
francophones have been historically unhappy with British symbols,
many of the changes in the symbol system designed to make them more
comfortable, have now alienated anglophones who feel estranged from
their own national society. If the English language was alienating francophones from English-speaking Canada (language, of course, is the
most powerful symbol), so the insistence on the use of French in
Quebec has had an alienating effect on anglophones. In a similar
manner, the shift away from the imperial system to the metric system,
and the devaluation of British symbols in public ceremony, have created
an environment in which continuity with the past is broken in favour of
a transformation to a new collective identity. In the long run, these
changes in the symbolic order may be significant in the production of a
new societal identity, but they have initially resulted in new conflict
within the national society.

Each of these five factors are important background issues in the
articulation of a societal identity. Because the society is dynamic rather
than static, considerable evidence has been given to suggest that the old
sponsored society is undergoing large-scale change which is clearly
producing a very different societal shape and tone. While the economic
foundations of the society demonstrate little change, it is clear that the
national collectivity is struggling with the desires of its component units
to evolve political and cultural solutions that are uniquely Canadian;
and in doing so, a national identity continues to emerge.

Nationalism: The Crystallization of a National Identity

The intensification of feelings about primary allegiance to the national society and its well-being is known as *nationalism*. Much like other words that end in "ism" (like communism or capitalism), nationalism implies a set of beliefs, convictions, and a worldview pertaining to the defense and advocacy of the society contained within a political jurisdiction. It is possible to be a resident of a nation-state but yet not be nationalistic. Nationalism emerges out of strong feelings about the collectivity as a whole (rather than individuals), and the belief that the welfare of the group, as determined by established boundaries, be a first principle in any action within the society.

One of the biggest dilemmas with nationalism is that different definitions of the boundaries of a national group may coexist within the same society. In Canadian society, segmentalists may limit their boundaries of nationhood to the French or the Dene. This view may challenge, or at least compete with, the pan-Canadian view of the population within all of Canada as being a national society. Furthermore, not everyone agrees that loyalty to the nation-state ought to be a priority, and they may opt for an individualistic or local group approach to life in society. Consequently, nationalist sentiment is highly variable over time, and is usually only a primary objective for a minority. Nationalism may be widespread for a short period, or it may be adopted by interest groups who find the supporting principles personally intriguing or beneficial.

For the majority of the population, loyalty to the nation-state is one of a chain of identities (e.g., family, ethnicity, religion) which they hold. The sheer experience of exposure to the news, for example, sensitizes persons to the national context in which they live, and leads to the assumption that a minimal level of national consciousness inevitably will be present in all residents. Particular events, e.g., the Canada-Russia hockey series, national elections, disasters or wars, or travel abroad, may heighten one's consciousness of being part of a national fabric, and this may evoke strong positive sentiments or attitudes towards one's country which is the substance of *patriotism*.

The strongest conception of nationalism assumes that individuals should subordinate all other interests and loyalties to the nation-state. This type of "full-blown nationalism" particularly lends itself to socialist societies, or to societies with a strong central government.[25] A more moderate perception of nationalism is that it is a belief in the right of societal self-determination. In this view, the society is expected to support a flexible program of actions and policies that maintain and sustain the independence and integrity of the society as a whole. Obviously, considerable differences of opinion will prevail about how flexible a national society can afford to be. Any looser conceptions of the nation-state (such as the concept that the state is only a framework for cultural and economic activities) suggests a more federated society such as exists in Switzerland, where only minimal societal cohesion prevails. While this concept of the nation-state is a recurring theme in Canada, nationalism has become a common synonym for beliefs related to societal self-determination.

Patriotism or love of country is an age-old phenomenon. Most people have always identified with, and been loyal to, their place of birth or place of residence. History demonstrates that people have always been conscious of the group to which they belonged, and commitment to that group has always been valued; however, the idea that loyalty is not just to a geographic locale or a social group, but to a political state, is a more recent phenomenon. This loyalty to the state was first clearly expressed in the latter half of the 18th Century during the French Revolution.[26] In post-revolutionary France, the state attempted to create a society or sense of nationhood out of all people living within the borders of the state, regardless of other subgroup allegiances. A single language and culture was imposed on all regions of the country, thereby breaking down barriers and aiding the creation of a single nation. Thus an ideal of the national society was established, whereby other forms of group identity were to be submerged to a single united ideal focussed on the state.

The principle that the state now serves as the basis of society, establishes the boundaries of the society, and blends its people into a nationality, is now almost assumed to be a foundation of world order. Nationality has become a part of personal identity much like gender or skin colour, and has become much more significant than earlier types of socio-political organization. In large measure, its legitimacy is hardly questioned, though we occasionally hear of ethnic groups who possess a sense of nationhood and who rebel against their subordinate position of submergence within the society of the nation-state.[27] Instances of this phenomenon were discussed in Chapter 6, and Canadian society has its own examples as has been noted in this book numerous times.

The Evolution of Canadian Nationalism

It is clear that at the time of Confederation in 1867, there was little sense of a Canadian nationality. Many residents of Canada had little concept of a society of the nation-state because of intense local attachments, warm sentiments towards the Mother Country, identities more closely related to a foreign place of origin, or even an ambivalence about this new political creation known as Canada. Confederation was based on the idea that a strong central government would be needed to establish a national society, but considerable latitude was given for the expression of regional uniqueness; e.g., the Catholic school system in Quebec. The "Canada First" movement of the 1870's was a short-lived campaign to forge a nationalism based on British culture.[28] Generally speaking, Canadian nationalism has been perceived with some suspicion because it has been viewed as a tool of ethnic assimilation, and it has been viewed with particular suspicion in Quebec where francophone residents possessed their own sense of nationhood.

Integration theories that explain the emergence of nationalism suggest that over time, traditional group loyalties will break down due to processes such as industrialization and urbanization, and people will be drawn into the larger collectivity.[29] In fact, it has been argued that nationalism is rooted in the economy of industrialization which requires centralization, and one form of communication. Further, some believe that industrialization itself helps create a homogeneous dominant culture.[30] Nationalism has also been linked to secularization (i.e., the decline of traditional religious attachments), so that the state becomes the new object of loyalty and devotion, almost as a form of surrogate religion. In other words, nationalism can be viewed as the product of a variety of trends contributing towards greater national unity.

It is perhaps true that the industrialization of Canada and the accompanying social and cultural changes which it produced have contributed to a growing nationalist spirit. As population shifted to Central Canada (particularly Ontario) because of the attractiveness of industrial growth, as new technologies brought East and West closer together, and as a consequence of higher educational levels among the population that had shifted from rural to urban residences, old attachments and ethnocentrisms slowly began breaking down. Rather than producing a pan-Canadian nationalism, however, these same processes also contributed to the rise of Quebecois new nationalist spirit. Instead of integrating Canadian society, therefore, nationalism or regionalism has erupted in sub-units of the society which has enhanced rather than reduced societal conflict.

In contrast to integration theories of nationalism, *conflict theories* explain the development of nationalism as a response to foreign domination. This domination may have its source in the strength of powerful nations that impose their will on weaker nations, and frequently, nationalism is a reaction to this external control.[31] Undoubtedly, concern over American control is a major impetus to nationalist thought and action in Canada, and it is for this reason that nationalism demonstrates a strong relationship with anti-Americanism. From the conflict theory perspective, therefore, nationalism is a response to the stress within the society caused by attempts to preserve the self-image and integrity of the society.[32]

Both integration and conflict theories provide key ideas in understanding the slow evolution of Canadian nationalism. Industrial change and communication technologies have brought residents of the society closer together in recent years, and have created an environment in which the sense of a national society can be developed. Similarly, repeated efforts at differentiation from American society provides the other building block for a growing sense of nationality.

It is generally agreed that in the late 1960's and 1970's, a new wave of nationalism manifested itself in Canadian society. Conflict theories of nationalism suggest that nationalist ideologies may not only be useful to thwart external control, but that nationalism may assist the capitalist class within a nation to support policies that are useful to them. For example, the Canadian Manufacturer's Association has historically been ardently nationalist in the sense that protective tariffs and the preferred purchase of Canadian manufactured goods have been promoted as the legitimate expression of good citizenship.[33] Nationalist policies in this later period also have a new source of support in the expanding middle class. Just as the rising new middle class in Quebec has been instrumental in the promulgation of Quebec nationalism (see chapter 5), so the new rising middle class in the rest of Canada realize that their own interests are distinctly related to strong national development.[34] It is this large group of young well-educated persons of long heritage in Canadian society, who have articulated a new defense of nationality and feeling of national pride. As a consequence, new markets have emerged in films, literature, educational materials, business opportunities, professional associations, and travel exchanges, that were previously weakly developed. It is from this basic change in the class structure of Canadian society that support for a new societal identity has emerged.

Stimulants of Nationalist Sentiment

Nationality is at least partially related to place of birth. Where one is born determines in large measure one's nationality because, barring other intervening factors of personal election, place of birth usually is the basis for determining citizenship. This correlation, however, does not imply that nationality is inborn. A national identity is something that is acquired through social learning. Learning the expectations,

REAL PEOPLE 7.2

Nationality as Personal Identity

"Hey Linda, what's your nationality?"

"Well my mother is German and my father is Polish. Actually he was German but was part of a German community that was living in Poland so he was considered Polish. My mother sort of considered herself kind of English too, as she worked as a nanny in England for several years before coming to Canada. Both of my parents became Canadian citizens after residing here for several years, but they still spoke the German language, and maintained their German and Polish citizenships as well."

"Me? Well I was born in Canada but my mother registered me with the German government as a citizen from abroad so that I would have dual citizenship. That was before she was naturalized as a Canadian. Does that make me a dual citizen?"

"I went to the United States for graduate study. There I met an American fellow and we got married. We decided to go overseas to Africa to work with the nationals there on a development project. While residing in Nigeria our children were born. They are considered Nigerian but we also registered them with the Canadian and American governments as born to citizens abroad. I think that gives them three different nationalities."

"What a mess! Does nationality matter anyhow?"

Questions to Consider

Given the increasing mobility of people, is nationality really that important? Why is the determination of citizenship considered so significant? If the United Nations proposed to establish a category "citizen of the world," would that be a preferable choice to narrower nationalities?

---

attitudes, and behaviour demanded by a society through interaction is known as the process of *socialization*.

It is through the basic institutions of a society (i.e., school, church, government, media) that one learns about, and develops attitudes towards, the society to which one belongs. The Canadian problem is not only that the society must teach its younger members about their relationship to the societal unit, but also that it must *resocialize* many of its older members into identification with the national society.

Perhaps the most important stimulant of nationalist sentiment is the *educational system* for it socializes the young into the societal tradition. It is here where students receive a sense of societal history and geography, and an awareness of what constitutes significant societal events. School assemblies begin to develop patriotic fervor through the learning of songs that reflect the societal heritage. In addition, the classroom provides a setting in which students may acquire a sense of familiarity with other aspects of a society's culture. In other words, the school system is expected to teach not only spelling and mathematics, but all of the basics of good citizenship.

Two observations about the role of schools in inculcating this nationalist sentiment can be made. First, one of the historic problems has been the lack of Canadian classroom materials in English-Canada. The use of British or American materials meant that it was more difficult to create an understanding of Canadian history and culture. In recent years, however, enormous developments have occurred in the publication of Canadian materials, which provide students with a greater degree of societal awareness. Second, because education is a provincial matter rather than a federal matter, the basic textbooks that are used begin with an orientation to the national society through provincial eyes. Nowhere is the implication of this fact more noticeable than in Quebec, where language differences combine with Quebec nationalist views to produce a markedly different perception of Canadian society.

Lamy speaks of the differences in the educational experiences of English and French adolescents as "socialization into discord."[35] In other words, French students acquired more positive feelings toward the provincial society, whereas anglophone students were more favourably oriented toward the federal level. One of the problems cited by the Royal Commission On Bilingualism And Biculturalism was that two different views of Canadian history were presented in the textbooks of the two languages.[36] The French language textbooks stressed the survival of French-Canadian society, with special emphasis placed on the period prior to the English Conquest. Succeeding events, including Confederation itself, were presented from the point of view of a minority facing English domination. English language textbooks, on the other hand, stressed the Conquest as a beginning rather than an ending, and glorified the historical significance of Confederation as the emergence of a new strong single entity — Canadian society. The result of this difference in socialization was that when school children were asked to identify national heroes, francophones and anglophones each identified with prominent figures of their own language group, and there were few "reconciliation symbols" which they shared.[37] Thus, the schools might be viewed as perpetuating a rift in Canadian society, rather than presenting a realistic view of the basis of national unity. Since public school texts are frequently written for and approved by provincial educational authorities, it is not surprising that school children in Newfoundland or British Columbia will also first learn about their national society through provincial eyes.

Schools clearly have a pivotal role in creating a knowledge base about the national society, and in developing positive attitudes towards it. The influence of schools on a child begins at an early age, and it can therefore be assumed that perceptions of Canadian society established here will be formative for later life.

Studies of nationalism have concluded that a necessary condition for the development of nationalist sentiment is the emergence of an *intelligentsia*, our second stimulant. The intelligentsia are a group of well-educated or learned persons who help to articulate the substance of the national idea primarily through their writing, which often receives widespread acclaim.[38] The intelligentsia include authors, journalists, professors, and even artists who are depicted as helping to uncover the core of nationality or the essence of the national experience.

The work of historians has a special role in formulating national feeling. In researching, writing, and interpreting a society's history, historians uncover the pivotal events in Canadian history which contribute to a greater sense of awareness of the society's legacy. Literary figures write about the land and its people in novels and verse which may develop romantic or thought provoking images that reflect a sense of nationhood. These persons are frequently celebrated in the media, their work is cited, and a general familiarity with their work is promoted through the schools. Sometimes these writers address the nationalist sentiment indirectly, but sometimes they become leaders in directly articulating nationalist fervor. In Canada, such persons include anglophones such as Northrop Frye, Stephen Leacock, Robertson Davies, Margaret Atwood, Pierre Berton, and francophones such as Michel Brunet, Roch Carrier, Marie-Claire Blais, Hebert Jacques Ferron, and Roger Lemelin among others. Other forms of more popular culture which reflect collective assumptions and values back to members of the society, include performers like Wayne and Schuster and the Mackenzie brothers. Intellectuals and media commentators can also serve as critics of the society, and their work may stimulate widespread debate.

Two further observations should be made about the role of the intelligentsia. First, since literary culture is conveyed in a specific linguistic form, it is clear that the two language groups will each have their own literature which may (unless people are fully bilingual) reinforce the idea of the two solitudes. Second, since literary culture is such a critical vehicle in sustaining the nationalist sentiment, many people vociferously advocate the development of cultural nationalism. *Cultural nationalism* is the advocacy and defense of Canadian culture whether in print, in drama, or in music. Cultural nationalists feel that indigenous forms of culture should be given priority, financial support, and special recognition, perhaps even to the extreme of the exclusion or control of foreign cultural products. Clearly, this perspective creates considerable debate within the society, but at its root is the argument that the intelligentsia and the artistic community both provide invaluable service in the articulation of the national identity.[39]

A third stimulant of nationalist sentiment emerges from *citizens for whom nationalist policies are personally advantageous.* Nationalism clearly has the potential of being an ideological weapon in the hands of the ruling class. This is because nationalism can be either a means to obtain power, or a vehicle to legitimate power already held. By establishing a rationale and a feeling of support for the collectivity, nationalism can serve as an effective mechanism of societal control. S.D. Clark points out that in Canada's early years, there was little support for nationalist sentiment among the people. Nevertheless, in this era, Canada's "most ardent patriots" were her dignitaries — business leaders, bishops, ministers of the Crown, and military officers — whose well-being and superior positions were connected to the independent existence of Canada, and to a strong Canadian society.[40] Earlier it was shown that business entrepreneurs who depend on the Canadian market may become strong economic nationalists because their livelihood is dependent on their survival in that market. Many members of the bourgeoisie may also be cautious nationalists, or even anti-nationalists particularly when opportunities for expansion open up in other countries. In general, *economic nationalism* is most typical when businesses or labour groups are struggling for survival, and feel that they need protection.

In the new wave of recent nationalism, it has been the expanded middle class, or new petty bourgeoisie of salaried professionals (many of whom are working for the state), or budding professionals still in training in universities and concerned about employment opportunities, who are the most nationalistic.[41] This social class is vocally supportive of policies that protect and enhance the national economy in matters that deal with technologies, research, management decisions, and corporate policies; i.e., matters of industrialization that specifically relate to white collar jobs. The significant increase in government expenditures in recent years has also led to the growth of a large cohort of professional government employees who help create and regulate policies aimed at the strengthening of the national society. The dwindling significance of farmers, miners, and fishermen in the economy reduces the overall power of this working class whose product, in many instances, is oriented to international markets. Industrial unions are becoming more nationalistic in recent years as they realize that life in the workplace is greatly affected by the intimate relationship between national policies and corporate policies.

Nationalism itself has no class connotations, but is a set of beliefs and attitudes that can be taken up by people who find those beliefs relevant to their well-being. In making this assertion, however, it is not to be assumed that nationalist fervor is necessarily something sinister or based only upon self-interest; but it does suggest that one of the most effective stimulants for a nationalist sentiment comes from those whose personal interests are most vitally at stake.

A fourth stimulant of nationalist sentiments comes from *institutional linkages* that bind the society together. These institutions such as nation-wide banks, railroads, churches, and various forms of communications, allow the member of the society to become more conscious of the boundaries of the society and aspects of the society which are held in common.[42] Not only do institutions like the Royal Bank of Canada, CP Rail, the United Church of Canada, and the Southam newspaper chain, have a high profile within the society as distinctly Canadian institutions; they also have a large number of employees and clients who support them, and this heightens a consciousness of the ties that bind members of the society together within a social and economic framework. The typical pattern of organizational structure from local to regional to national implies that whether identifying corporations (sales meetings, seminars, transfers, etc.), professional organizations, leisure clubs, or amateur sport competitions, members of the society are increasingly made aware of the national context in which their specific activity takes place.

Perhaps no institution has a more powerful role in forging national unity than that of broadcasting. While it was argued at the time of Confederation that it was to be the railroads that would provide "the ties that bind," in the modern era it is broadcasting that has this unique role. The print media should also not be ignored, for organizations like the Canadian Press gather stories from all parts of the society and disseminate them daily throughout the society through newspapers. Nevertheless, radio and television broadcasting are even more pervasive because they communicate not only news but entertainment; i.e., the substance of the culture of a society through music, drama, and documentaries. Also not to be overlooked are national advertising campaigns which frequently refer to the useage of products in a national context. Note, for example, how television weather maps acquaint the audience with the geography and weather differentials in different parts of the society. While the nationalist impetus is usually more implicit than explicit in all of these institutional examples, their significance is that they help frame a societal or national consciousness in the minds of members of the society.

The fifth stimulant of nationalist sentiment emerges from the *political process*, particularly from political leaders and political parties. Many people join political parties, take positions on national issues, and recruit people to their point of view. Others are less directly involved in the political world, but are made conscious of important political figures through the media. The media are continally soliciting reactions from politicians on virtually every issue that arises, whether that politician is part of the government or in opposition. Through the controversies articulated by political leaders, citizens are drawn into these issues and made aware of their national implications. Therefore, whether it is in electoral battle for leadership of a national or provincial party, or whether it is the articulation of positions on issues of national consequence, the political process reinforces the national context of the society in spite of disagreements or different levels of participation. In sum, political activities serve as constant reminders of the contours of Canadian society.

Conclusion

It would be an overstatement to say that these integrating forces contributing to national unity are more compelling, or have overwhelmed disintegrating forces within the society. The previous chapters have discussed many dilemmas, conflicts, contradictions, and forces of disunity for which no immediate resolution appears attainable, and which have significant implications for the emergence of a sense of society. For example, it is debatable whether a societal identity can ever crystallize without a common culture, a common language, or a common sense of history. At the same time, however, modern societies are not static homogeneous entities in which a sense of commonality will necessarily supercede individual preferences and/or local identities.

One of the problems with talking about a national society is that we bring our notions of small-scale communities to discussions of national belonging. The sociologist Ferdinand Tonnies distinguished a *community* from a *society* by noting that the intensity of social relationships was much stronger in a community, and much more distant, remote, and bureaucratic, in a society.[43] When nations were smaller self-contained ethnic groups or subgroups, it might have been possible to talk about the typical face-to-face interactions that created a sense of community. Now, however, political states are frequently formed by welding a diversity of ethnic groups together into a national polity. The result has been to create societies in which feelings of unity are superficial and social bonding is weak. Because the members of even the smallest modern nation will never know most of their fellow citizens, contemporary national societies are best referred to as "imagined communities."[44] A sense of society then begins in the mind, where the image of a level of a common identity produces an ephemeral unity that may never correspond to the hard facts of social reality. It is left to institutions such as governments, corporations, and other large organizations to give this identity a more tangible expression.

With this framework for a national society, it should not be expected that such a society will ever be a single unified entity. In contrast to an *ethnocentric nationalism*, where exclusive power is given to the pursuit of one national ideal, and where differences and divisions are viewed as defects in the society, the Canadian experience has evidenced a greater tendency toward a *polycentric nationalism*, with a tolerance of contending ideals, and openness to others, and a freely self-critical spirit.[45] The common acknowledgement that acceptance of the Canadian state should not necessarily threaten other identities such as ethnicity or region, for example, has undoubtedly contributed to several different levels of belonging that serve to structure the national society. Perhaps for this reason, the national society has for many generations resisted the insistence on a pan-Canadian solidarity. Increasing unity has focussed, however, on the use of the state as a vehicle for societal self-determination. It is upon this political desire for self-determination that a more integrated society could be built.

A Nationalist Test

If you saw a tag on a product in a store that read "Made In Canada" or "Buy Canadian," would you choose it over other products? — even if it was more expensive — even if it was of poorer quality?

Would you choose a product with an international brand name even if the Canadian product was less well known? — was cheaper, — and maybe even of better quality?

Further Exploration

1. What are the advantages and disadvantages of the expression of nationalist feeling? Do you think that more nationalist sentiment would be good in Canadian society? Is the growth of nationalism good for the world?
2. What are the factors that you think are most important in holding Canadian society together? Is it really necessary for the society to have a feeling of belonging together?
3. Do a content analysis of what you see and hear on television to determine whether it contributes to or detracts from a national identity?
4. Is nationalism a necessary quality of good citizenship?

Selected Readings

Susan Crean and Marcel Rioux, *Two Nations*, (Toronto: James Lorimer, 1983).

William Christian and Colin Campbell, *Political Parties And Ideologies In Canada*, 2nd Edition, (Toronto: McGraw Hill Ryerson, 1983).

Ronald Wardhaugh, *Language And Nationhood: The Canadian Experience* (Vancouver, New Star, 1983).

Landmark Canadian Document V

Document:	*A Future Together: Observations And Recommendations Of The Task Force On Canadian Unity*, Minister Of Supply And Services Canada, 1979.
Issue:	Regional tensions, and the increased disaffection of regions with their place in Canada, produced a growing awareness that the continued existence of Canadian society could not be taken for granted. The Task Force On Canadian Unity was established both to analyze these grievances and divisive problems, and to advise the federal government on means to facilitate greater unity.
Quotation:	"Sometimes the country seemed to us to be composed of a multiplicity of solitudes, islands of self-contained activity and discourse disconnected from their neighbors and tragically unaware of the whole which contained them all." (p. 6).

Context: The efforts of the 1960's to draw French-Canadians and their language more directly into the mainstream of Canadian life were producing contradictory results. In spite of the great strides that were made through a variety of policies such as bilingualism, the 1976 election of the Parti Quebecois in Quebec threatened the unity of the Canadian state through its separatist aspirations. But not only was the existence of the country challenged from Quebec, but other Canadians, and particularly those in the West, also began to articulate their grievances more loudly. Indeed, it was perceived that Canadian society was in the midst of a crisis in which special attention needed to be paid to opinions throughout the nation and to presenting a course of remedial action to the federal government. The anticipation of the Quebec referendum on independence gave the work of the Task Force a deep urgency.

Procedure: The Federal government created the Task Force On Canadian Unity on July 5, 1977, with eight members from different parts of the country. The Task Force, under the co-chairmanship of Jean-Luc Pepin and John P. Robarts, held hearings in 15 cities across Canada from the fall of 1977 to the spring of 1978. Individual members also appeared at numerous other meetings and on radio and television shows and sought a variety of opinions within their respective regions. The hearings themselves were covered extensively by the media and representatives of citizen organizations were encouraged to make presentations before the Task Force.

The Report: The Task Force found that the problem of national unity was of crisis proportions, and that there was a real problem regarding public attitudes towards the state. As the means of changing those attitudes, it was concluded that there must be significant institutional and policy reform. In general, the Task Force suggested that confrontations be replaced by open, fresh, and innovative accommodation.

The Report of the Task Force pointed out that Canadian society need not be a homogeneous mass in which diversity is submerged, but that diversity should be encouraged to coexist harmoniously. Diversity should be viewed as a national resource, rather than as a social problem. The Task Force was somewhat supportive of Quebec rights to self-determination, but expressed the hope that important changes could be made so that Quebec would feel more a part of Confederation while retaining her uniqueness.

The three principles of French-English duality, support for regionalism, and the commitment to the mutual sharing of benefits and powers, were the cornerstone of the Report. Among many other recommendations, some of the changes advocated included a Council Of The Federation, in place of the Senate, to which members would be appointed by the provincial governments; the elimination of the federal ability to disallow provincial legislation; electoral reform, and referendums on constitutional amendments that require majority support within each region. In general, the Task Force supported a more clarified distribution of powers between the federal and provincial governments and in particular the granting of greater control in certain areas to the provinces as a means of defusing regional discontent.

Assessment: The Task Force did its work in the shadows of the impending Quebec referendum, which coloured the disposition of the Report. Since then, the call for greater provincial controls and animosities towards the federal government have increased considerably. It is one thing to make general statements about the need to clarify and make adjustments to federal-provincial powers in the case of accommodating Quebec; it is quite another thing to make the same adjustments regarding the implications of such demands from the resource-rich Western provinces. It is precisely the difficulty of making such distribution of power adjustments that have become so cumbersome.

In the light of what has happened in the Western and Atlantic provinces since the work of the Task Force, it is also possible that the committee took anglophone commitment to Canada too much for granted. In any case, the issue which prompted the creation of the Task Force has continued to grow in its seriousness, and the concrete structural changes which the Report advocated have been slow to evolve. But even here, the Report sounds a note of pessimism in remarking that changes in the constitution will probably be easier to make than they will easily create unity among Canadians.

Further Readings: Two other documents were published by the Task Force. One is entitled *A Time To Speak: The View Of The Public*, containing summary statements, and a wide range of public opinion made in presentation to the committee. The second document, *Coming To Terms: The Words Of The Debate*, is a useful glossary and background discussion of critical social and political terms which are important to understanding the issues involved.

ENDNOTES

[1]Stanley Morse, "National Identity From A Social Psychological Perspective: A Study of University Students In Saskatchewan," *Canadian Review Of Studies In Nationalism* 7(1980): 299-312.

[2]Herschel Hardin, *A Nation Unaware* (Vancouver: J.J. Douglas, 1974), p. 12.

[3]This distinction was initially made by Albert Breton and Raymond Breton in *Why Disunity? An Analysis Of Linguistic And Regional Cleavages In Canada* (Montreal: Institute For Research On Public Policy, 1980), pp. 58-59 and is developed further here.

[4]This is essentially the point of W.L. Morton, *The Canadian Identity* (Madison: University of Wisconsin Press, 1965), p. 111.

[5]See Keith Banting and Richard Simeon, *And No One Cheered: Federalism, Democracy, And The Constitution Act* (Toronto: Methuen, 1983), Chapter 1; and David Milne, *The New Canadian Constitution* (Toronto: James Lorimer, 1982).

[6]R. Kenneth Carty and W. Peter Ward, *Entering The Eighties: Canada In Crisis* (Toronto: Oxford University Press, 1980).

[7]John Sloan Dickey, *Canada And The American Presence* (New York: New York University Press, 1975), p. 7.

[8]*Travel Between Canada And Other Countries*, Statistics Canada 1982, Catalogue 66-201.

[9]Dallas Cullen, J.D. Jobson, and Rodney Schneck, "Anti-Americanism And Its Correlates," *Canadian Journal Of Sociology* 3 (1978): 103-120.

[10]*Gallup Report*, March 5, 1983 and March 1, 1984.

[11]George Barnett and Thomas McPhail, "An Examination Of The Relationship Of United States Television And Canadian Identity," *International Journal Of Intercultural Relations* 4(1980): 219-232.

[12]S.D. Clark notes that anti-Americanism is frequently the means whereby this societal differentiation occurs. "Canada And Her Great Neighbor," *Canadian Review of Sociology And Anthropology* 1(1964): 193-201.

[13]See David Bell and Lorne Tepperman, *The Roots Of Disunity* (Toronto: McClelland Stewart, 1979), pp. 211-213.

[14]Herschel Hardin refers to this phenomenon as American ideology-in-Canada in which Canadian objectives are coloured by American standards and patterns. *A Nation Unaware*, p. 55.

[15]Neil Nevitte, "Nationalism, States And Nations," in Elliot J. Feldman and Neil Nevitte, eds., *The Future Of North America: Canada, The United States, And Quebec Nationalism* (Cambridge: Center For International Affairs, 1979), p. 354.

[16]See Mel Watkins, "Dene Nationalism," *Canadian Review Of Studies Of Nationalism* 8(1981): 101-113.

[17]Joseph G. Jabbra and Ronald G. Landes, *The Political Orientations Of Canadian Adolescents: Political Socialization And Political Culture In Nova Scotia* (Halifax: St. Mary's University, 1976), p. 101.

[18]Grace Skogstad, "Adolescent Political Alienation," in Elia Zureik and Robert M. Pike, eds., *Socialization And Values In Canadian Society*, Vol. I. *Political Socialization* (Toronto: McClelland and Stewart, 1975), pp. 185-208.

[19]James Overton discusses the neo-nationalism of regions opposing the centralization of power "Towards A Critical Analysis of Neo-Nationalism In Newfoundland," in Robert J. Brym and R. James Sacouman, eds., *Underdevelopment And Social Movements In Atlantic Canada* (Toronto: New Hogtown Press, 1979), p. 219-249.

[20]These ideas are an adaptation of a theme developed by Jeffrey Reitz, "Immigrants, Their Descendants, And The Cohesion Of Canada," in Raymond Breton, Jeffrey G. Reitz, and Victor Valentine, *Cultural Boundaries And The Cohesion Of Canada* (Montreal: Institute For Research On Public Policy, 1980), pp. 400-406.

[21]Ronald L. Watts, "Federalism, Regionalism And Political Integration" in David Cameron, ed., *Regionalism And Supranationalism* (Montreal: Institute For Research On Public Policy, 1981), p. 3.

[22]A related point has been made by Susan Crean and Marcel Rioux in *Two Nations* (Toronto: James Lorimer, 1983), p. 15.

[23]The stormy debate over the adoption of the maple leaf as the national flag is recorded in Blair Fraser, *The Search For Identity* (Toronto: Doubleday, 1967), Chapter 23.

[24]Raymond Breton, "The Production And Allocation Of Symbolic Resources: An Analysis Of The Linguistic And Ethnocultural Fields In Canada," *Canadian Review Of Sociology And Anthropology* 21(1984): 123-144.

[25]This concept of nationalism is developed by W. Christian and C. Campbell, *Political Parties And Ideologies In Canada* (Toronto: McGraw Hill Ryerson, 1974). See also Chapter 6 for a good study of Canadian nationalism in historical development.

[26]Anthony D. Smith, *Nationalism In The Twentieth Century* (Oxford: Martin Robertson, 1979), pp. 1-3.

[27]The concept of "submerged nations" has been developed by Vatro Murvar, *Submerged Nations: An Invitation To Theory* (Milwaukee: University of Wisconsin — Sociology, 1982).

[28]A.G. Bailey, *Culture And Nationality* (Toronto: McClelland and Stewart, 1972), Chapter 9.

[29]Theories of nationalism are discussed in Anthony D. Smith, *Theories Of Nationalism* (New York: Harper and Row, 1971).

[30]Ernest Gellner, *Nations And Nationalism* (Oxford: Basil Blackwell, 1983), p. 140.

[31]Silvia Brucan, "The Nation-State: Will It Keep Order Or Wither Away?" *International Social Science Journal* 30(1978): 9-30.

[32]Abraham Rotstein, "Is There An English-Canadian Nationalism?," *Journal Of Canadian Studies* 13(1978): 114.

[33]For a discussion on the CMA and nationalist sentiment as a long-standing phenomenon, see S.D. Clark, *The Canadian Manufacturers' Association: A Study In Collective Bargaining And Political Pressure* (Toronto: University of Toronto Press, 1939).

[34]Patricia Marchak, "Nationalism And Regionalism In Canada," *Canadian Review Of Studies In Nationalism* 7(1980): 26.

The explanation of nationalism developed here is actually built from modernization theories which point to a new educated class and their expanding influence on the rest of the society.

[35]Paul G. Lamy, "Political Socialization Of French And English Canadian Youth: Socialization Into Discord," in Zureik and Pike, eds., *Socialization And Values In Canadian Society*, Vol. I. *Political Socialization*, pp. 263-280.

[36]*Report Of The Royal Commission On Bilingualism And Biculturalism Book II: Education*, p. 275.

[37]Jean Pierre Richert, "The Impact Of Ethnicity On The Perception Of Heroes And Historical Symbols," *Canadian Review Of Sociology And Anthropology* 11(1974): 156-163.

[38]Anthony D. Smith, ed., *Nationalist Movements* (London: Macmillan, 1976), pp. 21-24.

[39]For a discussion of the relationship between Canadian literature and national identity, see Paul Cappon, ed., *In Our Own House: Social Perspectives On Canadian Literature* (Toronto: McClelland and Stewart, 1978).

[40]S.D. Clark, "Canada And Her Great Neighbor," p. 195.

[41]Philip Resnick, *The Land Of Cain: Class And Nationalism In English Canada* (Vancouver: New Star, 1977), pp. 147ff.

[42]For an interesting discussion of factors promoting the integration of Canadian society, see Douglas Cole, "The Integration Of Canada: An Overview," *Canadian Review Of Studies In Nationalism* 7(1980): 4-13.

[43]Ferdinand Tonnies, *Fundamental Concepts of Sociology* (New York: American Books, 1940).

[44]Benedict Anderson, *Imagined Communities: Reflections On The Origin And Spread of Nationalism* (London: Verso, 1983), p. 15.

[45]See Anthony D. Smith, *Theories Of Nationalism*, p. 158-159 and S.M. Crean, *Who's Afraid Of Canadian Culture?* (Don Mills: General Publishing, 1976), pp. 277-278.

Select Bibliography

Adams, I. et al. *The Real Poverty Report*. Edmonton: Hurtig, 1971.

Adams, W. (ed.). *The Brain Drain*. Toronto: Macmillan, 1968.

Alexander, D. *Atlantic Canada and Confederation*. Toronto: University of Toronto Press, 1983.

Anderson, A.B., and J.S. Frideres. *Ethnicity in Canada: Theoretical Perspectives*. Toronto: Butterworths, 1981.

Anisef, P. and N. Okihiro. *Losers and Winners: The Pursuit of Equality and Social Justice in Higher Education*. Toronto: Butterworths, 1982.

Armstrong, P. and H. Armstrong. *The Double Ghetto*, Revised Edition. Toronto: McClelland and Stewart, 1984.

Arnopoulos, S.M. *Voices from French Ontario*. Montreal: McGill-Queen's University Press, 1982.

Arnopoulos, S.M. and D. Clift. *The English Fact in Quebec*. Montreal: McGill-Queen's University Press, 1980.

Axline, A. et al. *Continental Community: Independence and Integration in North America*. Toronto: McClelland and Stewart, 1974.

Banting, K. and R. Simeon. *And No One Cheered: Federalism, Democracy, and the Constitution Act*. Toronto: Methuen, 1983.

Barr, J.J., and O. Anderson, eds. *The Unfinished Revolt*. Toronto: McClelland and Stewart, 1971.

Beattie, C. *Minority of Men in a Majority Setting*. Toronto: McClelland and Stewart, 1975.

Beattie, C., J. Desy, and S. Longstaff. *Bureaucratic Careers: Anglophones and Francophones in the Canadian Public Service*. Ottawa: Information Canada, 1972.

Beaujot, R. and K. McQuillan. *Growth and Dualism: The Demographic Development of Canadian Society*. Toronto: Gage, 1982.

Bell, D. and L. Tepperman. *The Roots of Disunity: A Look at Canadian Political Culture*. Toronto: McClelland and Stewart, 1979.

Bellamy, D.J., J.H. Pammett, and D.C. Rowat, eds. *The Provincial Political Systems: Comparative Essays*. Toronto: Methuen, 1976.

Bercuson, D.J., ed. *Canada and the Burden of Unity*. Toronto: Macmillan, 1977.

Berkowitz, S.D. *Models and Myths in Canadian Sociology*. Toronto: Butterworths, 1984.

Berkowitz, S.D. and R.K. Logan, eds. *Canada's Third Option*. Toronto: Macmillan, 1978.

Bowles, R.T., ed. *Little Communities and Big Industries: Studies in the Social Impact of Canadian Resource Extraction*. Toronto: Butterworths, 1982.

Breton, A. and R. Breton. *Why Disunity? An Analysis of Linguistic and Regional Cleavages in Canada*. Montreal: Institute for Research on Public Policy, 1980.

Breton, R., J.G. Reitz, and V.F. Valentine. *Cultural Boundaries and the Cohesion of Canada*. Montreal: Institute for Research on Public Policy, 1980.

Brym, R.J. and R.J. Sacouman. *Underdevelopment and Social Movements in Atlantic Canada.* Toronto: New Hogtown Press, 1979.

Caldwell, G. and E. Waddell. *The English of Quebec: From Majority to Minority Status.* Quebec: Institut Québecois De Recherche Sur La Culture, 1982.

Cameron, D.M., ed. *Regionalism and Supranationalism.* Montreal: Institute for Research on Public Policy, 1981.

Canadian Council on Social Development. *Not Enough: The Meaning and Measurement of Poverty in Canada.* Toronto: James Lorimer, 1985.

Cappon, P., ed. *In Our Own House: Social Perspectives on Canadian Literature.* Toronto: McClelland and Stewart, 1978.

Card, B.Y., ed. *Perspectives on Regions and Regionalism.* Edmonton: University of Alberta Press, 1969.

Carty, R.K. and W.P. Ward. *Entering the Eighties: Canada in Crisis.* Toronto: Oxford University Press, 1980.

Christian, W. and C. Campbell. *Political Parties and Ideologies in Canada,* Second Edition. Toronto: McGraw-Hill Ryerson, 1983.

Clairmont, D.H. and D.W. Magill. *Africville: The Life and Death of a Black Community.* Toronto: McClelland and Stewart, 1974.

Clark, S.D. *The New Urban Poor.* Toronto: McGraw-Hill Ryerson, 1978.

___ *Canadian Society in Historical Perspective.* Toronto: McGraw-Hill Ryerson, 1976.

___ *The Social Development of Canada.* Toronto: University of Toronto Press, 1942.

___ *The Canadian Manufacturers' Association: A Study in Collective Bargaining and Political Pressure.* Toronto: University of Toronto Press, 1939.

Clement, W. *Class, Power, and Property: Essays on Canadian Society.* Toronto: Methuen, 1983.

___ *Hardrock Mining: Industrial Relations and Technological Change at Inco.* Toronto: McClelland and Stewart, 1980.

___ *Continental Corporate Power.* Toronto: McClelland and Stewart, 1977.

___ *The Canadian Corporate Elite: An Analysis of Economic Power.* Toronto: and Stewart, 1975.

Clement, W., and D. Drache. *The New Practical Guide to Canadian Political Economy.* Toronto: Lorimer, 1985.

Coleman, W.D. *The Independence Movement in Quebec 1945-1980.* Toronto: University of Toronto Press, 1984.

Conway, J.F. *The West: The History of a Region in Confederation.* Toronto: James Lorimer, 1983.

Crean, S.M. *Who's Afraid of Canadian Culture?* Don Mills: General Publishings, 1976.

Crean, S. and M. Rioux. *Two Nations.* Toronto: James Lorimer, 1983.

Dacks, G. *A Choice of Futures: Politics in the Canadian North.* Toronto: Methuen, 1981.

Dahlie, J., and T. Fernando, eds. *Ethnicity, Power and Politics in Canada.* Toronto: Methuen, 1981.

Darling, H. *The Politics of Freight Rates.* Toronto: McClelland and Stewart, 1980.

Davis, M., and J.E. Krauter. *The Other Canadians: Profiles of Six Minorities.* Toronto: Methuen, 1978.

Dickey, J.S. *Canada and the American Presence.* New York: New York University Press, 1975.

Djao, A.W. *Inequality and Social Policy: The Sociology of Welfare.* Toronto: John Wiley, 1983.

Doern, G.B., and R.W. Phidd. *Canadian Public Policy: Ideas, Structure and Process.* Toronto: Methuen, 1983.

Doran, C.F., and J.N. Sigler. *Canada and the United States.* Englewood Cliffs: Prentice-Hall, 1985.

Dosman, E.J. ed. *The Arctic in Question.* Toronto: Oxford University Press, 1976.

Driedger, L., ed. *The Canadian Ethnic Mosaic.* Toronto: McClelland and Stewart, 1978.

Elkins, D.J., and R. Simeon, eds. *Small Worlds: Provinces and Parties in Canadian Political Life.* Toronto: Methuen, 1980.

Elliott, J.L., ed. *Two Nations: Many Cultures: Ethnic Groups in Canada,* Second Edition. Toronto: Prentice-Hall, 1983.

English, H.E., ed. *Canada-United States Relations.* New York: Praeger, 1976.

Feldman, E.J., and N. Nevitte, eds. *The Future of North America: Canada, The United States, and Quebec Nationalism.* Cambridge: Center for International Affairs, 1979.

Forbes, E.R. *The Maritime Rights Movement, 1919-1927: A Study in Canadian Regionalism.* Montreal: McGill-Queen's University Press, 1979.

Forcese, D. *The Canadian Class Structure,* Second Edition. Toronto: McGraw-Hill Ryerson, 1980.

Forcese, D. and S. Richer, eds. *Social Issues: Sociological Views of Canada.* Scarborough: Prentice-Hall, 1982.

Fournier, P. *The Quebec Establishment.* Second Revised Edition. Montreal: Black Rose, 1976.

Fraser, Blair. *The Search for Identity.* Toronto: Doubleday, 1967.

Frideres, J.S. *Native People In Canada: Contemporary Conflicts.* Second Edition. Scarborough: Prentice-Hall, 1983.

Fry, J.A., ed. *Contradictions in Canadian Society: Readings in Introductory Sociology.* Toronto: John Wiley, 1984.

Gagan, D.P., ed. *Prairie Perspectives.* Toronto: Holt, Rinehart and Winston, 1970.

Gagnon, A.G. *Quebec: State and Society.* Toronto: Methuen, 1984.

Gardner, R.C. and R. Kalin, eds. *A Canadian Social Psychology of Ethnic Relations.* Toronto: Methuen, 1981.

Gibbins, R. *Conflict and Unity: An Introduction to Canadian Political Life.* Toronto: Methuen, 1985.

__ *Prairie Politics and Society: Regionalism in Decline.* Scarborough: Butterworths, 1980.

__ *Regionalism: Territorial Politics in Canada and the United States.* Toronto: Butterworths, 1982.

Glenday, D., H. Guindon, and A. Turowetz, eds. *Modernization and the Canadian State.* Toronto: Macmillan, 1978.

Goldenberg, S. *Men of Property: The Canadian Developers who are Buying America.* Toronto: Personal Library, 1981.

Goldstein, J.E. and R. Bienvenue, eds. *Ethnicity and Ethnic Relations in Canada.* Toronto: Butterworths, 1980.

Grant, G. *Lament for a Nation.* Toronto: McClelland and Stewart, 1978.

— *Technology and Empire: Perspectives on North America.* Toronto: House of Anansi, 1969.

Gray, Earle. *Super Pipe: The Arctic Pipeline.* Toronto: Griffin House, 1979.

Hamelin, L.E. *Canadian Nordicity.* Montreal: Harvest House, 1979.

Hardin, H. *A Nation Unaware.* Vancouver: J.J. Douglas, 1974.

Harp, J., and J.R. Hofley, eds. *Structured Inequality in Canada.* Toronto: Prentice-Hall, 1980.

Hartz, L. *The Founding of New Societies.* New York: Harcourt, Brace and World, 1964.

Harvey, D. *Christmas Turkey or Prairie Vulture? An Economic Analysis of the Crow's Nest Pass Grain Rates.* Montreal: Institute of Research for Public Policy, 1980.

Heap, J.L., ed. *Everybody's Canada: The Vertical Mosaic Reviewed and Re-examined.* Toronto: Burns and MacEachern, 1974.

Henry, F. *Forgotten Canadians: The Blacks of Nova Scotia.* Don Mills: Longmans, 1973.

Hiller, H.H. *Society and Change: S.D. Clark and the Development of Canadian Sociology.* Toronto: University of Toronto Press, 1982.

Hiller, J., and P. Neary. *Newfoundland in the Nineteenth and Twentieth Centuries: Essays in Interpretation.* Toronto: University of Toronto Press, 1980.

Himmelfarb, A., and C.J. Richardson. *Sociology for Canadians: Images of Society.* Toronto: McGraw-Hill Ryerson, 1982.

Hindley, M.P., G.M. Martin, and J. McNulty. *The Tangled Net: Basic Issues in Canadian Communications.* Vancouver: J.J. Douglas, 1977.

Hughes, D.R., and E. Kallen. *The Anatomy of Racism: Canadian Dimensions.* Montreal: Harvest House, 1974.

Hunter, A.A. *Class Tells: On Social Inequality in Canada.* Toronto: Butterworths, 1981.

Hutcheson, J. *Dominance and Dependency.* Toronto: McClelland and Stewart, 1978.

Innis, H.A. *The Cod Fisheries.* Toronto: University of Toronto Press, 1940.

— *The Fur Trade in Canada.* Toronto: Univerity of Toronto Press, 1930.

— *Problems of Staple Production in Canada* Toronto: Ryerson Press, 1933.

Irving, J.A. *The Social Credit Movement in Alberta.* Toronto: University of Toronto Press, 1959.

Jabbra, J.G., and R.G. Landes. *The Political Orientation of Canadian Adolescents: Political Socialization and Political Culture in Nova Scotia.* Halifax: St. Mary's University, 1976.

Jackson, E., ed. *The Great Canadian Debate: Foreign Ownership.* Toronto: McClelland and Stewart, 1975.

Jones, R. *Community in Crisis: French-Canadian Nationalism in Perspective.* Toronto: McClelland and Stewart, 1972.

Joy, R. *Languages in Conflict: The Canadian Experience.* Toronto: McClelland and Stewart, 1972.

Kalbach, W.E., and W.W. McVey. *The Demographic Basis of Canadian Society.* Second Edition. Toronto: McGraw-Hill Ryerson, 1979.

Kallen, E. *Ethnicity and Human Rights in Canada.* Toronto: Gage, 1982.

Lavoie, Y. *L'émigration des Canadiens aux Etats-Unis avant 1930.* Montreal: University of Montreal Press, 1972.

Levine, M., and C. Sylvester. *Foreign Ownership.* Toronto: General Publishing, 1972.

Li, P.S., and B.S. Bolaria, eds. *Racial Minorities in Multicultural Canada.* Toronto: Garamond Press, 1984.

Lipset, S.M. *Agrarian Socialism: The Cooperative Commonwealth Federation in Saskatchewan.* New York: Doubleday, 1968.

___ *Revolution and Counter-Revolution: Change and Persistence in Social Structures,* Revised Edition. Garden City: Doubleday, 1971.

Little Bear, L., M. Boldt, and J.A. Long, eds. *Pathways to Self-Determination: Canadian Indians and the Canadian State.* Toronto: University of Toronto Press, 1984.

Litvak, I.A. and C.J. Maule. *The Canadian Multi-Nationals.* Toronto: Butterworths, 1981.

Lucas, R. *Minetown, Milltown, Railtown: Life in Canadian Communities of a Single Industry.* Toronto: University of Toronto Press, 1971.

Lumsden, I., ed. *Close the 49th Parallel: The Americanization of Canada.* Toronto: University of Toronto Press, 1970.

MacKie, M. *Exploring Gender Relations: A Canadian Perspective.* Toronto: Butterworths, 1983.

Macpherson, C.B. *Democracy in Alberta: Social Credit and the Party System.* Toronto: University of Toronto Press, 1953.

Marchak, M.P. *Ideological Perspectives on Canada.* Second Edition. Toronto: McGraw-Hill Ryerson, 1981.

___ *In Whose Interests: An Essay on Multinational Corporations in a Canadian Context.* Toronto: McClelland and Stewart, 1979.

Marsden, L.R., and E.B. Harvey. *Fragile Federation: Social Change in Canada.* Toronto: McGraw-Hill Ryerson, 1979.

Matthews, R. *The Creation of Regional Dependency.* Toronto: University of Toronto Press, 1983.

___ *There's No Better Place Than Here: Social Change In Three Newfoundland Communities.* Toronto: Peter Martin, 1976.

Matthews, R., and J. Steele. *The Struggle for Canadian Universities.* Toronto: New Press, 1969.

McRoberts, K., and D. Posgate. *Quebec: Social Change and Political Crisis,* Revised Edition. Toronto: McClelland and Stewart, 1980.

Milne, D. *The New Canadian Constitution.* Toronto: James Lorimer, 1982.

Milner, H. *Politics in the New Quebec.* Toronto: McClelland and Stewart, 1978.

Milner, S.H., and H. Milner. *The Decolonization of Quebec.* Toronto: McClelland and Stewart, 1973.

Moniere, D. *Ideologies in Quebec: The Historical Development.* Toronto: University of Toronto Press, 1981.

Murray, J., ed. *Canadian Cultural Nationalism.* New York: New York University Press, 1977.

Morton, W.L. *The Canadian Identity.* Madison: University of Wisconsin Press, 1965.

— *The Progressive Party in Canada.* Toronto: University of Toronto Press, 1957.

Niosi, J. *Canadian Capitalism: A Study of Power in the Canadian Business Establishment.* Toronto: James Lorimer, 1981.

Olsen, D. *The State Elite.* Toronto: McClelland and Stewart, 1980.

Ostry, S., ed. *Canadian Higher Education in the Seventies.* Ottawa: Economic Council of Canada, 1972.

Ossenberg, R.J. *Canadian Society: Pluralism, Change and Conflict.* Scarborough: Prentice-Hall, 1971.

—, ed. *Power and Change in Canada.* Toronto: McClelland and Stewart, 1980.

Palmer, H., ed., *The Settlement of the West.* Calgary: University of Calgary Press, 1977.

Panitch, L., ed. *The Canadian State: Political Economy and Political Power.* Toronto: University of Toronto Press, 1977.

Paterson, D.G. *British Direct Investment in Canada 1890-1914.* Toronto: University of Toronto Press, 1983.

Peacock, D. *People, Pereguines, and Arctic Pipelines.* Vancouver: J.J. Douglas, 1977.

Perry, R.L. *Galt U.S.A.: The American Presence in a Canadian City.* Toronto: Maclean-Hunter, 1971.

Phillips, P. *Regional Disparities.* Toronto: James Lorimer, 1982.

Phillips, P., and E. Phillips. *Women and Work: Inequality in the Labour Market.* Toronto: James Lorimer, 1983.

Ponting, J.R., and R. Gibbins. *Out of Irrelevance: A Socio-Political Introduction to Indian Affairs in Canada.* Toronto: Butterworths, 1980.

Porter, J., M. Porter, and B.R. Blishen. *Stations and Callings: Making it Through the School System.* Toronto: Methuen, 1982.

Porter, J. *The Vertical Mosaic.* Toronto: University of Toronto Press, 1965.

Pratt, L., and G. Stevenson, eds. *Western Separatism: The Myths, Realities, and Dangers.* Edmonton: Hurtig, 1981.

Putnam, D.F., and R.G. Putnam. *Canada: A Regional Analysis.* Toronto: J.M. Dent, 1970.

Ramcharan, S. *Racism: Non-Whites in Canada.* Toronto: Butterworths, 1982.

Rawlyk, G.A. ed. *The Atlantic Provinces and the Problems of Confederation.* St. John's, Newfoundland: Breakwater, 1979.

Rea, K.J. *The Political Economy of the Canadian North.* Toronto: University of Toronto Press, 1968.

Reitz, J.G., *The Survival of Ethnic Groups.* Toronto: McGraw-Hill Ryerson, 1980.

Resnick, P. *The Land of Cain: Class and Nationalism in English Canada.* Vancouver: New Star, 1977.

Richards, J., and L. Pratt. *Prairie Capitalism: Power and Influence in the New West.* Toronto: McClelland and Stewart, 1979.

Richmond, A. *Post-War Immigrants in Canada.* Toronto: University of Toronto Press, 1970.

Rioux, M., and Y. Martin, eds. *French-Canadian Society*, Vol. I. Toronto: McClelland and Stewart, 1971.

Ross, D.R. *The Canadian Fact Book on Poverty, 1983.* Toronto: James Lorimer, 1983.

Rotstein, A., and G. Lax. *Getting it Back: A Program for Canadian Independence.* Toronto: Clarke Irwin, 1974.

Ryan, T.J. *Poverty and the Child: A Canadian Study.* Toronto: McGraw-Hill Ryerson, 1972.

Schwartz, M. *Politics and Territory: The Sociology of Regional Persistence in Canada.* Montreal: McGill-Queen's University Press, 1974.

Shapiro, D.M. *Foreign and Domestic Firms in Canada.* Toronto: Butterworths, 1980.

Sitwell, O.F.G., and N.R.M. Seifried. *The Regional Structure of the Canadian Economy.* Toronto: Methuen, 1984.

Smiley, D. *Canada in Question: Federalism in the Seventies*, Second Edition. Toronto: McGraw-Hill Ryerson, 1976.

Stanley, G.F.G. *The Birth of Western Canada: A History of the Riel Rebellion.* Toronto: University of Toronto Press, 1978.

Starks, R. *Industry in Decline.* Toronto: James Lorimer, 1978.

Stevenson, G. *Unfulfilled Union: Canadian Federalism and National Unity*, Revised Edition. Toronto: Gage, 1982.

Stone, L. *Migration in Canada: Regional Aspects.* Ottawa: Statistics Canada, 1969.

Thomson, D.C., ed. *Quebec Society and Politics: Views from the Inside.* Toronto: McClelland and Stewart, 1973.

Tupper, A., and G.B. Doern, eds. *Public Corporations and Public Policy in Canada.* Montreal: Institute for Research on Public Policy, 1981.

Ujimoto, V., and G. Hirabayashi. *Visible Minorities and Multiculturalism: Asians in Canada.* Toronto: Butterworths, 1980.

Valliere, P. *White Niggers of America.* Toronto: McClelland and Stewart, 1971.

Wade, M. *Regionalism in the Canadian Community 1867-1967.* Toronto: University of Toronto Press, 1969.

Wardhaugh, R. *Language and Nationhood: The Canadian Experience.* Vancouver: New Star, 1983.

Warkentin, J. *Canada: A Geographical Interpretation.* Toronto: Methuen, 1968.

Watkins, M. *Dene Nation: The Colony Within.* Toronto: University of Toronto Press, 1977.

Yeates, M. *Main Street: Windsor to Quebec City.* Toronto: Macmillan, 1975.

Zimmerman, C.C., and G.W. Moneo. *The Prairie Community System.* Ottawa: Agricultural Economics Research Council of Canada, 1970.

Zureik, E., and R.M. Pike, eds. *Socialization and Values in Canadian Society,* Vol. I., *Political Socialization.* Toronto: McClelland and Stewart, 1975.

Index

Please return or renew by
latest date below

Printed in Canada